Ripley's Believe It or Not!

Executive Vice President, Intellectual Property Norm Deska
Vice President, Exhibits and Archives Edward Meyer
Senior Director of Publishing Amanda Joiner

Editorial Manager Carrie Bolin
Editors Jessica Firpi, Jordie R. Orlando
Junior Editor Emily Libecki
Researcher Sabrina Sieck
Text Geoff Tibballs
Feature Contributors Jessica Firpi, Emily Libecki, Jordie R. Orlando, Sabrina Sieck
Factchecker James Proud
Indexer Yvette Chin
Proofreader Rachel Paul
Special Thanks to Ripley's Cartoonist, John Graziano

Designers Rose Audette, Luis Fuentes
Reprographics *POST LLC
Cover Artwork Rose Audette, Christopher Bigelow, Ron Fladwood

ISBN 978-1-60991-217-8

For more information regarding permission, contact:
VP Intellectual Property
Ripley Entertainment Inc.
7576 Kingspointe Parkway, Suite 188
Orlando, Florida 32819
publishing@ripleys.com
www.ripleys.com/books

Manufactured in China in May 2018 by Leo Paper
First Printing

Library of Congress Control Number: 2018936372

PUBLISHER'S NOTE
While every effort has been made to verify the accuracy of the entries in this book, the Publisher cannot be held responsible for any errors contained in the work. They would be glad to receive any information from readers.

WARNING
Some of the stunts and activities are undertaken by experts and should not be attempted by anyone without adequate training and supervision.

Ripley's Believe It or Not!

A CENTURY OF STRANGE!

Ripley
PUBLISHING

a Jim Pattison Company

A Century of STRANGE

> One hundred years ago, a young Robert Ripley pondered how to fill the space assigned to him as a cartoonist for the *New York Globe*. Little did he know, the choice he was about to make would be the start of an amazing adventure that lives on today.

1918

» On December 19, 1918, the first *Believe It or Not!* cartoon was published, initially called *Champs and Chumps* and featuring a collection of sports oddities Ripley had saved.

1922

» In December 1922, Ripley embarked on his first around-the-world trip and returned on April 7, 1923. He published his travel journal in installment form.

1929

» The first *Believe It or Not!* book was published.

» On July 9, Ripley joined Hearst's King Features Syndicate and the *Believe It or Not!* cartoon went from being published in just 17 papers to worldwide distribution.

1930

» Ripley began his 17-year run on radio.

NOTE TO EDITORS—Here are the first six daily instalments of "Ripley's 'Round the World" Series. Matrix of the two-column cut of Ripley was mailed you last week together with other suggested advertising matter.

'ROUND THE WORLD WITH RIPLEY

A NEW AMAZING
BELIEVE IT OR NOT
Starring
ROBERT L. RIPLEY

THE HORNED

THE CHILD CYCLOPS

THE BOY WHO DIED OF OLD AGE BEFORE
HE WAS SEVEN YEARS OLD

VITAPHONE
SHORT SUBJECT

Ripley

THE MOST
INTERESTING
MAN IN THE
WORLD

The New
Believe it
or Not!
Ripley

1931

» The second
Believe It or Not! book
was published.

» Ripley created
movie shorts for
Vitaphone Pictures
made by Warner Bros.

1933

» The first Odditorium opened in
Chicago, Illinois, at the Century of
Progress World's Fair.

1949

» Robert Ripley died on
May 27 after collapsing
on the set of his weekly
television show.

100 YEARS

Ripley

Ripley

Believe It or Not Believe It or Not

SEE SHARKEE & BREMNER HERE!

1950

» The first permanent *Believe It or Not!* museum opened in St. Augustine, Florida, which still operates in its original location at Castle Warden.

1997

» The first Ripley's Aquarium opened in Myrtle Beach, South Carolina.

1980–84

» Successful national *Ripley's Believe It or Not!* TV show was broadcast for 82 episodes, starring Jack Palance.

2000

» Ripley's Aquarium of the Smokies opened in Gatlinburg, Tennessee.

» New *Ripley's Believe It or Not!* TV show, starring Dean Cain, premiered. It ran for 88 episodes, four seasons, before going into successful worldwide syndication.

100 YEARS!

2018

» 30 Ripley's Believe It or Not! Odditoriums
» 10 Ripley's Moving Theaters
» 9 Ripley's Marvelous Mirror Mazes
» 9 Ripley's LaseRaces
» 5 Ripley's Haunted Adventures
» 4 Louis Tussaud's Wax Works
» 3 Ripley's Aquariums

. . . and more!

2004

» Ripley Publishing was launched with the New York Times bestseller Ripley's Believe It or Not! annual.

2018

RIPLEY'S® EST. 1918

» **30,000 exhibits!**

» **Millions of books sold annually!**

» **Home of the oldest, continuously run comic panel in history!**

WOW!

BELIEVE IT OR NOT!

COOL STUFF STRANGE THINGS

LEECH FACIAL

WOMEN IN CAKES

» Ripley's newest YouTube series *COOL STUFF STRANGE THINGS*, hosted by Ripley's lead researcher Sabrina Sieck, brings you the most bizarre and odd stories with a twist of humor. Check out the latest episode on YouTube and head over to page 176 for one bloody story!

YOUTUBE SERIES WITH A TWIST!

» In today's world, many misconceptions have been perpetuated—becoming modern day "facts"—when, in reality, myths and hearsay have taken over. In this weekly column, Ripley's puts those delusions to the test, turning your world upside down, because you can't always. . . Believe It!

...OR NOT!

DEAD MEN TELL NO TALES, WE TELL TRUE TALES. PLANKS AND BURIED TREASURE WERE BOGUS!
PIRATES WOULD HAVE WISHED THE PLANK WAS AN OPTION!

TWINKIES AREN'T THE IMMORTAL SNACK CAKES YOU THINK THEY ARE
DO YOU LIKE TWINKIES?

ripleys.com

Ripley's Rarities

» Unlocking the Cabinet of Curiosities, *Ripley's Rarities* takes you up close and personal with some of the most interesting exhibits collected by Ripley's Believe It or Not! since the days of Robert Ripley himself.

RARITY № 18640
C. 1930
EMBALMING PUMP
PUMP USED BY MORTICIANS TO PRESERVE THE DEAD.

Ripley's WEIRD MINUTE

» Add 60 seconds of fun facts to your day with Ripley's *WEIRD MINUTE* through Amazon's Alexa, iTunes, Google Play, and Stitcher.

PRO-TIP: Once you have enabled the Ripley's Weird Minute skill, say "Alexa, what's my Flash Briefing?" or "Alexa, what's in the news?"

Hollywood Christmas Parade

➤ On December 15, 2017, Ripley's participated in the 86th annual Hollywood Christmas Parade!

Ripley's guided two larger-than-life gingerbread balloons along the Hollywood Boulevard parade route.

Leading the balloons was Ripley's lead researcher and YouTube host Sabrina Sieck in a classic car. Alongside her were a great variety of performers—from a contortionist to acrobatic roller skater!

Ripley's donated more than $100,000 worth of books to Toys for Tots. To represent this donation, we constructed a stunning 12-ft-tall (3.7-m) Christmas tree of books!

To get in the Hollyweird holiday spirit, Ripley's had three-time National Gingerbread House Competition winner Patricia Howard create a 5-foot-tall gingerbread house for the lobby of the Hollywood Odditorium.

BEHAVIOR DISCOUNT ▶ Antonio Ferrari gives a 5 percent discount to families whose children are well-behaved while they are eating at his restaurant in Padua, Italy.

PUB CRAWL ▶ In March 2017, a 200-year-old tavern was moved in its entirety from Southborough, Massachusetts, to Guilford, Connecticut, about 100 mi (160 km) away. The nine-room Woodbury Tavern, which dates back to 1808, had been dismantled and stored since 2006 in a barn. After it was put up for sale online, it was spotted by Bill Butterly, who bought it and plans to rebuild it as a home on his property in Guilford.

CHEESE PIZZA ▶ Vito Iacopelli, owner of a pizzeria in Hollywood, California, crafted a gluten-free, breadless pizza crust entirely out of mozzarella cheese. He began by flattening the mozzarella into a round base and then topped it with basil, tomatoes, oregano, sea salt, and more mozzarella.

SHORT FLIGHT ▶ In 2016, Austrian regional airline People's Viennaline introduced a regular international flight that takes just eight minutes. The service connects St. Gallen-Altenrhein in Switzerland with Friedrichshafen in southern Germany. To travel between the two towns by road takes about an hour.

DUCK STORE ▶ The Duck Store in Amsterdam, the Netherlands, sells nothing but rubber ducks. Thousands of toy ducks line the shelves, ranging from doctor, astronaut, and ninja ducks to Batman and Spider-Man ducks. The store also has a little pond where customers can test the ducks before buying them.

FLYING BATHTUB ▶ Charlesetta Williams and her son Ricky, of Marion County, Texas, were lifted off the ground and spun into the air by a 130 mph (208 kmph) tornado on January 21, 2017, while sitting in their bathtub. When they saw the tornado approaching, they sought refuge in the bathtub, believing that its weight would prevent the twister from sweeping it away. Instead the tornado sucked the bathtub through the roof before depositing it in the yard, with Mrs. Williams still inside it. Ricky was thrown out and landed about 20 ft (6 m) away. Although their home was destroyed, they suffered only minor bruises and scratches.

LEISURELY THRILLS ▶ The first rollercoaster in the United States—the Switchback Railway, which opened in Coney Island, New York, in 1884—had a top speed of only 6 mph (9.6 kmph).

TREE DWELLER ▶ After climbing to the top of a 90-ft-tall (27-m) sequoia tree in Seattle, Washington, and refusing to come down for 25 hours, Cody Lee Miller was accused of causing $8,000 worth of damage and was told he must have no future contact with the tree.

POLICE TREATS ▶ The Boston Police Department in Massachusetts added an ice cream truck to its patrol fleet in 2016 as part of a community policing initiative that has distributed more than 120,000 free ice cream cups since 2010.

WATERING CANS ▶ The outside of Bruno Geyer's florist shop in Rougemont le Château, France, is decorated with more than 800 watering cans that hang from the walls and roof.

PEN FORFEIT ▶ After losing a bet in 1981, a 14-year-old boy named Wang paid the forfeit by swallowing two ballpoint pens. They remained inside his body for 36 years until doctors in Suzhou, China, surgically removed them. Wang said he had completely forgotten about swallowing the pens until they showed up on an X-ray.

PAPER DISGUISE ▶ A burglar who broke into a drug store in Huaibei City, China, carefully wrapped his head in toilet paper to avoid being identified on surveillance camera—but was arrested because he did not realize that the camera had already caught his face before he put on his disguise.

Blood FALLS

> Blood Falls is a slow, 50-ft-high (15-m) trickle of crimson water seeping from an opening in the Taylor Glacier onto the frozen surface of Lake Bonney in Antarctica.

The falls were first discovered in 1911, but the cause of the geological phenomenon remained a mystery for 106 years until a study used echolocation technology to investigate the large saltwater lake that had been trapped under ice for one million years. The falls get their reddish tint from the subglacial lake and a network of subglacial rivers, all filled with iron-rich brine.

57 FLOORS UP!

LONGEST INFINITY POOL ▶ On the 57th floor of Singapore's Marina Bay Sands Hotel, guests can gaze out at the city skyline from an infinity pool that stretches 492 ft (150 m) long—the size of three Olympic swimming pools!

LARVAL INVASION ▶ After Radhika Mandloi, a four-year-old girl from Madhya Pradesh, India, complained of an earache, doctors removed 80 maggots from her left ear. A blow fly had invaded her body and laid its eggs in her ear. If she had not been treated, the insects could have eventually eaten her brain.

HEALTHY PROFIT ▶ An authentic 1950s green jacket from Augusta National Golf Club that was bought in 1994 for $5 from a thrift store in Toronto, Ontario, Canada, sold at auction in 2017 for $139,000—a profit of nearly three million percent.

HIDDEN TREASURE ▶ A man who inherited a house in Évreux, Normandy, France, from a dead relative found that it contained a hidden stash of gold bars and coins worth nearly $4 million. He discovered the secret treasure, which included 5,000 gold pieces, when he began clearing out the old furniture.

BAREFOOT TREK ▶ After disappearing from his home in Vancouver, British Columbia, Canada, in 2012, Anton Pilipa was found nearly five years later 6,500 mi (10,400 km) away in the Amazon rainforest in Brazil. With no money, no possessions, and no passport, he had walked barefoot across 10 countries and two continents. He had survived by searching through the trash for food and clothes, picking fruit, and relying on the kindness of strangers.

PROM INVITE ▶ Using a GPS tracking app to mark out his route, Joran Fuller, a 17-year-old student at Findlay High School, Ohio, ran 5.5 mi (8.8 km) to spell out "Prom?" as an invitation to girlfriend Claire Short.

WHITE STRAWBERRY

» White strawberries are real! Called pineberries, these strawberries are white inside and out and covered in red seeds. Although they cannot be produced in large quantities because of their small size, farmer Yasuhito Teshima, of Karatsu, Japan, sells "extraordinarily white and big" varieties of his "white jewel" strawberries for $10 each.

PATIENCE REWARDED ▶ Rosemary Loveland, of Boise, Idaho, played the same lottery numbers for 27 years, and her patience finally paid off in 2016 when they won her a $390,000 jackpot.

MEDICAL MYSTERY ▶ Dactylolysis spontanea is a mysterious medical condition that causes toes and sometimes fingers to fall off in a process known as "autoamputation."

KEEP CALM AND MOW ON

> On June 2, 2017, dad Theunis Wessels was snapped casually mowing his lawn despite a raging tornado swirling behind the family home in Three Hills, Alberta, Canada.

His wife Cecilia captured the silly sight after he refused to stop cutting the grass, later saying he was "keeping an eye on it." Although the twister seems much closer in the photo, it was about 1.25 mi (2 km) from their house.

CASUALLY MOWING LAWN

NAILED IT

» Artist M. Narahari of India paints miniature images on his clipped fingernails. Famous landmarks, people, and beautiful scenes cover the artist's homegrown canvases, which take up to a year and a half to prepare. He started 27 years ago and currently has 100 nail paintings!

BUTLER BOOM ▶ The popularity in China of British TV series *Downton Abbey* has led to a huge increase in the number of young Chinese men training to become professional butlers. Each year, thousands of hopefuls study at a six-week butler training school in Beijing, where they learn everything from serving tea to packing luggage and opening car doors.

SYMBOLIC CALF ▶ Up to 100 people a day visited Khim Hang's home in Kratié, Cambodia, in 2017 to see a young calf that she believes is the reincarnation of her husband, Tol Khut, who died the previous year. She says the calf has the same mannerisms as her late husband and even walks up the long staircase that leads into the house just like he did. Once the calf is inside, she feeds it, washes it, and puts it to bed with the fluffy pillow on which Tol Khut used to sleep.

CARDBOARD COLLECTION ▶
Kosuke Saito, from Osaka, Japan, has spent more than 10 years collecting empty Amazon cardboard boxes. After discovering that Amazon packages come in different shapes and sizes and with varying serial numbers, he began ordering specific products so that he could acquire every type of box. He has collected nearly 80 different boxes, his most prized possession being a rare XY36 model, which is only used for thin articles such as cutting mats.

OVERSIZED PASSENGER ▶ Trying to save the cost of hiring a removal van, an Australian man ended up paying a fine of nearly $200 for taking a refrigerator onto a passenger train in Queensland. With the help of a dolly, the man rolled the heavy fridge through the train doors at Bowen Hills station but was immediately ordered to remove it by security guards and was fined for taking an oversized item onto a train.

ATM PRISONER ▶ Customers at an ATM outside a Bank of America branch in Corpus Christi, Texas, found several notes sent through the receipt slot saying that someone was trapped inside. They dismissed it as a prank until one decided to call 911, and when the police arrived, they heard a faint voice and realized that a repairman really was stuck behind the machine. He had gone into the room housing the ATM to fix a broken door lock but was unable to get back out because he had left his swipe card—and his cell phone—in his truck.

SUGAR RUSH ▶ On January 16, 2017, a police officer in Sanxia Square, China, was stabbed by an angry street vendor with what she was selling—sugarcoated haw on a stick! The officer was attacked after trying to escort the 45-year-old woman because she was illegally operating her street vending business. The snack comes from the fruit of the Chinese hawthorn tree and is boiled in sugar, which gives it a sweet, delicious flavor.

LIVING GHOSTS
of BENIN

> The Egungun of Benin, West Africa, are a secret society filled with costumed men thought to be living ghosts and capable of killing villagers with a single touch.

Locals believe contact between an individual and an Egungun will result in the symbolic death of both parties, so they are protected by a "minder," a person wielding a large stick to beat away anyone who tries to touch an Egungun. To hide their identity, the Egungun are covered with colorful funeral quilts and masks, which allow them to act as faceless links between the living and the dead. They speak using high falsetto voices and channel ancestral spirits, passing absolute judgement on disputes in the Benin community.

Hairplay

Q *What inspired you to sculpt your hair?*

A An Instagram photo album that I saw a year ago. That album presented the hairstyles that women wore long ago in some African tribes. These were really impressive and artistic, and it made me want to use hairstyles as one of my means of expression.

Q *Do you use any materials other than your own hair?*

A I use many things! It depends on what I want to do. I can use thread, needle, fabric, wire, wool, hair extensions. When I imagine a new hairstyle, I try objectively to imagine what I will need.

Q *How long does it take you to sculpt?*

A It depends on what I want to do. Some take me just 20 minutes, while others take over 2 hours!

Q *Is there any shape or image that you want to try sculpting?*

A No! When ideas come, I try to do them.

Q *Do you ever go out in public with your hair art?*

A To be honest, no! I do these hairstyles just for a photoshoot 'cause they are not very comfortable. But I'm able to go out with it. Haha, you just gave me the idea to do it!

> Twenty-one-year-old fashion designer Laetitia Ky, from Abidjan, Côte d'Ivoire, Africa, took social media by storm after posting her new photo series where she sculpts her hair into all kinds of shapes and gestures!

21

Beauty Blogger

› Marimar Quiroa of California was born with a facial growth that prevents her from eating, breathing, or talking through her mouth, but that hasn't stopped her from following her passions—including hosting a makeup video blog with millions of views.

Marimar has a fluid-filled tumor, known as a cystic hygroma, on both sides of her face, requiring her to breathe and eat through tubes in her throat and stomach, respectively. She communicates in American Sign Language, through which her sassy attitude and confidence shines, earning her nearly 350,000 subscribers on YouTube. She is currently in her early 20s, teaches a Zumba class, attends makeup school, and is studying education so she can follow her dreams of teaching deaf children.

PANDA PEBBLE

» A stone found in a river in Shiyan, China, bears an uncanny resemblance to a panda! The finder was offered more than $1,500 for the small chunk of quartzite but turned it down.

FELL OVERBOARD › While on a five-day luxury cruise from Shanghai, China, to South Korea and Japan in 2016, a 32-year-old Chinese woman, Ms. Fan, fell overboard and survived without a lifejacket in jellyfish-infested water for 38 hours before being rescued by fishermen. She had fallen 70 ft (21 m) from the fourth deck of the ship after leaning over too far, but when she was eventually found having drifted at sea, her only injuries were blisters on her arms caused by jellyfish stings.

POKER SUCCESS ▶ Libratus, an Artificial Intelligence machine built by Carnegie Mellon University, beat four of the world's leading professional poker players in a tournament in Philadelphia, Pennsylvania. At the end of the 20-day poker marathon, the machine had amassed more than $1.7 million worth of chips. One of the reasons behind its success was that it can out-bluff humans.

PANDA COLLECTION › Celine Cornet, of Haccourt, Belgium, has a collection of more than 2,200 panda-related items. She started the collection in 1978 when her truck driver husband Andre brought her back a toy panda from a trip to Italy.

"To me, beauty means to accept yourself for who you are."

TOOLS OF THE TRADE

SEWING MACHINES ▶ Jim Young, from Mount Isa, Queensland, Australia, has a collection of 120 treadle sewing machines—but he is unable to use any of them because he can't sew. He has American, English, German, and French models, the oldest dating back to 1862, and keeps them all in a specially built tin shed.

GIRL POWER ▶ Ikram Salhi, a 15-year-old girl from Casablanca, Morocco, can pull two cars a distance of 33 ft (10 m) along the road with her hair. She dragged the cars, which together weighed about 2.5 tons, by attaching one end of the rope to the fronts of the vehicles and the other end to her ponytail. Her inspiration is her uncle, Aziz Salhi, a well-known strongman who discovered his niece's special talent when she was just seven.

LAST PICK ▶ Just three years after earning the dubious title of "Mr. Irrelevant," the nickname given to the player picked last in the annual NFL draft, Marty Moore played in a Super Bowl. He was selected by the New England Patriots as the last pick of the 1994 draft and went on to appear for them in the 1997 showpiece against the Green Bay Packers, the first "Mr. Irrelevant" to ever play in a Super Bowl.

LAKE SWIM ▶ On October 6, 2016, Sarah Thomas, of Conifer, Colorado, swam 82 mi (131 km) across Lake Powell, which runs along the Arizona-Utah border, in 56 hours. She swam mostly freestyle but occasionally switched to backstroke or breaststroke to loosen her muscles. She was accompanied by a support crew of 13 who traveled by houseboat and gave her food every half hour via a water bottle tied to a cord.

AMBIDEXTROUS SCHOOL ▶ All 300 students at Veena Vandini School in Madhya Pradesh, India, can write with both their right and left hand—and some are able to do both at the same time and in different languages. Outside of this school, only 1 percent of the world's population is ambidextrous.

GALLOPING GRANNY ▶ Deirdre Larkin, a retired concert pianist from Johannesburg, South Africa, only took up long-distance running in 2010 after being diagnosed with osteoporosis, but she already has more than 500 medals to her name. She ran 65 races in 2016 at age 84 and regularly competes in half-marathons.

YOUR UPLOADS

So Many Spoons

Canadian René Martin has collected more than 33,500 spoons from around the world! He could use a different one every day for 95 years and still have plenty to spare.

23

FISH
VORTEX

> Swarms of schooling fish behave as one, moving and shape-shifting to feed and escape danger!

Photographer Alex Voyer captured this remarkable phenomenon while swimming in the Pacific off the Galápagos Islands with free diver Gianno Haro. Haro can be seen bravely swimming into the synchronized school of fish despite it looking like a black hole!

ALSO KNOWN AS A BAIT BALL, A SWARM LIKE THIS IS SHORT LIVED—TYPICALLY LASTING NO LONGER THAN 10 MINUTES!

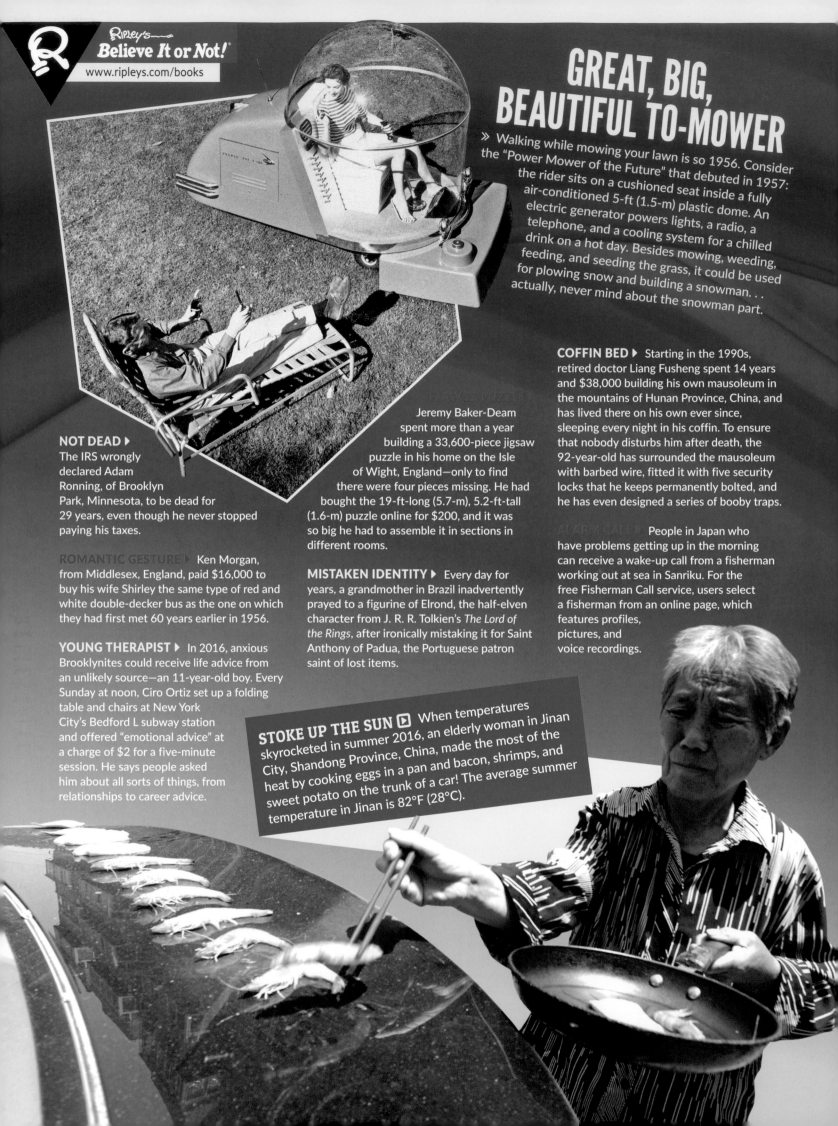

GREAT, BIG, BEAUTIFUL TO-MOWER

» Walking while mowing your lawn is so 1956. Consider the "Power Mower of the Future" that debuted in 1957: the rider sits on a cushioned seat inside a fully air-conditioned 5-ft (1.5-m) plastic dome. An electric generator powers lights, a radio, a telephone, and a cooling system for a chilled drink on a hot day. Besides mowing, weeding, feeding, and seeding the grass, it could be used for plowing snow and building a snowman... actually, never mind about the snowman part.

NOT DEAD ▶

The IRS wrongly declared Adam Ronning, of Brooklyn Park, Minnesota, to be dead for 29 years, even though he never stopped paying his taxes.

ROMANTIC GESTURE ▶

Ken Morgan, from Middlesex, England, paid $16,000 to buy his wife Shirley the same type of red and white double-decker bus as the one on which they had first met 60 years earlier in 1956.

YOUNG THERAPIST ▶

In 2016, anxious Brooklynites could receive life advice from an unlikely source—an 11-year-old boy. Every Sunday at noon, Ciro Ortiz set up a folding table and chairs at New York City's Bedford L subway station and offered "emotional advice" at a charge of $2 for a five-minute session. He says people asked him about all sorts of things, from relationships to career advice.

Jeremy Baker-Deam spent more than a year building a 33,600-piece jigsaw puzzle in his home on the Isle of Wight, England—only to find there were four pieces missing. He had bought the 19-ft-long (5.7-m), 5.2-ft-tall (1.6-m) puzzle online for $200, and it was so big he had to assemble it in sections in different rooms.

MISTAKEN IDENTITY ▶

Every day for years, a grandmother in Brazil inadvertently prayed to a figurine of Elrond, the half-elven character from J. R. R. Tolkien's *The Lord of the Rings*, after ironically mistaking it for Saint Anthony of Padua, the Portuguese patron saint of lost items.

COFFIN BED ▶

Starting in the 1990s, retired doctor Liang Fusheng spent 14 years and $38,000 building his own mausoleum in the mountains of Hunan Province, China, and has lived there on his own ever since, sleeping every night in his coffin. To ensure that nobody disturbs him after death, the 92-year-old has surrounded the mausoleum with barbed wire, fitted it with five security locks that he keeps permanently bolted, and he has even designed a series of booby traps.

ALARM CALL ▶

People in Japan who have problems getting up in the morning can receive a wake-up call from a fisherman working out at sea in Sanriku. For the free Fisherman Call service, users select a fisherman from an online page, which features profiles, pictures, and voice recordings.

STOKE UP THE SUN ▶

When temperatures skyrocketed in summer 2016, an elderly woman in Jinan City, Shandong Province, China, made the most of the heat by cooking eggs in a pan and bacon, shrimps, and sweet potato on the trunk of a car! The average summer temperature in Jinan is 82°F (28°C).

ABM

CAR VENDING MACHINE

> Singapore is home to a 15-story vending machine that dispenses luxury cars—the largest of its kind in the world.

Autobahn Motors runs the unconventional showroom, where customers simply buy their car on a tablet device before the vehicle is delivered to them on the ground floor within a couple minutes via a moving platform elevator. The futuristic structure holds up to 60 high-end cars, including Bentleys, Ferraris, Porsches, Lamborghinis, and even classics like a 1955 Morgan Plus 4.

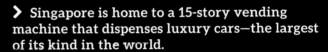

BELIEVE IT!

27

SPAGHETTI DONUT

BOY DRIVER ▶ Desperate for a cheeseburger, an eight-year-old boy from East Palestine, Ohio, took his four-year-old sister for a ride in his father's van and drove it to the nearest McDonald's restaurant. The boy drove about 1 mi (1.6 km) to the restaurant, through intersections and across railroad tracks, without mishap. He said he learned to drive by watching YouTube videos.

WOODEN MOSAIC ▶ Residents of Gresham, Oregon, teamed up to create a painted mosaic that used 14,400 wooden blocks and covered an area of 1,238 sq ft (115 sq m).

TIME TWIST ▶ Twins Samuel and Ronan Peterson were born in Cape Cod Hospital on November 6, 2016, to parents Emily and Seth, of West Barnstable, Massachusetts. Samuel was born at 1:39 a.m. and Ronan arrived 31 minutes later, but by the time Emily had given birth to Ronan, the clocks had gone back one hour due to daylight saving time. So Ronan's official time of birth became 1:10 a.m., making him the older brother even though he was born half an hour after Samuel.

NAIL GUN ▶ While carrying out construction work at his house in Peshtigo, Wisconsin, Doug Bergeson accidentally shot a 3.5-in (8.75-cm) nail into his heart—but despite coming close to death, he managed to drive himself 12 mi (19 km) to a hospital and even parked his pickup truck in the lot before walking into the emergency room. If the nail had gone any deeper, it would have pierced a main artery.

》 Luigi Fiorentino, of Brooklyn, New York, owner of Pop Pasta, serves savory spaghetti donuts. The dish is based on a traditional Neapolitan recipe called *frittata di spaghetti*, or spaghetti pie. Fiorentino bakes the spaghetti in round donut shapes and sells them in a range of flavors such as red sauce, carbonara, zucchini, and Bolognese.

SWOLLEN LIPS ▶ Tamara Bennett, from Tasmania, Australia, suffers from a rare condition that makes her lips swell up to three times their normal size. She was born with an unusual birthmark, caused by a vascular malformation, which causes her lips to fill with blood and means that she can only eat liquidized food through a straw.

ORGAN BAG ▶ Eighty-year-old Lan Guo'e, from Wuxue, China, has lived for more than 20 years with her intestines in a plastic shopping bag hanging out of her body. When an operation went wrong in the 1970s, the surgery wound split, causing her intestines to fall from her body. As she was unable to afford further treatment, she began storing them in a bag, which she keeps around her waist. She washes them daily with lukewarm water.

HELPING HANDS ▶ In May 2017, artist Lorenzo Quinn completed a large-scale sculpture of human hands rising from the waters to support the Ca' Sagredo Hotel building in Venice, Italy. The hands were transported via canal boat and then lifted and dropped into place. Titled *Support*, the installation comments on climate change and the rising sea levels impacting the iconic city.

ANIMAL ARSON

In 2017, a **HAWK** eating a large **SNAKE** in Black Eagle, Montana, completed a circuit atop a set of power lines and started a 40-acre blaze.

According to the National Fire Protection Association, **PETS** start 700 to 1,000 home fires **EVERY YEAR.**

A **PIGEON** dropped a burning cigarette butt into a London **ROOFTOP NEST** and started a building fire in 2014.

In 2014, a **RAVEN** flew into a transmission tower in Canada, causing a local power outage and a 37-acre wildfire.

Henry the **TORTOISE** and his lover Alice knocked over a **HEATER** and set fire to their conservatory home in England, sadly killing both.

In 2014, a **DOG** chewing on a box of **MATCHES** started a house fire in Yukon Territory, Canada.

SOLE STUDENT ▶ North Ronaldsay Primary School in Orkney, Scotland, was forced to close in 2017 after its only student—12-year-old Teigan Scott—reached the age where she graduated to a higher school.

DOOM DISORDER ▶ The sting of the venomous box jellyfish, *Carukia barnesi*, induces Irukandji Syndrome, a disorder whose symptoms include hypertension and feelings of impending doom.

COIN FLIP ▶ When a 2017 election for president of the village of Colp, Illinois, ended in a tie, Tammy O'Daniell-Howell defeated opponent Bryan Riekana by the flip of a coin.

MOON DUST ▶ A small white bag containing particles of moon dust collected by Neil Armstrong during NASA's *Apollo 11* mission in 1969 sold at auction in 2017 for $1.8 million.

FAKE BEARD ▶ A woman who tried to rob a bank in West Danville, California, disguised herself as a man by painting on a fake beard.

SLUG SLIME ▶ Scientists at Harvard University have created a new super-tough medical glue based on the slime secreted by the common garden slug.

BURGER BABIES ▶ On back-to-back days in September 2017, two women gave birth to babies in the parking lot of the same Burger King restaurant in Denville, New Jersey.

NEW WORDS ▶ On average, a new word is created in the English language every 98 minutes—that's nearly 15 new words every day.

MOSQUITO REPELLENT ▶ South Korean manufacturer LG has released a smartphone that uses ultrasonic sound waves to repel mosquitoes.

HELPING HAND ▶ Sian Berry gave birth to baby Mia in the passenger seat of her car while stuck in a traffic jam in Oxford, England—with the help of Dr. Ioannis Spiliotis, who happened to be in one of the cars in line behind her.

In Great Britain, dried or mummified cats are sometimes found hidden within walls, chimneys, and roofs, originally placed there to bring good luck or to ward off evil.

CRUSTY CAT

▶ While building an extension to his home in Wigan, England, father-of-two Adam White demolished the roof of a shed—and found a mummified cat that may have been there for 30 years.

White had lived in the house all his life, and he initially thought the feline mummy was a piece of expanding foam or some type of ornament, but the teeth and rib cage were a dead giveaway. His requests for help and subsequent search to find the former owner of the crusty cat have yielded no leads.

Taking FLIGHT

> It took mankind just 65 years to advance from the Wright brothers achieving 12 seconds of flight to the Apollo 11 astronauts landing on the Moon. The evolution of aviation happened, and is still happening, at breakneck speeds. Explore this timeline to find out more about the unbelievable history of flight.

December 17, 1903

The Wright Stuff

Brothers Orville and Wilbur Wright were the first people to achieve sustained, controlled flight of a heavier-than-air aircraft. It took years of work, building their own engine and designing the first efficient airplane propeller. After flipping a coin to decide who would fly first, Wilbur made a failed attempt on December 14. Three days later, Orville successfully flew for 12 seconds, going 120 ft (36.6 m). Their groundbreaking achievement was only reported in four newspapers the next day.

30-LB (13.6-KG), 5-GAL (19-L) CONTAINER OF GASOLINE!

DANGEROUS IN-FLIGHT SERVICE!

November 12, 1921
Heart-Stopping Gas Pumping

Less than 20 years after the Wrights took flight, pilots called "barnstormers" were entertaining the masses with their dangerous aerial stunts. Barnstormer Wesley May performed the first ever midair refueling by pulling himself and a 30-lb (13.6-kg) container of gasoline up from the wing of one biplane onto another. Refueling nowadays is much more practical.

1930s
Business Is Booming

In the thirties, the American aviation industry saw a transition from carrying mostly mail to carrying passengers. In the year 1930, there were only 6,000 passengers, but by the end of the decade, there were more than 1.2 million flying annually.

Some early passenger planes had wicker seats!

When an aircraft nears the speed of sound in humid atmospheres, it drastically changes the pressure and temperature to create a "vapor cone."

FIRST TO TRAVEL FASTER THAN THE SPEED OF SOUND!

October 14, 1947
Breaking Barriers

U.S. Air Force Captain Charles "Chuck" Yeager was the first person to travel faster than the speed of sound, creating a sonic boom over the Mojave Desert in California. Believe it or not, the speed of sound changes with altitude! Yeager broke the sound barrier flying 700 mph (1,127 kmph) at 43,000 ft (13,000 m) above sea level. To do the same at sea level would require a speed of 761 mph (1,225 kmph).

GLAMOROUS GLENNIS

Captain Chuck Yeager with the plane used to break the sound barrier, the Bell X-1 *Glamorous Glennis* (named after his wife).

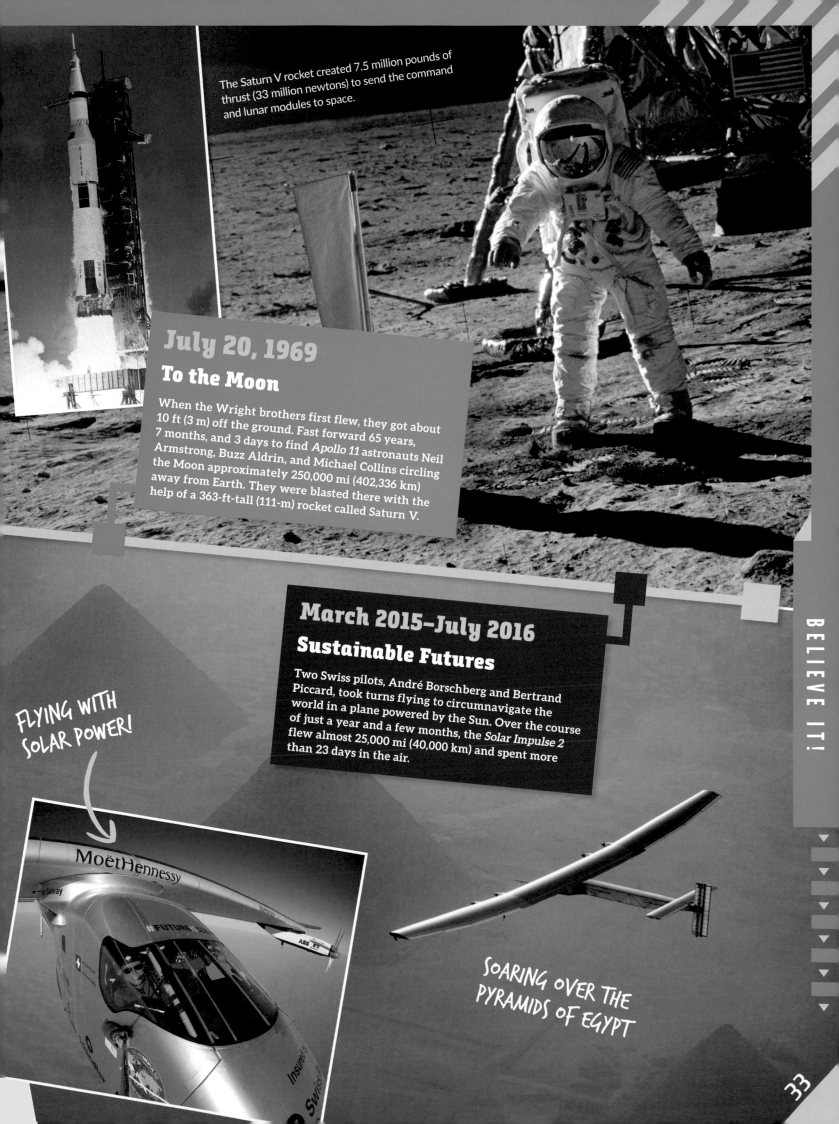

The Saturn V rocket created 7.5 million pounds of thrust (33 million newtons) to send the command and lunar modules to space.

July 20, 1969
To the Moon

When the Wright brothers first flew, they got about 10 ft (3 m) off the ground. Fast forward 65 years, 7 months, and 3 days to find *Apollo 11* astronauts Neil Armstrong, Buzz Aldrin, and Michael Collins circling the Moon approximately 250,000 mi (402,336 km) away from Earth. They were blasted there with the help of a 363-ft-tall (111-m) rocket called Saturn V.

March 2015–July 2016
Sustainable Futures

Two Swiss pilots, André Borschberg and Bertrand Piccard, took turns flying to circumnavigate the world in a plane powered by the Sun. Over the course of just a year and a few months, the *Solar Impulse 2* flew almost 25,000 mi (40,000 km) and spent more than 23 days in the air.

FLYING WITH SOLAR POWER!

SOARING OVER THE PYRAMIDS OF EGYPT

JAR HEAD

> In 1841, Portugal's very first serial killer Diogo Alves's head was severed from his body after execution and preserved in a jar for scientists to study—and it's still on display!

University of Lisbon's Faculty of Medicine once researched the pickled head when phrenology was first popularized in the 19th century. Although they didn't identify criminal personality traits by the shape of his head, Alves, who murdered an estimated 70 people between 1836 and 1839, peacefully watches over the university's anatomical theatre to this day.

HOOKED

» Out of devotion, a man hangs fruit and holy water from his flesh using hooks during the Aadi Festival in Tamil Nadu, India. The Hindu celebration occurs between mid-July and mid-August, marking the start of the monsoon season. Several smaller festivals occur during the holy month, but the most prominent is "Aadi Perukku," which honors the life-giving properties of water.

ACTION BRIDE ▶ When Sarah Ray's father and grandparents were involved in a car crash on the way to her wedding reception in Clarksville, Tennessee, the off-duty paramedic responded by rushing to the scene of the accident in her wedding dress.

PIZZA DIET ▶ New York City chef Pasquale Cozzolino lost 101 lb (46 kg) by eating pizza every day for seven months. He used to wear pants with a 48-in (122-cm) waist, but by adopting a pizza diet, his weight went from 370 lb (168 kg) to just under 270 lb (122 kg).

CLOUD SEEDING ▶ The Russian government spent $1.3 million on cloud seeding technology to ensure perfect weather in Moscow for its 2016 May Day celebrations. The process involved spraying a solution of granulated carbon dioxide, liquid nitrogen, and cement from an airplane to encourage clouds to release precipitation before they reached the city. When the same method was used for Russia Day 2008, the cement dropped from an airplane failed to fragment as planned when falling through the air and instead crashed as a solid lump through the roof of a Moscow home.

GOLDEN PILLOW ▶ Dutch inventor Thijs van der Hilst has created a $57,000 pillow. The luxury pillow is made of silk, Egyptian cotton, and 24-karat gold fabric, while its zipper is studded with four diamonds and a large sapphire. By using 3-D scans and an algorithm, he can design a pillow that perfectly fits each customer's upper body shape.

An accident at a local factory caused several tons of pink fruit juice to flood the streets of the Russian town of Lebedyan in April 2017 and flow into the Don River.

PATIENCE REWARDED ▶ Photographer Louis-Marie Préau waited on a riverbed for two to three hours a night for four years to get the perfect picture of a beaver. Wearing snorkeling gear and weights to keep him anchored to the bottom of the river, he lay motionless night after night in the same spot in the Loire region of western France.

VIDEO TOOTHBRUSH ▶ Dr. Craig S. Kohler, a dentist from Wilmette, Illinois, has invented a high-tech toothbrush that allows users to stream and review film of the insides of their mouths as they brush. The Prophix brush employs Wi-Fi and Bluetooth technology to send video to smartphones so that users can monitor their oral health.

DEALERSHIP BIRTH ▶ Amanda Sherman gave birth at an auto dealership in South Hills, Pennsylvania, while the oil in her husband's pickup truck was being changed. She went to the restroom to use the toilet, but three minutes later she was holding daughter Heather Lynn. She was then helped by husband Adam and a registered nurse who happened to be a customer in the shop at the time.

HITLER'S PHONE ▶ Adolf Hitler's personal telephone, engraved with his name and found in the Berlin bunker where he committed suicide in 1945, sold at auction in Maryland in 2017 for $243,000. The red phone was used by the Nazi leader to issue many of his deadly orders during World War II.

BROTHERLY LOVE ▷ Elias Blomdahl, a seven-year-old boy from Kvelia, Norway, extracted a loose tooth by tying one end of a piece of string to it and the other end to the handlebars of a motocross bike. He then asked his older brother Henning to ride past, and when he did, the tooth flew out.

BULLET SURPRISE ▶ Michael Blevins, of Deltona, Florida, did not realize that he had accidentally shot himself in the arm while cleaning his gun until he changed his long-sleeved shirt two days later and noticed the bullet's entry and exit wounds.

PET PERFORMANCES ▷ Actors Alex Bailey and Krõõt Juurak travel around Austria, Germany, and the United Kingdom putting on theatrical shows exclusively for pets. By crawling around on all fours and making nonhuman noises, they try to encourage the animals to participate in the performance. Although cats usually leave the room first, they always return and make the best audiences.

GLOBETROTTING DUCK ▶
An oversized rubber duck that was mysteriously stolen from outside Jennifer Troiano's home in Hampton, New Hampshire, in 2011 was returned to her in 2016, along with a suitcase full of mementos from the bath toy's adventures in 20 different countries and numerous U.S. cities. During Gale Ducky's five-year absence, her unknown abductor posted pictures of her travels to Europe, Africa, and Asia on Ducky's own Facebook page.

IMPERSONATED MOTHER ▷
In Smith Falls, Ontario, Canada, a 39-year-old woman was charged with impersonating her 73-year-old mother so that she could take her driving test for her. The instructor's suspicions were aroused by the young candidate's strange wig, glasses, and clothes.

PEOPLE WALKER ▶ Chuck McCarthy charges $7 per mile (1.6 km) to walk people around the streets of Los Angeles, listening to their problems or simply making conversation. The enterprise has proven so successful that he has hired five more people walkers to cover other areas of the city. He originally considered walking dogs to make money but didn't want to pick up dog poop.

STRESS RELIEF ▷ For about $65, over-stressed Japanese office workers can hire a handsome man to wipe away their tears. They can select from six such men from Tokyo-based company Ikemeso Danshi.

THE Mapparium

> **You can stand in the middle of Earth inside a library in Boston, Massachusetts!**

The Mapparium at Mary Baker Eddy Library is a three-story, stained-glass globe with a 30-ft-long (9.1-m) bridge going through the center. The bridge, built in 1935, gives visitors a perspective impossible to recreate with flat maps, which are generally inaccurate when it comes to the size and scale of landmasses. The continents on the Mapparium, however, are reproduced perfectly to scale. Fun fact: The Mapparium is a whispering gallery, meaning two people can whisper at opposite ends of the bridge and hear each other loud and clear!

YOUR UPLOADS

Crafted Corpse

Canadian textile artist Shanell Papp sent us these photos of her life-size needlework version of a human body. Titled *LAB*, the impressive piece includes a skeleton stuffed with organs, as well as unseen details like bone marrow and half-digested food in the stomach—all created with yarn!

NAKED WALK ▶ A man who could not pay his drinks bill in Prerov, Czech Republic, left his clothes at the bar as collateral and, in the middle of the day, walked across town naked—apart from a pair of socks—to obtain some cash.

COFFIN ARRIVAL ▶ New Jersey student Megan Flaherty, 17, arrived at Pennsauken High School's junior prom in an open coffin. As the coffin slid out the back of a hearse, Flaherty stepped out on the arm of her date. She hopes to become a funeral director one day.

TOUCH PLAY ▶ Kevin Rhomberg, a left fielder with the Cleveland Indians baseball team in the early 1980s, had a superstition whereby if somebody touched him, he had to touch that person back. An umpire once had to halt a game between the Indians and the New York Yankees because the Yankees players refused to stop touching Rhomberg.

Pink Mountain

▶ Mount Yoshino in Japan is home to 30,000 flowering cherry trees, earning it the nickname "The Pink Mountain."

For centuries, the Japanese have appreciated the cherry, or "sakura," tree blossoms, which last only a week or so and signal the start of warm spring weather. The traditional custom of viewing the delicate flowers is known as "hanami."

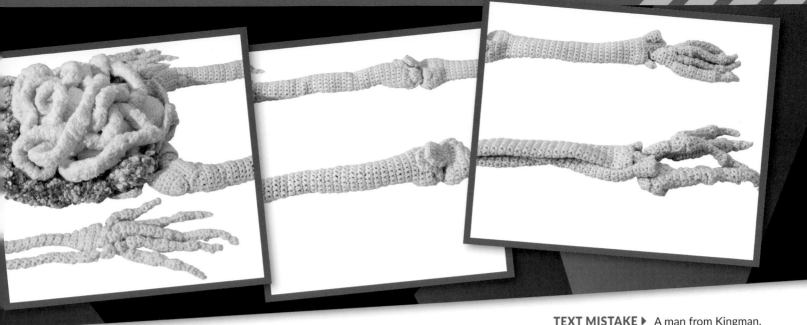

HOCKEY SUPERSTITIONS ▶ Before every game, former Montreal Canadiens hockey goaltender Patrick Roy would skate toward the net at full speed before turning around at the last second because he believed it made the goal shrink. He also used to talk to the goalposts during a game, especially after they made a save for him.

DANCING COP ▶ Kunwar Ranjeet Singh, a traffic cop in Indore, India, dances his way through his daily work routines at one of the city's busiest intersections. The self-confessed Michael Jackson fan manages the traffic with a range of dance moves, including the moonwalk. He has become so popular that people sometimes drive past his intersection just to see him in action.

TEXT MISTAKE ▶ A man from Kingman, Arizona, was arrested after he sent a text message about a drug deal to his parole officer by mistake.

HEALTH PROBLEM ▶ About 70 staff members of the New Mexico Department of Health became gastrointestinally sick after their 2016 Christmas party in Santa Fe.

MUMMIFIED CHAMELEON!

MOWER MAYHEM ▶ A 67-year-old man from Bristol, Vermont, was arrested on suspicion of driving a lawnmower while under the influence of drugs. He was stopped after driving the John Deere mower down the town's main street.

ODD DONATIONS ▶ Among the items handed in to U.K. charity shops in December 2016 were a sheep's head, a prosthetic leg, a live ferret, and a ventriloquist's dummy.

SUPERHERO RESCUE ▶ When a kitesurfer got into trouble in the sea off West Sussex, England, he was rescued by two men dressed as Batman and Robin. Derren Guile (Batman) and David Schneider (Robin) had been kayaking in their costumes for a Superhero Paddle event when they spotted the kitesurfer being dragged helplessly across the beach.

MACABRE MUMMIFICATION

≫ A chameleon in India was mummified alive by the intense tropical sun while trying to drink from a water pipe that had been turned off. The thirsty reptile died while desperately clutching the spigot and was then quickly mummified by the blazing sun, its dried body preserved by ants that ate its innards.

SOME CORPSES STILL HAVE THEIR HAIR AND SKIN INTACT!

NAZCA
SKELETONS

> Just 20 mi (32.2 km) south of the city of Nazca, Peru, lies an ancient burial ground with well-preserved mummies dating back roughly 1,000 years.

Chauchilla Cemetery exhibits corpses and heads from the 9th century and only recently has been restored as close to its original state as possible—it was a victim of Peruvian grave robbers until government protection in 1997. The bodies are preserved so well because of the dry climate of the Peruvian Desert, as well as the burial practices used, which include clothing the bodies in cotton and painting them with resin. Mysteriously, many of the skulls have holes drilled into the back, and some even have rope threaded through the holes, but no one is sure why.

BABY BLUES

» Hitachi Seaside Park in Hitachinaka, Ibaraki Prefecture, Japan, boasts a host of seasonal flowers that attract visitors from all over the world, but between April and May, an astonishing 4.5 million nemophila flowers steal the show. Also known as "baby blue eyes," the flowers cover the hills, turning the ground into the color of the sky.

SHAKING ISLAND ▶ The currents surging through the Nakwakto Rapids in the narrow entrance to Seymour Inlet, off the coast of British Columbia, Canada, are so strong at peak tides, sometimes reaching 20 mph (32 kmph), that they cause a small island in the middle of the inlet to shake. Consequently, the island, Turret Rock, is also known as Tremble Island.

SHORT ESCALATOR ▶ The Puchicalator, a down escalator in the basement level of More's Department Store in Kawasaki, Japan, has only five steps and a descent of just 32.8 in (83.4 cm).

RUNWAY GRAVES ▶ Beneath the tarmac on Runway 10 at Savannah International Airport, Georgia, lie the graves of Richard and Catherine Dotson, who both died in the late 19th century—nearly two decades before the Wright brothers completed their first flight. While other bodies in the graveyard were moved to accommodate the expanding airport, the Dotson family refused permission, and now the couple's final resting place is marked by two flat headstones inserted into the runway, only yards from where planes take off and land.

LOST CITY ▶ English history fan Stuart Wilson spent his life savings of $50,000 to buy a field in South Wales, and when he dug it up, he found the buried remains of a lost city, Trellech, which in the 13th century had a population of 10,000 people, making it one of the biggest cities in Britain.

GOLDFISH FOR HIRE ▶ Hotel Charleroi Airport in Belgium rents a goldfish in a bowl to lonely guests for $4.17 a night.

MUMMIFIED HAND ▶ Visitors to the basement of St. Michan's Church, Dublin, Ireland, can lightly shake the mummified hand of an 800-year-old crusader. The wooden coffin in which his body is kept has disintegrated over the centuries, allowing his right hand to protrude. Touching his desiccated fingers is said to bring good luck.

WORLD MAP ▶ Working until his death at age 81, farmer Søren Poulsen spent 25 years building Verdenskortet, a scale map of the world made from stones and grass, on land at Lake Klejtrup, Denmark. Some of the stones that he single-handedly moved to the site weigh more than 2 tons, and his map covers an area of more than 43,000 sq ft (4,000 sq m).

ONLY INHABITANT ▶ In 1989, Mauro Morandi's run-down catamaran was carried to Budelli, a small Italian island in the Mediterranean Sea between Corsica and Sardinia—and he has been the island's only resident ever since.

$10,000 DRINK ▶ A young Chinese man paid $10,000 for a small shot of whiskey at the luxury Waldhaus Hotel in St. Moritz, Switzerland. The 0.68-fl oz (2-centiliter) measure came from a prized 1878 bottle of Macallan, part of the hotel's collection of 2,500 different whiskies.

DEVIL FEARS ▶ Babies in Bali, Indonesia, are not allowed to touch the ground for the first three months of their life in order to prevent the devil penetrating their soul. They are carried everywhere until a priest performs a purifying ceremony, Tigang Sasih, at which their feet finally touch the ground for the first time.

TUDOR DEATHS

 IN TUDOR ENGLAND, DEATH CAME KNOCKING ON PEOPLE'S DOORS ALL TOO OFTEN AND ACCIDENTS COULD HAPPEN AT ANY TIME. HERE ARE SOME RATHER ODD WAYS TO GO...

In 1543, Elizabeth Browne was **CRUSHED TO DEATH** after the rope suspending four slabs of smoked **BACON** in the chimney above her broke.

On June 2, 1523, Cambridge baker George Duncan went out to use the **BATHROOM** but fell in backward, got stuck, and the stench **SUFFOCATED** him.

 In 1563, two women named **AGNES** were killed by bears—one by a **PET BEAR** when it broke loose and the other by a **RUNAWAY BEAR**.

 Fifty-six accidental deaths from people **STANDING** too close to **ARCHERY TARGETS** were reported during the Tudor period.

In 1557, a man walking through the fields in Lincolnshire was gored to death by a **MAD COW**. The victim's name? **ROBERT CALF**.

YIN YANG TOFU

» In May 2017, 30 cooks created a giant Tai Chi diagram made out of tofu! The sizeable snack measured about 26 ft (8 m) in diameter, weighed 5 tons, and was eaten in an hour to celebrate a Taoist festival.

DAILY SWIM ▶
To avoid the busy rush-hour traffic in Munich, Germany, Benjamin David swims to work each day. He leaves his waterfront apartment, jumps into the Isar River, and swims 1.2 mi (2 km) to his workplace, carrying his laptop, cell phone, and clothes in a waterproof bag. The bag is also designed to be a buoyancy aid so that he can simply float downstream if he feels tired. His daily commute takes him about half an hour.

PERSISTENT CLOCK ▶ An alarm clock owned by Jerry Lynn rang once a day, every day, inside the wall vent of his home in Ross Township, Pennsylvania, for 13 years. While trying to pass a TV cable through a hole in the wall in 2004, he accidentally dropped the clock down the vent and was unable to retrieve it. From then until it was finally pulled out by a specialist company in 2017, the clock went off daily at 6:50 p.m. (during standard time) or 7:50 p.m. (during daylight saving time), its battery never running out over all those years.

ROTTING CORPSE ▶ An elderly woman kept the rotting body of her son in the attic bedroom of her home in Brooklyn, New York, for eight years. Her son was in his forties when he died, but his body was only discovered when his mother was taken to the hospital following a fall.

RING CLUE ▶ A man who robbed a woman in her shop in Aba, Nigeria, made the mistake of still wearing her distinctive gold wedding ring on his index finger when he later stood before her in an identity lineup at a police station.

SPEED DETERRENT ▶ On weekends and holidays, Kelly Tufts deters speeding drivers by placing an aluminum cutout of a police patrol car at the end of his driveway in Lakeville, Massachusetts. He got the life-size Ford Crown Victoria sign from a friend who owned a salvage yard.

2,000 IVANS ▶ On July 30, 2017, a total of 2,325 people with the first name Ivan gathered in the town of Kupres, Bosnia and Herzegovina, beating the previous world record of 1,096 Mohammeds gathered in one place.

STOLEN TAXI ▶
After stealing a taxi in Philadelphia, Pennsylvania, a 65-year-old woman stopped to pick up a fare before she was finally arrested.

SLOW NUGGETS ▶ A customer at a drive-thru restaurant in Waco, Texas, called 911 to complain that it was taking too long to deliver her order of chicken nuggets.

SUSPECTED VAMPIRE ▶ Over the course of a decade, farmer George Brown, of Exeter, Rhode Island, lost his wife Mary and daughters Mary and Mercy to the same illness, now known as tuberculosis. In 1892, with son Edwin displaying similar symptoms, George and the villagers exhumed the three women's bodies to determine whether they were vampires preying on the family. The two Marys had been reduced to bones, but Mercy was suspiciously well-preserved, so, decreeing that she must be a vampire, the villagers cut out her heart, burned it, and mixed the ashes with water for the sick Edwin to drink. He died two months later.

CORN THERMOMETER ▶
Sanmenxia City, China, is home to a titan-sized, working vegetable thermometer. Standing 26 ft (8 m) tall, the corn-shaped instrument measures the internal and external temperature of a nearby home inside a cave.

GREASE LIGHTNING

> In November 1931, two women had slabs of bacon tied to their feet in Chehalis, Washington, to grease a massive pan used to cook a 7,200-egg omelette!

Holding a giant spatula for balance, the skillet skaters soared across the surface, which was 8 ft (2.4 m) in diameter.

REAL BACON!

CAN'T BE THAMED

This stunt was attempted once before in Los Angeles by someone else in 2006 but unfortunately ended in a crash.

❯ **On October 5, 2017, Travis Pastrana successfully completed the world's first barge-to-barge motorcycle backflip over the Thames River in London, England.**

The action sport icon and Nitro Circus ringleader battled high winds and rough waters as he flew between the two vessels, with the iconic O2 Arena rising in the background.

LATE RETURN ▶ A book of short stories titled *40 Minutes Late* was returned to San Francisco Public Library 100 years late. Phoebe Marsh Dickenson Webb had checked it out when she was 83, but died a week before it was due to be returned. Her great-grandchildren returned it a century later in 2017, by which time it would have racked up a $3,650 fine, but thanks to an amnesty program there was no charge.

ANCIENT FILLINGS ▶ Scientists discovered a set of dental fillings inside a pair of 13,000-year-old human front teeth near Lucca, Italy. The ancient fillings were made of bitumen, a semi-solid form of petroleum. Although bitumen is now commonly used in road construction and as a roof sealant, it was probably used then as an antiseptic.

MOVIE PROP ▶ When Darcy Fox received a badly damaged $20 bill from an ATM in Seattle, Washington, she studied it more closely and realized it was a movie prop. Instead of "United States of America," the fake bill read "Motion Picture Use Only." The bank later agreed to give her a real $20 bill.

EXTENDED FAMILY ▶ Sindhutai Sapkal has devoted over 40 years of her life to raising more than 1,400 abandoned children in her orphanages in Pune, India. Her work has earned her 750 awards and the title "Mother of Orphans."

GROWTH SPURT

≫ In January 2017, Mandy Atkinson of Coffs Harbour, Australia, found a strawberry with leaves growing on its surface. The phenomena, known as "vivipary," causes seeds to germinate while still attached to the mother plant. They sprout and leaves eventually breach the surface, giving it a feathery appearance. Although quite common in some plants, vivipary is rare in strawberries.

OIL RESCUE ▶ After dropping his cell phone down a narrow gap between two rocks on a jetty at Narragansett, Rhode Island, a man tried to retrieve it, only to become stuck headfirst. It took fire crews 2.5 hours to free him, which they eventually did with olive oil before the tide came in.

WALLET RETURNED ▶ A wallet belonging to Courtney Connolly that was stolen from her car in Wellfleet, Massachusetts, in 2009 was returned to her eight years later, and it still contained all of her cash—$141.

EIGHT WHEELIN' ▶ Massachusetts man Erik Kondo has modified a longboard in a way that allows him to ride it while in his wheelchair. By adding to the skateboard an electric motor and rails that lock his chair's wheels in place, Kondo can glide along on sidewalks and in skate parks with relative ease. He says he enjoys the experience because it allows him to use his balance to steer, rather than his hands.

MOLASSES FLOOD

> During the Great Molasses Flood of 1919, 21 people were killed as sticky molasses rushed through Boston at 35 mph (56.3 kmph).

In one of the world's most deadly food fatalities, a tank of molasses burst due to a quick change in temperature, and as much as 2.3 million gal (8.7 million L) exploded into the streets. Onlookers described it as an 8-ft-high (2.4-m) tidal wave that picked people up and carried them as if they were surfing. The nearby elevated railway's steel girders were even destroyed by the sticky mass, and to this day, residents claim you can still smell molasses at the site on hot days.

THROWING KNIVES!

> A master of the impalement arts, The Great Throwdini is the only person in the world known to successfully perform the Veiled Double Wheel of Death stunt—throwing knives onto a spinning wheel that has two people, hidden by a paper curtain, holding on.

Otherwise known as the Reverend Doctor David Adamovich, The Great Throwdini was introduced to knife-throwing by chance at the age of 50. Within five years, he was winning national and world championships and joined a circus. Now at 71 years old, Throwdini has more than 40 knife-throwing records under his belt for speed, distance, and accuracy—and he shows no signs of slowing down. Ripley's visited him to witness his performance of the Veiled Double Wheel of Death and ask him some questions about his career in the impalement arts.

Step 2: After a paper veil is placed in front of the assistants, Throwdini spins the Wheel and throws the knives!

Q *Have you ever missed your target?*

A Yes. Remember—I aim to miss! All kidding aside, with all those knives and at that speed, sometimes the margin of error is pushed to its limit. As a result, I've scraped my assistant on several occasions. Never had to pull a knife out of what you'd consider a stab.

Q *Is there a special kind of knife you use to perform your stunts?*

A My "bread and butter" knife used for most of my performance stunts and world records is "The Great Throwdini 'Signature Series' Professional Throwing Knife." It is a double-edged, diamond-shaped, 14-in (35.6-cm) knife weighing 12 oz (0.34 kg).

Q *When the wheel is spinning, how do you know when to throw the knives?*

A The precise "secret" to the Veiled Wheel of Death is understanding the timing of the throw against the paper veil. When I perform an unveiled Wheel, it takes about 1 second for the wheel to spin, and I throw two knives per second. Veiled is a bit more difficult, and even more so with two assistants behind the paper veil. The Double Veiled Wheel of Death spins slightly slower, so I take a fraction of a second longer to throw the knives.

Step 1: Two brave assistants, Lynn and Peggy, don fencing masks and climb aboard the Wheel of Death.

Step 3: The curtain is removed to reveal the knives stuck firmly into the Wheel, with both Lynn and Peggy unharmed.

Q *How did you convince people to get on the wheel?*

A It wasn't a matter of convincing. They all accept and understand each component of the act before I ever throw the first knife around any of them. There's a mutual trust we have in each other, very much like the flyer and catcher in a trapeze act. Each is a vital component of the performance. Without my assistant, there is no act.

Q *How long did you practice knife-throwing before bringing people into the mix?*

A I competed with the objective of hitting a bull's-eye for five years. Then, when switching over from competition to the impalement arts, my focus went from aiming-to-hit to aiming-to-miss! An old-time performer once said, with reference to throwing knives around human targets, "Aim to miss—they last a lot longer that way."

Q *Is there anything else about knife-throwing that you want people to know?*

A Yes, it's not a joke nor is it to be taken lightly. It's a serious and potentially dangerous circus act that requires a significant level of skill to be performed safely. Anyone considering the impalement arts should do so with the utmost respect for their assistant.

Ripley's EXCLUSIVE

Veiled Double
WHEEL OF DEATH

SPIKE CAN HOLD
WOODEN SPATULAS,
BUTCHER KNIVES,
AND MARKERS!

STAINLESS STEEL

Get a Grip

> A new artist has taken social media by storm, selling original art pieces at auction for hundreds of dollars. Meet Spike the stag beetle.

Owner Mandy, an American English teacher currently living in Japan, says beetles are common, low-maintenance pets in Japan and that it all started when she began documenting how Spike grabs onto objects, no matter what they are, if they're put in front of him. Using his strong mandibles, Spike can hold wooden spatulas, butcher knives, and of course, markers. Although the amateur artist started from humble beginnings, his fan base has grown to an astonishing 85,000 Twitter followers and 35,000 Instagram followers.

ROTATE AND BALANCE ▶ Michael Grab of Canada created a rock-balancing masterpiece in a shopping mall in Shanghai, China. Using absolutely no glue, cement, or nails, Grab vertically stacked rocks that held a life-size car at the top.

HIGHWIRE WEDDING ▶
Circus acrobats Mustafa Danguir and Anna Lebedeva got married on a narrow highwire 30 ft (9 m) above the ground during a show in Houston, Texas. The groom, wearing a white tuxedo, arrived by camel, while the bride, in veil and gown, entered the ring on a horse. After climbing ladders at either end, they walked to the center of the wire where they exchanged vows and rings.

UNLIKELY ROMANCE ▶ A year after 82-year-old Martha Potu, from North Sulawesi, Indonesia, accidentally phoned a complete stranger, 28-year-old warehouse worker Sofian Loho Dandel, she married him! The misdialed call conversation lasted nearly an hour, and afterward they kept in touch before Dandel traveled 75 mi (120 km) to meet his new love in person—and discovered that she was 54 years his senior. Undeterred, they married on February 18, 2017, having won over their respective families.

BULLDOZER BATTLE ▶
When workers from two rival construction companies in Hebei Province, China, had a falling out, they took to the streets for a brawl with bulldozers. At least six bulldozers took part in the fight, ramming each other with their shovels. Two bulldozers were toppled over and two drivers were injured in the battle, which only ended when police officers arrived on the scene.

INSURANCE SCAM ▶
A 30-year-old Vietnamese woman hired a friend to cut off her left hand and foot so she could claim a $180,000 health insurance payout. The woman wanted her injuries to make it look as if she had been hit by a train, so she paid her friend $2,200 to sever her limbs, but suspicious investigators found that her business was struggling and that she had bought a large health insurance policy shortly before the fake accident. The police decided not to charge either her or her accomplice with fraud because it would be difficult to find an appropriate law to charge the pair for this kind of fraud.

CART CARAVAN ▶ For years, homeless woman Sonia Gonzalez hauled a block-long caravan of overstuffed shopping carts around New York City. A habitual hoarder, she would collect recyclables plus other items she found on the street and load them into her collection of 20 grocery carts, 14 laundry carts, eight suitcases, two large crates, and one dolly. It would take her an hour just to move them all 20 ft (6 m). Each night, she made her bed somewhere in the carts.

GOLD SUSPECT ▶ A man arrested on suspicion of driving under the influence in Berkeley, California, had spray-painted himself gold from head to toe. A witness to three collisions on Interstate 80 had described the erratic driver as "gold," and when police caught up with 21-year-old Damaj Cook, they found that he lived up to the description, with his hair, face, arms, hands, feet, T-shirt, and shoes all sprayed gold. Inside the car, even the steering wheel was stained with gold spray paint.

EXTREME SHOPPING

» For two days in August 2017, a pop-up shop provided jackets, hoodies, socks, and other outerwear to around 70 people for free, but for one price—you had to climb 300 ft (61.4 m) up a sheer mountain face. The Cliffside Shop, as it was called, was installed on the Bastille, Eldorado Canyon outside Boulder, Colorado, and it took roughly six weeks to create the 6 × 10-ft (1.8 × 3-m) structure that dangled precariously from the cliff.

CLIFFSIDE SHOP

NEPTUNES

> Using specially designed instruments, Danish group AquaSonic is the first ensemble to perform music underwater and does so without using breathing apparatuses!

Members, who must resurface frequently to breathe, are submerged in water-filled tanks with hydrophones, microphones that pick up the band's haunting concertos.

HUMAN CATTLE ▶ People with the psychological disorder boanthropy believe themselves to be cows or oxen and may be seen crawling on all fours, eating grass. Scientists believe the disorder could originate in a dream before consuming the cognizant mind, too.

CRUEL IRONY ▶ American entrepreneur Gary Kremen, the founder of online dating site Match.com, lost his girlfriend to a man she met on Match.com. Although it hurt Kremen at the time, it proved to him that the site worked.

TANK TREASURE ▶ Military enthusiast Nick Mead, from Northamptonshire, England, bought an ex-Iraqi Army tank on eBay for $40,000, and when he opened one of its fuel tanks, he found five gold bars worth an estimated total of more than $2 million. The tank's previous owner had replaced its tracks and fixed its engine without ever discovering the treasure inside.

CAR COLORING ▶ To keep children entertained on long journeys, U.S. auto rental company Hertz created a car that has its interior seats, doors, and ceiling completely upholstered in coloring book print, featuring popular designs such as houses, animals, and flowers.

VAGUE ADDRESS ▶ A letter was successfully delivered in just a few days to Antony Wren, of Suffolk, England, even though the address on the envelope was nothing more precise than "somewhere near the sea in Suffolk."

HOLDING HANDS ▶ Identical twins Rowan and Blake Lampshire, from Oxfordshire, England, kept each other alive by cuddling and holding hands in mom Hayley's womb for up to 34 weeks. The twins were suffering from a rare condition where they shared an amniotic sac instead of having one each, meaning that if they moved around in the womb, their umbilical cords could have become tangled, cutting off their food and oxygen supply. The only way they could survive was to stay still, which, as regular scans showed, they did by holding hands.

POOP TIME ▶ All mammals— including humans, elephants, and mice—take an average of just 12 seconds to poop. This is primarily to guard against predators, which can be attracted by the smell of body waste.

DINOSAUR FOOTPRINT ▶ A recently discovered dinosaur footprint in Western Australia, measured 5.75 ft (1.8 m) long—the height of an average man. The footprint belonged to a sauropod, an order of long-necked, plant-eating dinosaurs, that would have stood nearly 18 ft (5.5 m) tall at the hips.

TWIN FLIGHTS ▶ Twin brothers Jeremy and Nick Hart retired as British Airways pilots by landing their final flights 30 seconds apart at London's Heathrow Airport on September 28, 2017.

LOST RING ▶ Jan Faircloth Kentros, of Peabody, Massachusetts, had her missing class ring returned to her in 2017, 46 years after her then-boyfriend lost it. Decades after the ring vanished in 1971, someone at Bishop Fenwick High School discovered it near the school's athletic track. School staff then looked through old yearbooks to track down the original owner, then known as Janet Faircloth, from the "JMF" initials engraved inside the ring. Her boyfriend has obviously been forgiven, because he has been her husband for more than 40 years.

BURROWING MAGGOTS ▶ When Marcus Johnstone of Bayou Vista, Texas, complained of pain and discomfort around his groin area, surgeons discovered two parasitic botfly larvae burrowing under the skin of his scrotum. The botfly had laid its eggs on a mosquito, and when that mosquito had bitten Johnstone, the parasite's eggs entered his body through the wound before developing into maggots.

TIMELY DEATH ▶ Jimmy Newell, of Devon, England, was born at exactly noon on October 11, 1913, and died at the same time on October 11, 2016—his 103rd birthday.

HOT
LAVA!

VOLCANO
Blues

> The lava at Indonesia's Kawah Ijen volcano appears to glow bright blue at night!

During the day, Kawah Ijen looks like a typical volcano, but when the sun goes down it becomes dark enough to witness the blue flames caused by high levels of sulfuric gas combusting when it touches the air surrounding the lava, the reaction causing air temperatures to skyrocket to 680°F (360°C) or more. Once the lava and sulfur have mixed, cooled, and hardened into yellow rock, workers brave the heat and fumes to collect the yellow rocks to sell down the mountain.

COCKROACH BREAD ▶ Brazilian food scientists Andressa Lucas and Lauren Oliveira have developed a flour made from cockroaches and have used it to bake bread. The insects—from a species called the lobster roach (*Nauphoeta cinerea*)—are sourced from a specialized breeder who only feeds them fruit and vegetables. The cockroach flour contains 40 percent more protein than regular wheat flour.

COOKIE BEER ▶ The Veil Brewing Company, of Richmond, Virginia, created Oreo-flavored beer. Hornswoggler Oreo is a chocolate milk stout that has been brewed with hundreds of pounds of Oreo cookies and even contains chunks of icing.

TALL SLIDE ▶ The Kilimanjaro water slide at the Aldeia das Águas Park Resort in Barra Do Piraí, Brazil, has a drop of 164 ft (50 m)—just 3 ft (0.9 m) less than the height of Niagara Falls. Riders reach speeds of nearly 60 mph (96 kmph) on their descent. On average, one in 20 people change their minds about riding the slide when they reach the top and look down.

CHANGING COURSE ▶ For most of the year, the Tonlé Sap River in Cambodia runs south from Tonlé Sap Lake to the larger Mekong River. But during summer monsoon rains, the Mekong River rises and its floodwaters push up the Tonlé Sap, forcing it to reverse its course and flow north instead.

SOURDOUGH HOTEL ▶ People in Stockholm, Sweden, who like to make their own bread can leave their precious sourdough at a special hotel while they are away on vacation, where it will be looked after for about $20 a week until it is able to be collected. The hotel promises to keep the dough in good shape by feeding it water and flour and giving it regular massages. If cared for properly, sourdough can last for more than 40 years.

BURIED JEEP ▶ A Jeep Wagoneer was stuck inside a sand dune in Truro, Massachusetts, for 40 years before finally being removed in 2017. The vehicle had been parked in a wooden shed on Ballston Beach in the 1970s, but over the decades, high winds had buried it in sand.

PALATIAL BLOCK ▶ Vladimir Chaika spent 15 years converting the staircase on the first three floors of his stark, Communist-era apartment block in Kiev, Ukraine, into a replica of an elegant 18th-century Russian palace. The retired construction worker covered the once gray walls and ceilings with reproductions of beautiful portrait paintings, ornate cherubs and flowers, and stylish plaster decorations. A perfectionist, Chaika redid the ceiling of the first floor four times before he was satisfied with it.

CHURCH BAR ▶ The residents of Brielen, Belgium, used to meet up for a beer following Sunday mass, but when the last bar in the village closed down, the local priest decided to keep the tradition going by turning the church into a bar. So as soon as the service is over, wooden chairs and tables with white cloths are brought out and a bar is set up—for churchgoers only.

LUCKY CATS ▶ The Gotokuji temple in Tokyo, Japan, is filled with more than 1,000 red and white cat figurines, which are supposed to bring good luck and happiness. Visitors to the Buddhist temple are encouraged to buy a figurine of the cat doll, Maneki Neko, and to return it as a sign of gratitude once their wishes have been fulfilled.

BANANA SPLIT ▶ At the 2017 Feast of the Senses Festival, the residents of Innisfail, Queensland, Australia, made a banana split that was more than 26,371 ft (8,040 m) long. Hundreds of volunteers spent almost 12 hours preparing the enormous dessert, which contained 40,000 bananas, 550 gal (2,500 l) of ice cream, and 440 gal (2,000 l) of topping.

BADGER DAMAGE ▶ The tiny village of Shingle Street, Suffolk, England, was virtually cut off from the outside world in April 2017 by a family of badgers who burrowed under a road, causing a huge sinkhole to open up. The road was the only one leading in and out of the village, and while small cars could get through, the village became temporarily inaccessible to delivery trucks.

SWINE STONE ▶
In April 2017, a strange exhibition debuted in Huaibei, China, with stones that looked just like slabs of pig flesh.

ROSE GROWERS ▶ Twenty-five million rose stems are flown out of Nairobi Airport every day, having been grown in huge nurseries in Kenya for export to customers all across Europe and Asia.

WINDING RIVER ▶ If all the bends in the 4,258-mi-long (6,853-km) Nile River were straightened out, it would flow from the Equator in Africa right up to the Scottish Highlands.

TROUT RIVER ▶
The lower Bow River running through Calgary, Alberta, Canada, is home to up to 2,500 brown and rainbow trout per mile.

KUNG FU NUNS ▶ Nuns at the Druk Amitabha Mountain nunnery in Nepal practice kung fu for two hours every day.

VERTICAL DROP ▶
Located on Baffin Island in the Canadian territory of Nunavut, Mount Thor has a sheer, vertical drop of 4,101 ft (1,250 m)—nearly four times the height of the Eiffel Tower—that angles inward at an average of 105 degrees.

DESERT
Billboards

❯ In early 2017, a unique billboard installation stretching alongside two Southern California roads "advertised" something totally bizarre—the local scenery.

Called *Visible Distance/Second Sight,* the outdoor exhibition was created by artist Jennifer Bolande, who wanted passersby to look twice at the neglected picturesque vistas. Bolande strategically placed the signs so that they camouflaged into the landscape, with some billboards aligning perfectly with the mountain range behind it.

1841

LAMAR

LAMAR

$25K TACO ENTRÉE

» In February 2017, the Grand Velas Los Cabos Resort in Cabo San Lucas, Mexico, gave the classic, simple, and low-cost Mexican taco an upgrade worth $25,000. Created by Chef Juan Licerio Alcala, the monstrosity consists of Kobe beef, caviar, chunks of lobster, black truffle-infused brie cheese, and 24-karat gold leaf. It's topped with a salsa infused with dried Morita chili peppers, tequila, and civet coffee (which is made from partially digested coffee cherries eaten by wild civets)—all served on a gold flake-infused corn tortilla.

SHORT PARADE ▶ In 2017, around 30 neighbors in Mequon, Wisconsin, held a 4th of July parade that stretched for only 264 ft (80 m) and lasted barely two minutes.

CAT WINE ▶ Businessman and cat lover Brandon Zavala, from Denver, Colorado, has developed a wine exclusively for cats. The founder of Apollo Peak wine has created a nonalcoholic drink that is a blend of organic catnip and water. Both the white and red varieties are colored with different types of beets.

BABY BOTTLES ▶ At Le Refuge des Fondus, a restaurant in the Montmartre region of Paris, customers are served wine in plastic baby bottles as a way to avoid paying the French tax on wine served in proper glasses.

CITY DOCUMENT ▶ From 1841 to 1994, aldermen in Halifax, Nova Scotia, Canada, signed their oath of office on the City of Halifax Aldermanic Scroll—a document that measures 21 ft (6.4 m) long.

MINE VORTEX ▶ The 1,722-ft-deep (525-m) Mir diamond mine in eastern Siberia has a diameter of nearly 1 mi (1.6 km). The vast crater creates such a powerful vortex that helicopters are banned from flying over it in case they are sucked down inside.

CHOCOLATE WATERFALL ▶ A 21-ft-tall (6.4-m) chocolate waterfall has been operating continuously inside the Candy Basket store in Portland, Oregon, since 1991, with 2,700 lb (1,226 kg) of chocolate cascading down the marble tower from top to bottom.

ROOFTOP GALLEON ▶ Unable to fulfill his dream of sailing around the world, carpenter Valeriy Vasilevich Kiku did the next best thing by building a replica of English sailor Sir Francis Drake's 16th-century galleon *The Golden Hind* on the roof of his workshop in Kupino, Russia. The towering wooden replica, which took more than six years to build, includes three masts, a crow's nest lookout point, captain's quarters, and a cargo hold. He hopes eventually to turn it into a museum to accommodate the dozens of smaller models of famous ships that he has built, ranging from Egyptian rowing boats to Russian cruisers.

SUN-COOKED CHICKEN ▶ Sila Sutharat, a street vendor from Phetchaburi, Thailand, cooks chicken with sunlight. He uses 1,000 mobile mirrors, which concentrate the natural sunlight into a powerful beam to replicate the heat of a 593°F (312°C) oven. He used to cook traditionally over a charcoal fire until one day he felt the heat from the sunlight reflected off the window of a passing bus and decided to harness that instead. By using only natural energy, he can cook a 3.3-lb (1.5-kg) chicken in less than 15 minutes.

GIANT TRUFFLE ▶ Sweet Shop USA, a chocolate manufacturer from Mount Pleasant, Texas, made a chocolate truffle weighing 2,368 lb (1,075 kg), measuring 3.5 ft (1.2 m) tall and 12.1 ft (3.7 m) in diameter.

OVAL OFFICE ▶ Glynn Crooks has built a life-size replica of the White House's Oval Office in a 2,000-sq-ft (185-sq-m) extension to his home in Prior Lake, Minnesota. A keen collector of presidential memorabilia, he designed his room with the iconic four curved doors, the same kind of desk used by the president, and even a copy of the Rembrandt Peale portrait of George Washington above the fireplace.

RAGING RIVER ▶ During the monsoon season, children living in the town of Chamba in the Himachal Pradesh region of northern India must cross a 50-ft-wide (15-m) raging river to get to school. It takes 40 minutes to cross the river, which rushes down the side of a mountain, and older children often carry younger ones across on their backs.

America on Wheels

Robert Luczun of Clifton, New Jersey, has covered his 1986 Chevrolet El Camino with paintings detailing the history of the United States of America. It took him two years to get to this point, drawing and painting up to 8 hours every day! He's left empty spaces to fill in as history unfolds.

YOUR UPLOADS

CLIMB TIME

> Mallakhamb is a traditional Indian sport dating back to the 12th century and consists of gymnastics performed on wooden poles and ropes.

There are three disciplines of mallakhamb: pole, hanging pole, and rope. Pole and hanging pole are traditionally performed by men and boys, who cover themselves in castor oil so they can easily glide up, down, and around a pole either coming up from the ground or hanging from a rope on a frame. Meanwhile, the rope is often for girls and women who seem to defy gravity, wrapping the rope around their bodies and gripping it between their toes to hold themselves up. Sometimes there are multiple athletes performing on one pole or rope, requiring extreme trust.

REGULAR CUSTOMER ▶ Nadine Baum, of Hanover, Pennsylvania, visited her local branch of McDonald's for lunch almost every day for more than six years—right up until her death at age 100.

RARE MUSHROOM ▶ *Chorioactis geaster*, an extremely rare mushroom, is only found in two places in the world—Texas and Japan—more than 6,000 mi (9,600 km) apart.

DROWNED VILLAGE ▶ The village of Geamana, Romania, was evacuated in 1977 to make way for a vast copper mine, and has since become slowly buried in 300 ft (90 m) of industrial waste sludge so that only a church spire is now visible above ground.

EGG COFFEE ▶ The Café Giang in Hanoi, Vietnam, serves coffee containing egg and cheese. A whole egg is whisked into steaming coffee, along with butter and cheese, to produce an extra rich, creamy froth.

BRIDAL KIDNAPPING ▶ If a man from Sudan's Latuka tribe wants to marry a woman, he kidnaps her from her home. Elderly members of his family then go and ask the girl's father for permission for the marriage to go ahead, and if the father agrees, he physically beats the suitor as a sign of his acceptance.

THICK ICE ▶ At up to 1.9 mi (3 km) thick, the ice in Greenland is so deep that six Empire State Buildings could stand on top of each other and still fit inside it.

IVORY PYRES

> In April 2016, anti-poaching activists lit 12 carefully arranged pyres containing 105 tons of elephant ivory and 1.35 tons of rhino horn from thousands of animal carcasses at Nairobi National Park, Kenya.

The mounds were 10 ft (3 m) high and took 10 days to build, destroying highly prized animal parts worth millions on the black market. This event marked Kenya's staunch wildlife conservation stance and memorialized animals lost to the cruelties of poaching.

CAVE DWELLER ▶
Zarko Hrgic has been living in a small mountainside cave on the banks of Bosnia's Babina River for more than 10 years. The former steelworker survives on food retrieved from dumpsters and on leftovers donated by kind local people. He shares his cave home with 13 stray dogs that he feeds every day with bones from a butcher's shop.

SEABED LIFTED ▶ An earthquake that struck the coast of New Zealand's South Island on November 14, 2016, was so powerful it raised the seabed around 6.6 ft (2 m), exposing seaweed-strewn rocks and leaving marine animals stranded above tide levels.

MISLEADING NAME ▶ Ironically, the Austrian town of Rottenegg is famous for the high quality of its clean, mountain air.

MASSIVE MOREL ➜ While out hunting mushrooms in Greene County, Indiana, 13-year-old Kayden Graber discovered a massive morel mushroom that was nearly 1 ft (30 cm) tall—three times the normal height.

1,000 PACK ▶ The Nokian Panimo brewery in Finland introduced a 1,000-pack of its Keisari beer for very thirsty customers. The giant pack sells for $2,346—just over $2 a beer.

101 CHEESES ▶ Scottie's Pizza Parlor in Portland, Oregon, created a pizza—the Centouno Formaggio—using 101 different types of cheese.

TABLET PLATES ▶
Instead of using conventional plates, Michael and Lindsay Tusk's San Francisco restaurant Quince serves food on Apple iPads, which play videos relating to the contents of the dish.

DANGEROUS DRIVERS ▶ In Aichi, Japan, elderly drivers are considered so dangerous that they are offered discounted funerals if they give up their driver's license.

TWO STRIKES ▶ During a violent snowstorm on February 27, 2017, lightning struck Seattle's Space Needle twice in one day—a rare phenomenon. Twenty-five lightning rods, including the spire itself, are scattered on the roof of the Needle in an attempt to protect the building from lightning strikes.

BAT BEER ▶ To mark the opening of the Atlanta Braves' new SunTrust Park stadium in 2017, the Georgia-based Terrapin Beer Company created a beer, called the Chopsecutioner Bat Wood Aged IPA, that was aged using leftover chips and shavings from the production of baseball bats, instead of using traditional wood chips.

$2,000 PIZZA ▶ New York City restaurant Industry Kitchen serves a $2,000 pizza. Its 24K Pizza consists of a crust made with black squid ink, topped with English Stilton cheese, foie gras, and truffles from France, Ossetra caviar harvested from the Caspian Sea, and then covered in flakes of edible 24-karat gold.

TISSUE REPAIRS ▶ Workers in the city of Littleton, Colorado, used toilet paper to help seal up cracks along more than 120 streets in 2016. The tissue was applied with a paint roller over the freshly laid tar that had been used to fill cracks in the asphalt. Before breaking down and disappearing altogether, the biodegradable paper absorbs the oil from the tar as it dries, allowing the road to reopen to traffic more quickly.

STRONG COFFEE ▶ With its increased caffeine content (58.4 mg per fluid ounce), Black Insomnia Coffee, made by the South African company of the same name, is almost five times stronger than average coffee.

SPACE BOOST ▶ In 2011, a vial of unmatured malt whiskey from Scotland's Ardbeg Distillery was sent to the International Space Station with pieces of charred oak, and after it returned in 2014, experts said it tasted much better than identical samples that had been kept on Earth.

BUDDHA STATUES ▶ There are more than 800 gray stone Buddha statues in the village of Fureai Sekibutsu no Sato (translated to "the village where you can meet Buddhist statues") near Osawano, Japan. The village founder, Mutsuo Furukawa, paid a Chinese sculptor around $60 million to create them in 1989, and in addition to the Buddhas, there are various statues depicting Furukawa's friends.

CHAND BAORI

▶ **There are 3,500 symmetrical steps leading 13 levels deep into the Chand Baori stepwell in Rajasthan, India.**

The famous structure was built more than 1,000 years ago as a way to collect precious water during monsoons, which was in short supply during the hot summers. Thousands of stepwells were built between the first and fifteenth centuries, but they have fallen out of use with technological advances. Luckily, some of the most impressive, like Chand Baori, have been preserved and can still be visited today.

Several scenes in the Batman movie *Dark Knight Rises* were filmed at Chand Baori.

> No matter where you go in the world, if you look hard enough, you are bound to find some unique architecture. Sometimes these buildings have historical significance, other times they are representations of the work that goes on inside, but some of them were built just for fun! Check out this collection of bizarre buildings from around the world.

BIZARRE BUILDINGS

GIANT DRAGON TEMPLE!

FITTING FISH

» Anyone trying to find the National Fisheries Development Board in Hyderabad, India, need only look for a giant fish. The four-story building is lit up by blue spotlights at night, making it appear as though it is swimming through the city.

DOG HOUSE ▶ Nestled comfortably in Tirau, New Zealand, this canine-themed building is made of corrugated iron and looks like a dog! The goofy creation is never lonely, as there are other animal-shaped corrugated buildings right next door, and they are especially treasured in Tirau's artistic community.

FIERCE FAÇADE

› Travel off the beaten path in Khlong Mai, Thailand, and you might stumble upon the Wat Samphran Temple—a cylindrical 17-story tower surrounded by a massive dragon.

The shocking pink building is filled with shrines and even includes an entrance into the hollow body of the dragon itself! The temple's history and meaning are shrouded in mystery, but people visit from all over the world to climb to the top and touch the dragon's beard.

GAS

FILL 'ER UP ▶

Believe it or not, this gas station was not built by a tea fanatic. Rather, it was built in 1922 to remind passersby of the Teapot Dome Scandal, which saw a politician of the time taking bribes from private oil companies. For a fill-up and a history lesson at the same time, head to Old Highway 12 in Zillah, Washington.

PINEAPPLE WITH A PAST

» A pineapple-topped building in Scotland may sound silly, but there is actually a reasonable(ish) explanation. When Europeans started bringing new foods back from the Americas, many travelers would place an exotic pineapple on their gatepost to signal their return home. Lord Dunmore took it one step further, and a year after his return as the last English governor of Virginia in 1777, this massive pineapple was installed atop his summer home in Airth, Scotland.

LIVING BUILDING ▶ The exterior walls of Edificio Santalaia, an 11-story building in Bogota, Colombia, are covered in 115,000 plants. The lush vegetation of the vertical garden is spread over an area of 33,000 sq ft (3,065 sq m) and helps insulate the building, keeping it warm in winter but cool in summer.

PLANE GROUNDED ▶ A packed Citilink Indonesia flight was grounded for 90 minutes at Kualanamu International Airport in September 2017 after a swarm containing thousands of bees landed on one of the plane's wings. The bees were eventually removed with jets of water.

FREE BURGERS ▶ In 2017, Burger King Argentina offered free burgers for life to anyone with the surname Parrilla, which means "grill" in Spanish.

SIDEWALK VASES ▶ Floral designer Lewis Miller turns the sidewalk trash cans of New York City into huge vases by filling them with dozens of flowers and decorative plants that have been left over from weddings.

LIGHTNING ENERGY ▶ A single bolt of lightning contains enough energy to toast 100,000 pieces of bread.

OLD TOWN ▶ Of the 2,000 people living in the small town of Acciaroli in southern Italy, about 300—15 percent—are centenarians, aged 100 or more. A fifth of these live to be at least 110 even though many smoke or are overweight.

RELAXATION CAFÉ ▶ Mr. Healing, a café chain in South Korea, encourages customers to lie down, relax, and even fall asleep. Each café has massage chairs where people can enjoy a short nap while listening to soothing music, and the concept has proved so popular that 50 branches have opened and customers need to make a reservation in advance.

BAD OMEN? ▶ Father-of-the-bride J. P. Nadeau was giving a toast at his daughter's wedding in Lower Woodstock, New Brunswick, Canada, when he was struck by lightning. He was holding a microphone, and as the electricity shot through the cable, his entire hand lit up. Incredibly, he wasn't hurt.

RAT CAFÉ ▶ The Black Rat Café, a pop-up coffee shop that opened at a tourist attraction called the San Francisco Dungeon in 2017, allowed visitors to sip their coffee surrounded by rats.

TECHNO TOWER

▶ The MahaNakhon skyscraper in Bangkok, Thailand, looks like a computer glitch in a virtual world.

The pixelated look is achieved with "sky boxes" that jut out of the building in seemingly random intervals. Light shows projected onto and from the building enhance its futuristic features.

CLOWN HOME ▶ A bungalow listed for sale in Brantford, Ontario, Canada, featured clown wallpaper, clown artwork, and more than 1,500 clowns that had been collected by the owner over a period of 25 years.

HIGH PIE ▶ To celebrate the 2016 World Pie Eating Championship, a group of enthusiasts in Wigan, England, launched a meat and potato pie 100,000 ft (30,000 m) into space attached to a helium-filled weather balloon.

FOOD STOP ▶ Runners in the Half and Half Marathon in Washington, D.C., must eat a chili dog and potato chips halfway to the finish.

SHARK ROOM ▶ More than 60,000 people entered an Airbnb contest to sleep in a bedroom in Paris, France, that was submerged in a huge tank containing 37 sharks. The temporary underwater room for two at the city's Shark Aquarium had a 360-degree transparent wall, which was all that separated the guests from the sharks.

DUCK DINNER ▶ The winning owner in an annual rubber duck race in Harvard, Massachusetts, gets a free dinner for two anywhere in the world. Past winners of the Ducky Wucky River Race on the Nashua River have dined as far away as Australia, Tokyo, South Africa, and Paris.

TRASH ISLAND ▶ Despite being an uninhabited island in the Pacific Ocean about 3,100 mi (5,000 km) from the nearest population center, Henderson Island is awash with around 37 million items of plastic debris. A magnet for trash carried on currents from South America, the island is covered in 17 tons of plastic, with 671 items per square meter, and every day more than 13,000 pieces of garbage wash ashore.

FLOWER FLUSH ▶ In an effort to change the country's infamously smelly and dirty public bathrooms, China has opened almost 70,000 upgraded toilet facilities, including these flower-shaped garden stalls at a park in Anlong County.

ROCK SMASHING ▶ At the annual Blessing of the Virgin of Urkupina religious celebration in Bolivia, thousands of Catholics try to smash large rocks with sledge hammers in the hope that it will make their dreams come true. According to local belief, if a rock is easily split, their wishes will soon be fulfilled.

HEARTS OF GLASS

» Spanish company Wedding Glass offers couples the option of walking barefoot on broken glass on their wedding day. For the ceremony, called "Crystals of Love," the couple walk carefully toward each other while their guests look on. The ritual is seen as a metaphor for married life, with the shards of glass representing the fears, challenges, and hardships that the newlyweds will need to overcome.

DANGEROUS GAME ▶ In the Colombian game of tejo, competitors lob 1.6-lb (0.7-kg) steel pucks at a circular target in a box packed with gunpowder. Any contact with the gunpowder can cause it to explode, which explains why many veteran tejo players have fingers missing.

MOUSETRAP MUSEUM ▶ A museum in Neroth, Germany, celebrates the town's most famous product—the mousetrap. Dozens of vintage traps are on display, along with a reconstruction of an old mousetrap maker's workshop. The industry sprang up in the 19th century to combat a rodent infestation in the region, and traveling trap sellers used to work in pairs, communicating with each other via their own secret language called Jenisch. In recognition of its importance to the local economy, a silver mousetrap is featured on Neroth's coat of arms.

TACTILE SIGNS ▶ More than 2,100 braille and raised-letter signs were installed at pedestrian crossings in Sydney, Australia, in 2016 to help visually impaired people—becoming the world's largest braille and tactile network. Placed next to push buttons, the aluminum panels feature street names and building numbers in both braille and large, raised lettering.

UPSIDE DOWN ▶ A three-story town house in Taipei, Taiwan, has deliberately been built upside down. All the furniture—including beds, tables, and bathtubs—is stuck to the ceilings, and a car and a bicycle hang from the roof of the garage. The house, which was created as a tourist attraction, took two months to construct at a cost of more than $600,000.

NOTABLE NOSES ▶ Sweden's Lund University displays a collection of more than 100 plaster casts of noses belonging to notable Scandinavians, including Sweden's first astronaut, Christer Fuglesang; its first female archbishop, Antje Jackelén; and the famous metal nose of 17th-century Danish astronomer Tycho Brahe.

FIRE TWISTERS ▶ When a small fire started in a farmer's field in Cornelius, Oregon, on August 12, 2016, strong, erratic winds whipped up a number of 200-ft-tall (60-m) firenados—tornados comprised of flames and smoke!

OFF THE RAILS

❯ In late 2017, the world's steepest railway opened in Switzerland.

Taking 14 years and $53 million to build, the railway transports passengers from the valley town of Schwyz up 328 ft (110 m) to the village of Stoos, allowing children to get to school and tourists to take in the alpine views. The best part of the experience is that the floors inside the barrel-like carriages tilt and adjust so passengers stay standing upright even at the near-vertical 110 percent gradient.

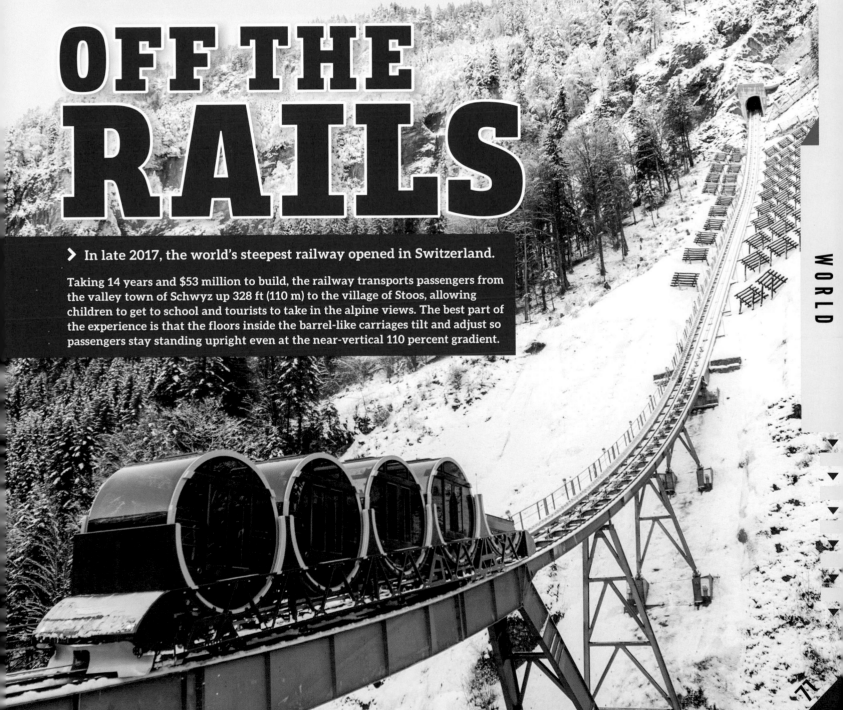

Flour FIGHT

> Every year on December 28, the town of Ibi, eastern Spain, celebrates the Els Enfarinats festival—a massive food fight for charity!

The 200-year-old tradition sees two sides bombard each other with flour, eggs, and firecrackers. One side declares and enforces absurd new laws, fining citizens that break them, while the other tries to regain control. After the battle is over, money collected from the fines gets donated to charity.

Els Enfarinats means "the floured ones" in the Valencian language.

TOWERS OF SILENCE

For more than 3,000 years, Zoroastrians in Iran and India laid their dead on a flat tower for them to be slowly picked apart by vultures. The tradition was done to prevent corpses from becoming impure or contaminated by demons. The bodies were exposed to the elements atop the desert *dakhmas*, arranged in concentric circles. Once the bodies were picked clean, the bones were placed near or inside of the towers of silence.

RIPPED *From* HISTORY

TOWER OF SILENCE — IN BOMBAY, India.
WHERE THE PARSEES FEED THEIR DEAD TO THE VULTURES.

In 1926, Ripley visited Mumbai (then Bombay), India, and sketched a tower of silence, releasing the cartoon December 21, 1930.

OLD ROSE ▶ A White Lady Banks rose that was planted at the Rose Tree Museum in Tombstone, Arizona, in 1885 still blooms for six weeks every year. Its trunk is now about 12 ft (3.6 m) in diameter, and its branches cover an area of 9,000 sq ft (836 sq m).

MOSQUITO BOOM ▶ In September 2017, a mosquito trap set up in Hernando County, Florida, after Hurricane Irma, caught 26,000 bugs in just 16 hours—more than 50 times the number of mosquitoes usually expected at that time of year. Ten different species of mosquitoes were caught overall.

HOT CHILI ▶ Farmer Mike Smith, from Denbighshire, Wales, grew a chili pepper, the Dragon's Breath, that registers 2.48 million on the Scoville heat scale, making it hotter than the pepper spray used by the U.S. Army and 500 times hotter than Tabasco sauce. Smith, who does not even like spicy food, says it is too hot for consumption, as anybody who tried to eat it would be at risk of dying from anaphylactic shock. However, its oil is so potent that it could be used in medicine as an alternative anaesthetic.

DIVORCE HOUSE ▶ Dutch design company Studio OBA has concepted a floating home that can split into two if a couple divorces. Each house is made up of two prefabricated units, which are constructed from lightweight carbon fiber and wood, and have a connecting mechanism that allows them either to slot together or detach, depending on the status of the owners' relationship.

$2,500 BURGER ▶ Diego Buik, chef at the South of Houston restaurant in The Hague, Netherlands, created a $2,500 burger. It consists of a Japanese dry-aged Wagyu and Black Angus beef patty, Oosterschelde lobster infused with gin, foie gras, white truffle, Remeker cheese, and caviar. It is served with a sauce made from 35 lobsters, Jamaican Blue Mountain Coffee, Madagascan vanilla, saffron, and Japanese soy.

LOCK COLLECTION ▶ The Museum of Physical Security at Nicholasville, Kentucky, houses 12,000 locks collected by the late Harry Miller, including a lock from a Russian nuclear warhead! Miller, who died in 1998, was an accomplished locksmith who managed to crack the burglar-proof safe at the White House after the only person who knew the combination had died. He was summoned to open the safe because then First Lady Eleanor Roosevelt needed her jewels for a state visit.

MOBILE PUB ▶ Ben Levy, from the West Midlands, England, converted his 1957 Volkswagen camper van into a mobile pub called The Dub Inn. It comes complete with bar stools, beer on tap, wine racks, disco lights, and a dartboard on the door.

VANISHING SNOW ▶ A patch of snow on the 4,250-ft-high (1,296-m) Braeriach mountain in Scotland melted in 2017 for the first time in 11 years. The snow is believed to have disappeared completely only seven times in the last 300 years.

WATER EXPERT ▶ German-born Martin Riese is the only professional water sommelier in the United States—with more than 40 natural waters on his water menu at Ray's and Stark Bar in Los Angeles. He has been fascinated by the different tastes of water since he was four, and whenever he went on vacation as a child, the first thing he did was try the local drinking water.

PINK CHOCOLATE ▶ Swiss chocolatier Barry Callebaut has created pink chocolate. His "Ruby" chocolate is made from a Ruby cocoa bean and has an intense, berry-like taste.

DRINK BLOOD ▶ Members of the nomadic Nenets tribe of Siberia drink the blood of freshly slaughtered reindeer to survive in temperatures of –49°F (–45°C).

PROSTHETIC SHRINE ▶ Visitors to the shrine at the Saint Roch Chapel in New Orleans, Louisiana, leave their old prosthetic body parts as an offering, including glass eyes, dental plates, crutches, and false limbs.

RICE
CRISPY TREES

> **At the start of spring, the people of the Dong village in Hubei Province, China, "feed" cooked rice to trees.**

Although little is known of the custom, the village elders slice the trunks of fruit and nut trees (like grapefruit, walnut, or loquat trees) and place cooked rice on the openings in the belief that feeding the trees will help them to bear more fruit.

ROBOT PRIEST ▶ Worshippers at a church in Wittenberg, Germany, can receive automated blessings in five languages from a robot priest called "BlessU-2." The robot has a touch screen chest, which prompts it to raise its arms, flash lights, and recite a Bible verse.

REMOTE RESTAURANT ▶ German pizza company Dr. Oetker opened a pop-up restaurant on Dirk Hartog Island, a remote location off the coast of Western Australia that is home to only two permanent residents.

BRIDGE ROLL ▶ Using 21,000 pieces of dried seaweed and 1,320 lb (600 kg) of rice, volunteers in Goheung County, South Korea, made a 4,408-ft-long (1,344-m) seaweed roll. They prepared the giant roll on tables erected on the bicycle lane of the Geogeum Bridge, which links Geogeum Island to Sorok Island.

DOLL SEATS ▶ Thai Smile Airways allows passengers to purchase seats for their Luk Thep "angel dolls," which are believed to possess the spirit of a child and bring good luck.

MARS LETTER ▶ According to NASA and Britain's Royal Mail, it would cost nearly $24,000 to send a letter to Mars—that's 18,416 first-class stamps.

FAKE VENICE ▶ The city of Dalian, China, has constructed a $756 million replica of Venice to lure tourists. The cloned Italian city features a gondola service along a specially built 2.5-mi (4-km) canal, which is surrounded by 200 European-style buildings adorned with copies of Renaissance paintings.

GEESE RACE

» Every summer around mid-June in Skanör, Sweden, an odd event takes place in the middle of the village—a goose race. Ironically not featuring actual geese, the race sees teams of six strap themselves to two wooden planks and race down the main street. The winning team gets the grand prize of a painting by late artist Hans Andersson and a pair of clogs. Why a goose race? Skanör is famous for geese and even has its own goose crossing.

POOH CLOUD ▶ In July 2016, a cloud shaped exactly like a reclining Winnie the Pooh appeared in blue skies over Dorset, England—during a charity event for children. The white fluffy cloud seemed to have the legs, arms, ears, and smiling face of A. A. Milne's popular children's story character.

DRINKING RACE ▶ In Beer Mile races, runners must drink four beers before each of the 400-meter laps, thus consuming a total of 16 beers during the race. The beers—either bottled or canned—must be at least 12 oz (355 ml) in volume and 5 percent alcohol, and competitors are advised to tip the container over their head afterward to confirm that it is empty. The Beer Mile originated among students in Canada in 1990, but has since spread to the United States and the U.K. and is now considered a major sports event, with more than 100,000 people having officially taken part.

DEEP WHIRLPOOL ▶ The Old Sow whirlpool between Deer Island and Indian Island, New Brunswick, Canada, can extend to a diameter of 250 ft (76 m) and a depth of 12 ft (3.7 m)—about the height of a telephone pole.

HOT SPRINGS ▶ The Nine Hells of Beppu on the Japanese island of Kyushu is home to more than 2,800 hot springs, and many of the pools are hot enough to boil eggs.

SNOW GOGGLES ▶ The Inuit people of the Arctic traditionally made snow goggles from carved caribou antlers and sinew.

LOW AIRPORT ▶ The runway of Bar Yehuda Airfield, a regional airport located in Israel's southern Judean Desert, is built 1,240 ft (378 m) below sea level.

DEADLY AVALANCHE ▶ A dry slab avalanche, caused when a large plate of snow suddenly slides away, can reach a speed of 80 mph (128 kmph) in only five seconds and can ultimately travel at up to 225 mph (360 kmph) with a force equal to that of a hurricane. Nearly all avalanche deaths in North America are caused by dry slab avalanches.

TO PEE, OR NOT TO PEE ▶ In early 2017, a set of colorful open-air urinals in Chongqing, China, were unveiled and quickly went viral online. Situated in a flashy (no pun intended) urban amusement park called Foreigners' Street, which caters to traveling tourists, the outdoor urinals feature a strategically placed arc-shaped plastic covering over the waist area and not much else. Pee afraid. Pee very afraid.

Windmill PARK

❯ In January 2017, fields decorated with more than 400,000 windmills attracted visitors to Chengdu City, China, for the colorful display.

DRIED LIZARD SOUP

» Among the fish bladders, bird's nests, and duck legs on display in Hong Kong, there's still some cuisine that intrigues every curious bystander—like, for instance, dried lizards on a stick. The dried lizards (sold in pairs—male and female) are used to make a soup, one of the most popular dishes in Hong Kong. The lizards are not eaten but simmered in a boiling broth for hours so the taste is released into the soup. Lizard soup is consumed for its supposed medicinal value, much like chicken soup is given to those in America with a slight cough or cold.

HOT SPOT ▶ The air temperature above Jupiter's Great Red Spot reaches at least 2,400°F (1,315°C), making it hotter than the hottest volcanic lava on Earth.

SECRET SLIDE ▶ To reach a secret water slide hidden away in Hawaii's Waipio Valley, thrill-seekers trek for hours through narrow mountain paths, jungle, and dark tunnels—a treacherous journey known as the White Road Hike. The 35-ft (11-m) slide is actually a cement pipe, part of a local irrigation system.

FIRST TAKEAWAY ▶ In 2017, the remote village of Inverie in the Scottish Highlands had its first ever food delivery—a box of pizzas that was delivered by helicopter and dropped in a nearby field. No roads lead to the village, which is otherwise accessible only by ferry.

DONKEY CHEESE ▶ Serbian tennis champion Novak Djokovic bought up almost the entire world's supply of donkey cheese for his new restaurant chain. Called "pule," donkey cheese is produced by only one farm in the world.

LARGE SLICE ▶ Wayne Duffy's Dulwich Bakery in Adelaide, South Australia, baked a vanilla slice that was 20 ft (6 m) long and weighed a colossal 1,770 lb (804 kg). It comprised 1,320 lb (600 kg) of custard, 330 lb (150 kg) of pastry, and 110 lb (50 kg) of icing.

ICE DISC ▶ In January 2017, a rare revolving ice disc appeared on the surface of the Snoqualmie River near North Bend, Washington. Spinning ice circles occur when cold air comes into contact with an eddy in a slow-moving river. The ice forms a thin circular disc, which sometimes keeps rotating as a result of the current it creates as it melts.

Beat the IRON BALL

360 STEEL NAILS!

❯ Every year, village residents in southeast China's Fujian Province gather for Da Tieqiu, or "Beat the Iron Ball"—a painful ceremony in which half-naked men beat their own backs with an iron ball covered in 360 steel nails.

The ceremony commemorates a national hero from the Ming dynasty who defended China from Japanese raids in the 16th century. Shirtless and barefooted, the men are carried aloft on seats made of knives and flay their backs with the urchin-shaped iron balls until they bleed. The event encourages the men to guard the safety of their home and country.

ZEBRA Crossing

> Instead of traffic cops, some cities in Bolivia have zebra crossings!

Part-time students, usually between the ages of 15 and 25, dress up in full-body zebra costumes to help direct traffic by dancing, helping pedestrians cross the street, and interacting with drivers, teasing them for breaking traffic rules. The program started with a small herd of just 24 zebras, but today there are more than 200 in multiple cities.

BURGER TATTOO ▶ Café 51, a burger restaurant in Melbourne, Australia, offered free burgers for life to any customer who got a life-size tattoo of one of its burgers anywhere on their body.

SKYSCRAPER CEMETERY ▶ The Memorial Necrópole Ecumênica cemetery in Santos, Brazil, stands 354 ft (108 m) tall. It has 32 floors and contains more than 25,000 burial tombs. When it was originally built in 1983, it was just a small building, but with burial space at ground level in short supply, it has steadily extended upward and is now one of the São Paulo region's major tourist attractions.

HOUSE MOVE ▶ In February 2017, a three-story brick house weighing 370 tons and covering an area of nearly 3,000 sq ft (279 sq m) was hoisted off its foundation, loaded onto a truck, and driven just 0.7 mi (1.1 km) to a new location in St. Louis, Missouri, to make way for the National Geospatial-Intelligence Agency's new campus. The short journey took almost six hours. The 122-year-old house is the home of 81-year-old Charlsetta Taylor, who has lived there since 1945.

SINKING CITY ▶ Parts of Mexico City have sunk by as much as 42 ft (13 m) over the last 100 years, and in some areas the city is currently sinking at a rate of 8 in (20 cm) a year. The main water supply for 21 million people is pumped from an aquifer (a layer of permeable rock) directly below the city, but the water is being siphoned more quickly than it is being replenished by natural sources such as rainfall, causing the city to sink.

PECULIAR PINEAPPLES

> Red pineapples (Ananas bracteatus), native to South America, grow a vibrant violet-red color. The unique pineapples are grown as ornamental plants or are used as protective home security hedges because of their spiny leaves.

Black-and-white painted crosswalks where vehicles must stop if a pedestrian needs to cross the road are known as "zebra crossings" in both Bolivia and the United Kingdom.

OPEN ROOM ▶ Perched 6,643 ft (2,025 m) up in the Swiss Alps, the $260-a-night Null Stern (meaning "No Stars") hotel room has no door, walls, or ceiling—just a king-size bed with an open, 360-degree view. Breakfast in bed is prepared for guests by a butler from a nearby wooden cabin, and the nearest toilet is a 10-minute walk away.

SCHOOLHOUSE MOVE ▶ In 2016, the old Orleans County Grammar School building in Brownington, Vermont, was moved back to the hilltop spot where it had first stood when it was built in 1823. The historic 105-ton, timber-frame schoolhouse was relocated nearer to town in 1869, but a team of 44 oxen, with assistance from a modern engine, succeeded in dragging and pushing it 0.3 mi (0.5 km) back up the hill to its original site.

ARCTIC DESERT ▶ Although it is located on the edge of the Arctic Circle, the Russian village of Shoyna is surrounded by sand dunes in what has been called the world's northernmost desert. The sand is whipped up by westerly winds with such force that entire houses can be buried in a single night. Consequently, villagers always leave their front doors open at night so they are not trapped inside the next morning. Some have even cut manholes into the roofs of their houses to use as front doors.

SMALL WORLD ▶ About one million Earths could fit inside the Sun. The Sun holds 99.8 percent of the solar system's mass and is roughly 109 times the diameter of Earth. Someone would need to explode 100 billion tons of dynamite every second to match the energy produced by the Sun.

GUESSING CONTEST ▶ Thousands of Alaskans take part in an annual contest to guess the precise time when the ice on the Tanana River will first move in spring. They pay $2.50 for a ticket, with the jackpot often exceeding $250,000. The winning time is determined when a cable attached to a tripod on the river ice trips a clock on shore.

HIGH SCHOOL ▶ Children from the Atule'er village in China's Sichuan Province had to climb a series of 17 vine ladders attached to a 2,624-ft-high (800-m) cliff in order to reach school. The village is perched on top of a mountain, with the Le'er Primary School at the bottom. Supervised by parents, children as young as six go up and down the cliff face with heavy packs strapped to their back, but the two-hour journey was so dangerous they only returned home twice a month. Recently, portions of the climb were updated to steel ladders.

WATER CHANNEL ▶ Using only hand tools, Huang Dafa and his team of 200 villagers spent 36 years digging a 6.25-mi-long (10-km) water channel through three mountains in order to bring water to their home settlement of Caowangba, buried deep in the mountains of China's Guizhou Province. Named the Dafa Channel in his honor, it was finished in 1995 and now supplies the 1,200 villagers with water, which also allows them to grow more than 880,000 lb (400,000 kg) of rice every year.

RECLUSIVE TRIBES ▶ There are about 500 indigenous tribes living in the Amazon rainforest, and of these, as many as 50 have never experienced any contact with the outside world.

CALENDAR CEMETERY ▶ The Bridge to Paradise Cemetery in Mexico's Xcaret Park is based on the structure of the Gregorian calendar, with seven levels representing the days of the week, a main entrance with 52 steps marking the weeks of the year, and 365 colorful external tombs depicting the days of the year.

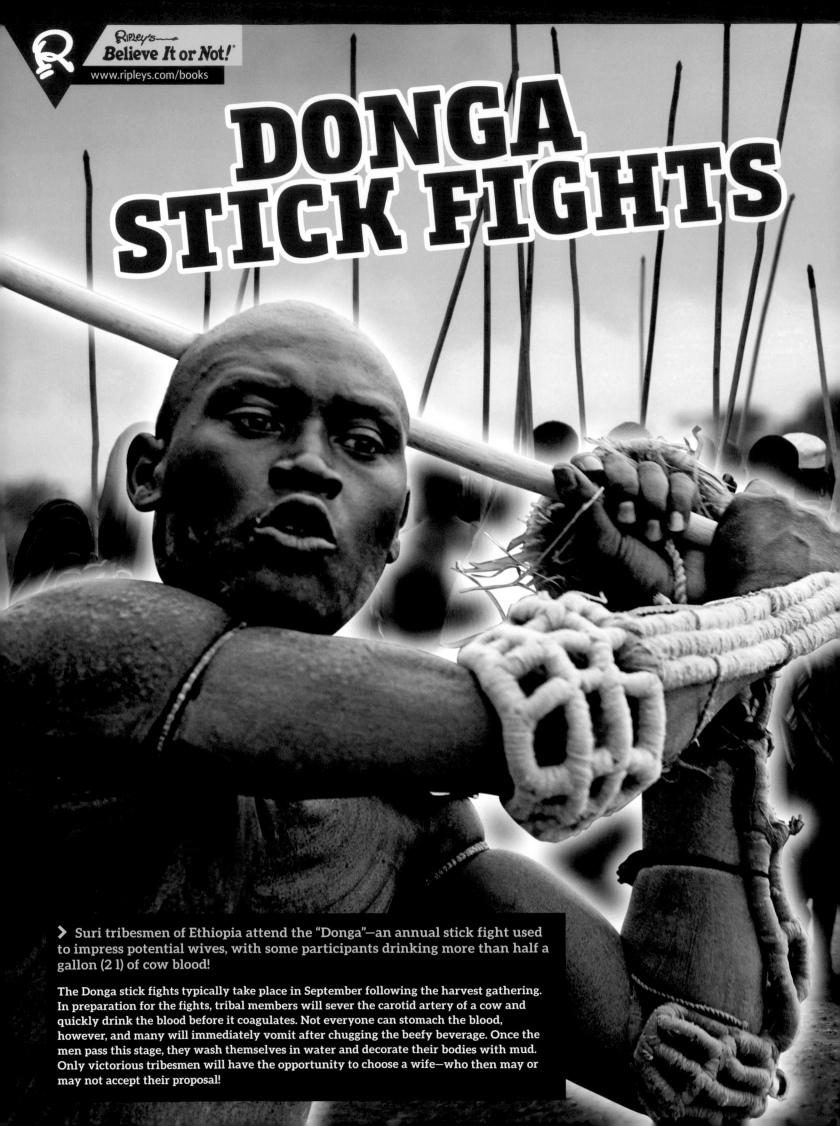

DONGA STICK FIGHTS

> Suri tribesmen of Ethiopia attend the "Donga"—an annual stick fight used to impress potential wives, with some participants drinking more than half a gallon (2 l) of cow blood!

The Donga stick fights typically take place in September following the harvest gathering. In preparation for the fights, tribal members will sever the carotid artery of a cow and quickly drink the blood before it coagulates. Not everyone can stomach the blood, however, and many will immediately vomit after chugging the beefy beverage. Once the men pass this stage, they wash themselves in water and decorate their bodies with mud. Only victorious tribesmen will have the opportunity to choose a wife—who then may or may not accept their proposal!

Say Cheese

> **Did you know that in England newborn babies were once passed through a cheese hole for good luck?**

The now-defunct tradition, known as groaning cheese, saw parents carve out a large hole in a 15-in-diameter (38-cm) wheel of cheese and then pass the baby through the cheese ring, sharing leftover cheese with family and friends to eat afterward. It was meant to symbolize the birth of the baby, with the "groaning" representing the groaning during childbirth.

BANANA CROSSING ▶ In Costa Rica, local workers transport bunches of bananas across plantations using a zip line pulley system, sometimes creating banana crossings with gates that come down to stop traffic while the bananas zip by, much like railroad crossings.

WIND MUSEUM ▶
An entire museum in Trieste, Italy, is devoted to a specific wind, the bora, which blows fiercely down the Adriatic coast, especially in winter, bringing gusts of 90 mph (144 kmph) or more. The Bora Museum contains songs and poems written about the wind, as well as a Hall of Wind—a room where visitors can experience the sensation of being on the receiving end of a blast from the bora.

BOX BEDROOM ▶ In March 2016, Peter Berkowitz paid $400 to live in a wooden box in a San Francisco apartment. The 25-year-old illustrator spent $1,300 on building the box—complete with a door, a bed, a fold-up desk, windows, and a skylight—and placing it in a corner of the living room of a friend's three-bedroom apartment. Whereas his roommates who lived in the regular bedrooms were paying $1,000 a month in rent, Berkowitz paid less than half that but still had access to all the amenities.

CORNY HOUSE

» In November 2017, Liu Hongcai of Jilin Province, China, built a farmhouse with more than 20,000 corncobs. Alongside 14 villagers, Liu attached the corncobs to frames of metal and wood. The property also housed a corn well, a corn waterwheel, and a corn fence. Hoping his creation will attract tourists, Liu has allowed a small population of local stray cats to live in the corn structure to ward off any pests.

DYING FORBIDDEN ▶ People are not allowed to die in the remote Arctic town of Longyearbyen on Norway's Svalbard Islands. The town has a small graveyard and it stopped accepting new burials more than 80 years ago because bodies never decompose in the cold climate. Instead they are so perfectly preserved by permafrost that when scientists recently removed tissue samples from a man who had died there, they found live traces of the influenza virus that had killed him in 1917. So anyone in Longyearbyen who is on the verge of death is transported to the mainland for the last days of their life.

HIDDEN DIAMONDS ▶ For one day only—on January 6, 2016—French husband-and-wife bakers Nicolas and Julie Lelut hid diamonds in their pastry products as a promotional scheme. Customers at their two patisseries in Paris and Custines had a 0.25 percent chance of winning a diamond worth around $750. To avoid the risk of anyone accidentally swallowing the prizes, the Leluts inserted much larger fake diamonds into the pastries, and these were then exchanged for real gems at the patisseries.

CURSED VILLAGE ▶ For more than 500 years, the Spanish village of Trasmoz has been the apparent subject of a curse so potent that only the current pope can lift it. Reacting to tales of witchcraft and pagan rituals in the area, the local Catholic Church abbot placed a curse on the entire village and its descendants in 1511, and the drastic measure was sanctioned by Pope Julius II. Trasmoz was once a bustling settlement with a population of around 10,000, but now, because of the "curse," there are just 30 permanent residents.

GAMERS' CONFUSION ▶ In 2016, Freddie's Restaurant and Pizzeria in Long Branch, New Jersey, had to add extra phone lines after receiving up to 200 calls an hour from people asking if it is Freddy Fazbear's Pizzeria, the setting for the video game *Five Nights at Freddy's*, a horror game in which the player is a security guard attacked by animatronic robots.

TIGER CAKE ▶ Zoe Fox, from Leicestershire, England, baked a lifelike cake in the shape of a full-sized tiger. It took her 300 hours to make the cake, which was hand-carved and made of ganache—a hard-setting chocolate and cream mix—then covered with fondant icing and airbrushed with edible paint. She was part of a team of bakers who prepared wildlife-themed cakes to highlight the plight of endangered animals. Their creations included an iguana, a slow loris, and a lowland gorilla, but the fiercest looking specimen was a Madeira cake in the shape of a crocodile by Irish baker Tanya Ross.

BROTH POPSICLE ▶ New York City restaurant Springbone Kitchen makes bone broth popsicles in summer. The broth, which is made by slowly boiling animal bones in water, was first served cold but proved too gelatinous, so they decided to mix it with coconut milk, raspberry puree, pomegranate juice, and maple sugar, and then freeze it and sell it as a popsicle.

PRESIDENTS' HAIR ▶ In July 2016, the Academy of Natural Sciences of Drexel University in Philadelphia, Pennsylvania, exhibited locks of hair from early U.S. presidents, including George Washington, Thomas Jefferson, John Adams, John Quincy Adams, and Andrew Jackson. A Philadelphia attorney collected the specimens, which were given to the museum after he died in 1860.

CAKE PROMISE ▶ According to Serbian superstition, if you accidentally bite your tongue, it means that your grandmother is planning to bake a cake for you.

FRUIT BAT SOUP ▷ All over the Asian and Pacific Rim countries, bats make their way onto plates as an exotic delicacy. But in Palau, Micronesia, it's taken one step further, with the furry little creatures served whole! Fruit bat soup consists of a steaming bowl of broth and an entire fruit bat, sometimes topped with coconut milk. Everything except the bones are eaten, including the eyes and wings, as the bat is a good source of protein.

The "ugly" Chläuse wear materials like twigs and furs along with creepy masks to scare away evil spirits.

A yodel group, or "Schuppel," of ugly-beautiful Chläuse dressed in pine and tree bark.

Silvesterchläusen

GIANT WOODEN HAT!

> From early morning to late at night, groups of elaborately costumed men yodel and dance their way from farmhouse to farmhouse during the Swiss winter festival Silvesterchläusen.

Every year on December 31 and January 13 in the Swiss state of Appenzell Ausserrhoden, these groups meet as early as 5 a.m. dressed in one of three kinds of costumes: the beautiful, the ugly, and the ugly-beautiful. They all carry large bells on their bodies, making the outfits weigh up to 66 lb (30 kg) each, and perform a wordless yodel unique to the region, called "Zäuerli," to scare off evil spirits. The families they visit offer them drinks and money in exchange for a firm handshake and well-wishes for the new year.

WORLD

A "beautiful" Chläuse wearing a traditional women's dress and an elaborate wooden hat, featuring a summer scene.

DOG CARRYING DAY ▶ Every year, the small Chinese village of Jiaobang celebrates a festival that sees a dog dressed up in human clothing being hoisted up in a sedan chair and paraded across a rice paddy. The Miao people observe this tradition to show respect for all creatures, worshipping the chosen dog as a god. According to local legend, the first settlers to the area were led to a water source by a dog and thereby saved from dying of dehydration.

SKATE PARK ▶ In 2017, 250 tons of granite slabs from LOVE Park, Philadelphia, Pennsylvania, which was once an unauthorized skateboarding venue, were shipped 4,000 mi (6,400 km) to Malmo, Sweden, for use in an official skate park.

TOILET CHASE ▶ Hurricane-strength winds in Moscow, Russia, on June 30, 2017, caused portable toilets dislodged from their positions to chase people down the streets.

SWEET DEAL ▶ Real estate agent Erin Allard offered her $390,000 four-bedroom, century-old home in Jackson, California, as first prize in a dessert contest. Each entrant had to pay a $100 fee, and the house was given to whoever came up with the best dessert recipe.

YELLOWSTONE QUAKES ▶ Each year, there are between 1,000 and 3,000 earthquakes in Yellowstone National Park—although most are too small to be felt. The region is one of the most seismically active in the United States, and can be affected even by distant quakes. In 2002, a 7.9 magnitude earthquake in Alaska 1,250 mi (2,000 km) away triggered hundreds of small tremors in Yellowstone.

LIBRARY DYNASTY ▶ The running of a library in Tamegroute, Morocco, has been handed down from father to son since the 17th century. The library is home to 4,000 (of an original 50,000) ancient books, including a 13th-century version of the Koran engraved on a patch of gazelle skin.

FINAL BREATH ▶ Thomas Edison's last breath is held in a vial at the Henry Ford Museum in Dearborn, Michigan. Eight test tubes were by Edison's bedside when he died in 1931, and afterward his son Charles asked the attending physician to seal them. Charles later gave one of the tubes to Ford.

AWESOME WINGSPAN ▶ Designed for launching satellites into space, the U.S.-built Stratolaunch carrier aircraft weighs about 250 tons and has a wingspan of 385 ft (117 m)—longer than a football field.

TOWN HERMIT ▶ The Austrian town of Saalfelden employs an official hermit. The unpaid job requires the hermit to greet pilgrims visiting the 350-year-old hermitage, which is built into a nearby cliff, has no heating or running water, and is only habitable between April and November.

HEY BABE.

COLOSSAL CARROT

» Chris Qualley, of Minnesota, grew the world's biggest carrot, weighing an impressive 22.4 lb (10 kg)! The dad-of-three spent the last two years cultivating the giant veggie, determined to outgrow the competition—the previous record holder weighed in at 20 lb (9.1 kg).

The local villagers have helped him make the stone blocks.

STONE CASTLE

> For the past 20 years, 78-year-old Song Peilun has been building a 50-acre (20-hectare) stone castle in a secluded valley outside Guiyang, China.

The professor-turned-artist quit his day job in 1996, devoting all his time to creating the exotic stone statues and pillars that make the massive castle such a standout. Song was inspired by the Crazy Horse monument in South Dakota and decided he wanted to honor the minority Nuo culture of southwest China in the artistic design of the castle.

ASARO
Mud Men

> The Asaro mud men from the Eastern Highlands of Papua New Guinea are known for caking their bodies with mud, wearing bamboo claws, and donning eerie clay masks decorated with wild pigs' teeth, tusks, and shells.

It's unclear why or when the Asaro began making their morbid mud masks, but it's believed that the practice has been around for centuries. The masks have played a huge role in intimidating and winning wars against enemy tribes, as their ghoulish appearance makes them look like evil spirits.

UNBELIEVABLE Birth

> A monkey born in 2017 was named Ripley in honor of the unbelievable fact that his mother is the oldest of her species to give birth at 22 years old!

Residents of the Memphis Zoo, Ripley and his mother, Tanah, are Francois' langurs, an endangered species found in southwestern China and northeastern Vietnam. Believe it or not, Francois' langur babies are born with bright orange hair, which gradually changes to black within a year.

SIDEWAYS BILL ▶ The wrybill, a small plover-like bird from New Zealand, has a bill that bends sideways to the right so that it can reach tasty mayfly larvae that are hiding under rocks along rivers.

CONTAGIOUS LAUGHTER ▶ The kea, a New Zealand parrot, has a particular call that sounds like human laughter. They only use it when they are engaging in playful activities with other keas and when other keas hear it they "laugh," too!

BEAR PIANIST ▶ A black bear that broke into a home in Vail, Colorado, was captured on the resident's security camera playing the piano in the lounge before raiding the kitchen for food and then leaving.

VENOMOUS PACKAGE ▶ A Los Angeles man was arrested on suspicion of smuggling king cobra snakes into the United States inside potato chip cans. Three live snakes—each about 2 ft (0.6 m) long—were found by Customs and Border Protection officers in a package that was mailed to his California home from Hong Kong.

FREED LEG ▶ Ten-year-old Juliana Ossa fought off an attack from a 9-ft-long (2.7-m) alligator by prying open its jaws and freeing her leg. The reptile had clamped down on the girl's calf and knee while she was swimming in shallow water at a lake in Moss Park, Orlando, Florida. At first she tried hitting it on the head, and when that didn't work, she stuck two fingers up its nose so that it was unable to breathe, forcing it to open its mouth and allowing her to pull her leg out.

EXTRA LEGS ▶ A Black Angus calf born on Gerald Skalsky's ranch near Beulah, North Dakota, in May 2017 had an extra pair of small legs attached to its neck. The calf was otherwise healthy, and the additional limbs were most likely caused by a genetic disorder.

DUELING MANTISES

> These female praying mantises may look like they're performing for the circus, but they're actually in the middle of an intense duel! Photographer Arif Avize spotted the pair while on a walk in Kahramanmaraş, Turkey.

EMERALD RETRIEVER

» A golden retriever in Golspie, Scotland, gave birth to a green puppy! This rare wonder is thought to be caused by a green pigment found in bile that got mixed with the amniotic fluid surrounding the unborn puppy, dying the fur green. The dye-job is temporary, though, meaning this emerald canine will be golden in no time.

TIGER TERROR ▶ In September 2017, 12 monkeys suffered simultaneous heart attacks after apparently being scared to death by a roaring tiger in a forest clearing in the Kotwali Mohammadi region of northern India.

DRIVING COMPANION ▶ In February 2017, police in Edmonton, Alberta, Canada, issued a ticket to a motorist for distracted driving—the person was wearing a live ferret around their neck.

NOT YOUR AVERAGE BEETLE ▷ When it comes to female trilobite beetles, everything about them is weird. Compared to the relatively normal males that reach about 0.2 in (5 mm) in length, females can be as much as 12 times larger, growing up to 2.4 in (6 cm) long. Despite that, they never grow past their larval form, which boasts armor covered in intimidating bumps and spikes. But don't expect all that to be proportional—their heads are extremely small in comparison and can be pulled inside their shell-like thorax for protection.

RIDICULOUSLY TINY HEAD!

PET DETECTIVE ▶ Abby, a bloodhound trained to find missing humans and pets around Jamestown, Rhode Island, reunited more than 80 pets with their owners over the course of her career. She once spent three months searching for a lost cat, Ivy, before eventually reuniting her with her 91-year-old owner.

NOSTRIL CONE ▶ In the opening of each nostril, the peregrine falcon has a small protruding bony cone—known as a baffle—which deflects shockwaves of air away from the bird and allows it to breathe in a controlled manner while diving at incredible speeds of 200 mph (320 kmph). The falcon's design has been copied by the airplane industry. When a jet flies at supersonic speeds, the engine can "choke." Air moving toward the engine appears to hit a wall of resistance and flows around, instead of through, the engine, causing it to stall. So manufacturers build a metallic cone—similar to the falcon's nostril—in the opening of the engine, enabling outside air to enter safely.

SWEET TOOTH ▶ A bear tore off the rear bumper of a car used to deliver doughnuts in Steamboat Springs, Colorado, and then tried to claw its way through the trunk to get inside. Although there were no donuts in the car at the time, the owner, café proprietor Kim Robertson, said the vehicle constantly smells like a bakery, even from the outside.

ANIMALS

Believe It or MOTH

❯ Hummingbird moths fly, move, and even sound just like hummingbirds!

The several species of the genus Hemaris fly suspended in the air as they sip flower nectar, emitting an audible hum. Some species lose the scales that cover their wings and so earn the common name "clearwing hummingbird moths." The next time you're in your garden, take a closer look at that hovering pollinator, because it might just be a moth.

LEMMING LOSS

» In July 2013, a snowy owl nest in the Ungava Peninsula, northern Quebec, Canada, was photographed surrounded by 70 slaughtered lemmings and eight voles. According to research biologist Jean-François Therrien, the unlucky rodents were brought back to the nest by the male owl to feed the mother and incubating chicks. As he usually sees up to three dead lemmings around nests, Therrien called the find "shocking." With an uptick in the Arctic lemming population every few years, there's more food for hungry owl chicks.

SOLE HABITAT ▶ The entire world population of the pygmy three-toed sloth is found in an area the size of New York City's Central Park. The sloth lives only on Isla Escudo de Veraguas, a small island off the coast of Panama.

TAIL EYES ▶ The golden sea snake (*Aipysurus laevis*), which lives in the Indo-Pacific, can see with its tail. It has a series of photoreceptors on its tail, allowing it to detect light variations while it is feeding in the dark crevices of coral reefs. This enables it to spot approaching predators such as sharks.

SKUNK DAMAGE ▶ After a skunk broke in and spent just three hours inside their home in Latrobe, Pennsylvania, it took Scott and Amber Gray and their family more than seven months and $30,000 to repair the damage caused by its noxious spray. The family had to strip the house down to its wood framing to get rid of the odor, throw away furniture, toys, and appliances, and move into a nearby apartment while they rebuilt. Even when they turned on the TV, they could smell the residue of the skunk's spray as the set heated up.

EYE SPY ▶ In 2017, a goat was born in Assam, India, with just one eye in the center of its head, like the mythical cyclops from ancient Greek legend. The condition that causes the birth defect is known as cyclopia and occurs when the two hemispheres of the embryo's brain fail to separate. Owner Mukhuri Das said villagers believed the strange animal was sacred and began to worship it.

STRESS RELIEF ▶ Oliver, an eight-year-old donkey, provided stress relief for students during finals week at Montana State University in Bozeman. Students petted and hugged him and took selfies with him to calm their exam nerves.

HORSE WARNING ▶ Horses kill more people in Australia than snakes and spiders combined. Between 2000 and 2013, horses were responsible for 74 deaths, compared to 27 from snake bites and zero from spiders.

RARE TURTLE ▶ When a Yangtze giant softshell turtle died in captivity in Vietnam in 2016 aged nearly 100, it reduced the world population of the species by a quarter. Scientists know of only three left on the planet—a male and a female at Suzhou Zoo, China, and one wild specimen living in a Vietnamese lake. Also called Red River turtles, they are the largest freshwater turtles in the world and can grow to almost 220 lb (100 kg).

MIRACULOUS RESCUE ▶ A cat thought to have been killed in a house fire at South Haven, Michigan, was rescued after being found alive two months later by the family dog. Christine Marr was certain that their cat, Ringer, had perished in the March 2017 blaze, but when she returned to visit the destroyed home in May of that year, their dog, Chloe, began frantically digging and scratching at the floor. When Chloe eventually found a hole, Marr heard meowing and lured Ringer out with food. Although he had lost half his body weight, the cat had miraculously survived under the floorboards of the burned-down house by eating bugs and spiders.

SHARKNADO

» A 5-ft-long (1.5-m) bull shark was found dead in a puddle about 8 mi (12.8 km) inland on a road near Ayr, Queensland, after Cyclone Debbie hit Australia in March 2017. The shark's body was only discovered when the floodwaters finally receded.

BEETLE INFESTATION ▶ After her dog Bailey refused to eat and began foaming at the mouth, Frances Jiriks took him to a veterinarian in Hoisington, Kansas, who removed up to 40 Asian lady beetles that had been attached to the roof of the dog's mouth. The beetles look like common ladybugs but have a mucus-like discharge that allows them to stick to the top of an animal's mouth.

TOUGH TURTLE ▶ A turtle in Florida miraculously survived despite being run over by one vehicle and then flung through the windshield of the car behind it in a 75 mph (120 kmph) impact. Nicole Bjanes was driving along Interstate 4 in Deltona when the speed of the turtle's collision with the vehicle in front of her sent it flying into the air and smashing through the windshield of her car before hitting the passenger seat and bouncing onto the dashboard. Bjanes was treated for minor cuts, but the turtle swam away unharmed after being placed in a nearby pond.

HEADBUTTING BEES ▶ When a scout honeybee finds what it thinks is a suitable nest location, it performs a "waggle dance" with its body, but if it keeps waggle dancing in favor of an unpopular nesting site, other worker bees headbutt it to help the colony reach a decision. With enough headbutts, a scout bee will stop its dance, demonstrating that there is no longer overwhelming support for that nest.

PYTHON MASSAGE ▶ Frank Doehlen, a hairdresser in Dresden, Germany, offers his customers neck massages by a 4-ft-long (1.2-m) ball python named Monty. The 13-year-old snake, which is 90 percent muscle, has to be booked by appointment only, as its terrarium is too large to fit in the shop permanently.

ALERT KITTEN ▶ Ivan McNamara, of Oldbury, Western Australia, was saved from stepping into a shoe in which a venomous snake was hiding thanks to the vigilance of his four-month-old rescue kitten. When McNamara saw the cat staring intently and lunging at the shoe, he took a closer look and saw a baby tiger snake inside the shoe with its head in a strike position. He eventually managed to capture the snake in a container and release it back into the wild.

RIPPED from HISTORY

Robert Ripley poses with a giant Japanese spider crab, mid-1930s.

SPIDER CRAB

The Japanese spider crab (Macrocheira kaempferi) has a leg span of up to 19 ft (5.8 m) from claw to claw—equal to the width of three cars!

MONKEY
Mommy

> Airocolina "Pinky" Janota from Beecher, Illinois, shares her home with six rescued monkeys, treating the primates like her own children.

The 53-year-old considers herself a mother to the three rhesus macaques, two marmosets, and one bonnet macaque, who are all named after cosmetic brands like Maybelline, L'Oreal, and Avon. Maybelline and co. were abused and abandoned by owners in the United States, with some even missing parts of their tails and ears, before finding their way to Pinky. Pinky keeps busy teaching them sign language, feeding them in their high chairs, and changing their diapers.

FIRST TWINS ▶ Two Irish wolfhound puppies born in Mogale City, South Africa, in 2016 are the first-ever confirmed case of identical twin dogs. Veterinarian Kurt de Cramer was performing a Caesarean section on the mother when he found two puppies—Cullen and Romulus—attached via umbilical cords to the same placenta. The other five puppies in the litter each had their own placenta, as is usual with dogs, and were not identical to the twins. Until then, it was thought that only humans and armadillos could give birth to genetically identical twins.

SCORPION STING ▶ Although the venom of the deathstalker, one of the most dangerous scorpions in the world, is life-threatening, it also has the potential to help treat brain tumors.

BEE SCARE ▶ While helping a beekeeper remove a hive from a tree outside her home, April Collins, of The Village, Oklahoma, ended up with thousands of bees falling on her head—but not one stung her.

PURRFECT LIFE ▶ Clive, a two-year-old Norwegian Forest cat owned by Tanya and Jonathan Irons, disappeared from his home in Nottinghamshire, England, in December 2014, and when he was found in February 2016, he had grown to twice his original size. It turned out that he had spent the intervening 14 months living in a nearby pet food factory.

URINE GUARD ▶ The slender loris of India and Sri Lanka rubs its urine over its hands, face, and feet to act as protection against its diet of toxic beetles and cockroaches. The urine coating defends the loris against any insect stings.

SURPRISE GUEST ▶ Cleaning staff at the Marriott Residence Inn of Worcester, Massachusetts, found a 5-ft-long (1.5-m) reticulated python in a drawer inside a hotel room that had recently been vacated.

COW BURIAL ▶ An American badger spent five straight days painstakingly burying an entire cow carcass in Utah's Great Basin Desert. Badgers like to bury their food so that it stays fresh when they come to eat it later—and a whole cow would be enough to feed the short, stocky mammal for almost two months.

SLOW PROCESS ▶ Sloths have large, slow-acting stomachs with multiple compartments, so it can take up to a month for a sloth to digest its food completely.

Fishy ANI-MOLE

> In May 2017, Missouri fisherman Monroe MacKinney reeled in a once-in-a-lifetime catch—a largemouth bass with a mole peeking out from its mouth.

Although it was too late to save the eastern mole, the 22-year-old was so startled he almost dropped the fish back in the pond. Largemouth bass are known to eat (by way of swallowing whole) pretty much anything, even the unfortunate, displaced mole.

MITTEN CRABS

» These freshwater crabs keep warm with mittens on their claws! Just kidding about the keeping warm part, but Chinese mitten crabs (*Eriocheir sinensis*) are indeed named for the mitten-like hairs covering their white-tipped claws. Interestingly, scientists aren't sure exactly what the hairy bristles (or setae) do. Also, as their name suggests, they are native to the Pacific coast of China and Korea but considered an invasive species everywhere else.

DOUBLE CATCH ▶ When 10-year-old Chipper Burman, of Hockley, Texas, reeled in a catfish, it came with a diamondback water snake attached. The unlucky fish had been caught by the snake and the boy at almost the exact same time.

LOCK PICKERS ▶ Raccoons can pick a lock in fewer than 10 tries and remember the solution for up to three years.

ORIENTATION FLIGHT ▶ Sand wasps fly backward out of the nest to make sure they can find their way home later. On exiting the ground-located nest, they perform an orientation flight, where they fly backward in a zigzag pattern, slowly getting higher and further away, so that they can familiarize themselves with the view they will have when they return.

THIRSTY COBRA ▶ When temperatures soared in parts of southern India in 2017, a video surfaced of a king cobra drinking from a water bottle in a village in Kaiga township. Saved by wildlife rescue workers, the venomous reptile was reportedly 12 ft (3.7 m) long and wandered into town in search of water—which unbelievably happens often during summer months.

YELLOW POOP ▶ The Egyptian vulture deliberately eats the yellow poop from piles of cow dung, partly because it contains nutrients and also because it emphasizes the bird's bright yellow beak, making it look healthy and more attractive to a potential mate.

DOG PASSENGER ▶ Whenever her owner Jeff Young, from Seattle, Washington, is too busy to take her to the park, Eclipse, a black Labrador-bull mastiff mix, catches the bus and goes there by herself. She has been taking the D-Line bus to the park for more than four years, and always occupies a window seat so that she knows when to get off.

DECADE AWAY ▶ Freda Watson, of Winnipeg, Manitoba, Canada, was reunited with her pet cat George after he had been missing from home for more than 10 years.

TALENTED SOW ▶ Pigcasso, a pig that was rescued from a slaughterhouse in South Africa, now creates paintings that sell for up to $2,000. Animal sanctuary manager Joanne Lefson first noticed the sow's talent after putting some paintbrushes in her pen, and Pigcasso has since become such a prolific abstract artist that her paintings are exhibited at her own gallery.

LICKI BRUSH

» Husband and wife Jason and Tara O'Mara, of Portland, Oregon, have designed the LICKI brush, a device that allows cat lovers to groom their pets with an artificial tongue. The tongue-shaped brush is held in the owner's mouth between the teeth and is used to lick a cat's fur in the same way that a cat would lick itself. Not only does it increase the bond with the pet; it also reduces the risk of cat hairballs.

ARTISTIC BEAR ▶ Juuso, a 17-year-old, 930-lb (423-kg) brown bear at the Kuusamo Predator Center in northern Finland, likes painting with his paws—and some of his artworks sell for more than $4,000! Keepers first noticed the bear's artistic tendencies when he got some paint in his paws and started to make marks with them. So now they leave non-toxic paint, plywood, and paper in his enclosure for his use and say red and blue are his favorite colors. A 2017 exhibition in Helsinki featured 11 of Juuso's paintings.

GLOWING SNAIL ▶ When it feels threatened, the clusterwink snail (*Hinea brasiliana*) defends itself by glowing a vibrant blue-green color. Its shell contains a carbonate mineral called aragonite that amplifies light and allows it to flash brightly for a few seconds at a time in the dark ocean waters where it lives off the coast of eastern Australia.

NASAL SNAKE ▶ Marian, a black cat from Mendocino County, California, had to have a snake removed from her nostril. Marian's owner noticed a few inches—including the head—of the tiny, non-venomous sharp-tailed snake dangling from her nose after she had apparently tried to eat it alive. He was able to pull the snake out through her nostril and the cat ran off unharmed.

MOTOR MUTT

» Lidiane Braga Carlos of Campo Largo, Brazil, was shocked when she lifted the hood of her car to find out why it had stopped running, only to see a dog pop up from inside the engine bay! With the help of some baffled passersby, she was able to safely remove the young pooch from the bizarre predicament. Miraculously, the dog was unharmed and the car started up just fine once it was canine-free.

RESOURCEFUL BEAR ▶ A 200-lb (91-kg) black bear accidentally locked itself inside a car in Roanoke County, Virginia, and honked the horn until it was freed by police.

REGULAR ROUTE ▶ For more than a year, Thor, a white Akita Inu dog, has retraced the daily walk that he and his owner, Claudio Cantarelli, used to take through the streets of Caçapava do Sul, Brazil, before Cantarelli's death in December 2015. He stops at all the places—including the lottery office—that he and his master regularly visited together for nearly a decade. People stop to pet him, and food and water bowls are always full outside one of his favorite landmarks, the shoe store.

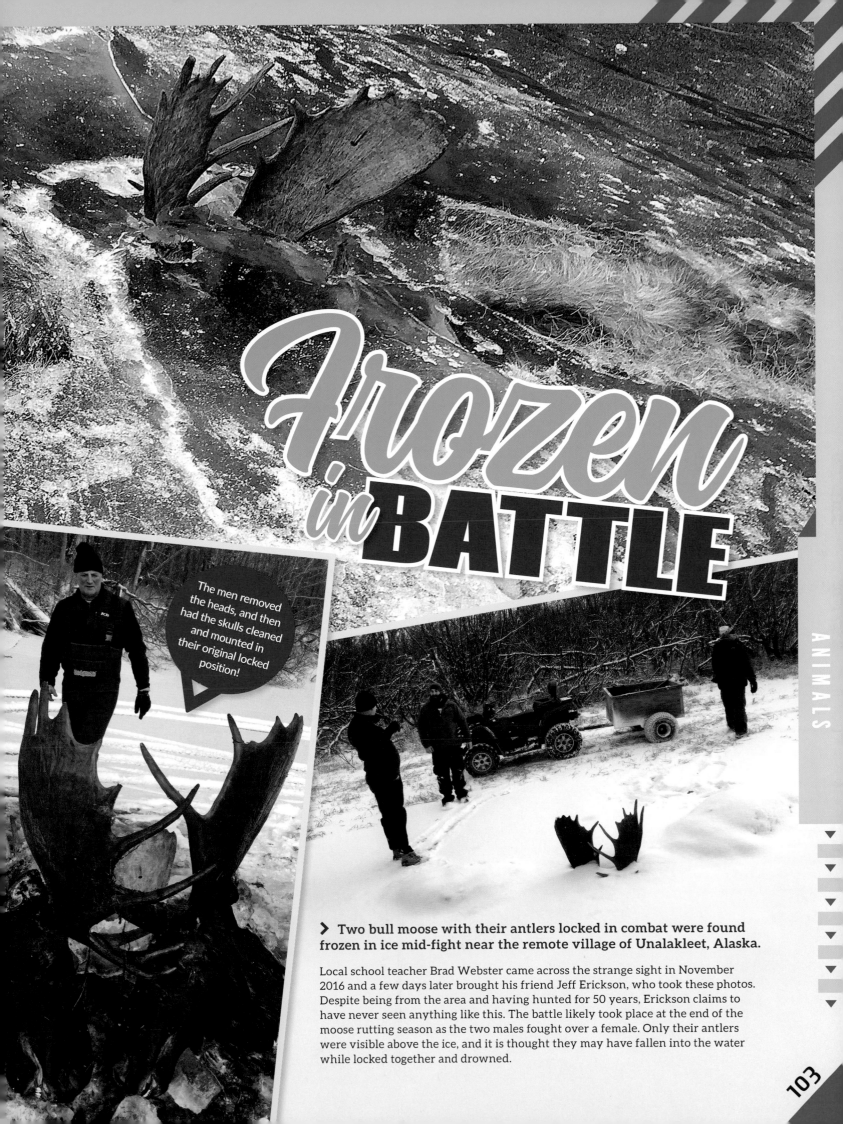

Frozen in BATTLE

The men removed the heads, and then had the skulls cleaned and mounted in their original locked position!

> Two bull moose with their antlers locked in combat were found frozen in ice mid-fight near the remote village of Unalakleet, Alaska.

Local school teacher Brad Webster came across the strange sight in November 2016 and a few days later brought his friend Jeff Erickson, who took these photos. Despite being from the area and having hunted for 50 years, Erickson claims to have never seen anything like this. The battle likely took place at the end of the moose rutting season as the two males fought over a female. Only their antlers were visible above the ice, and it is thought they may have fallen into the water while locked together and drowned.

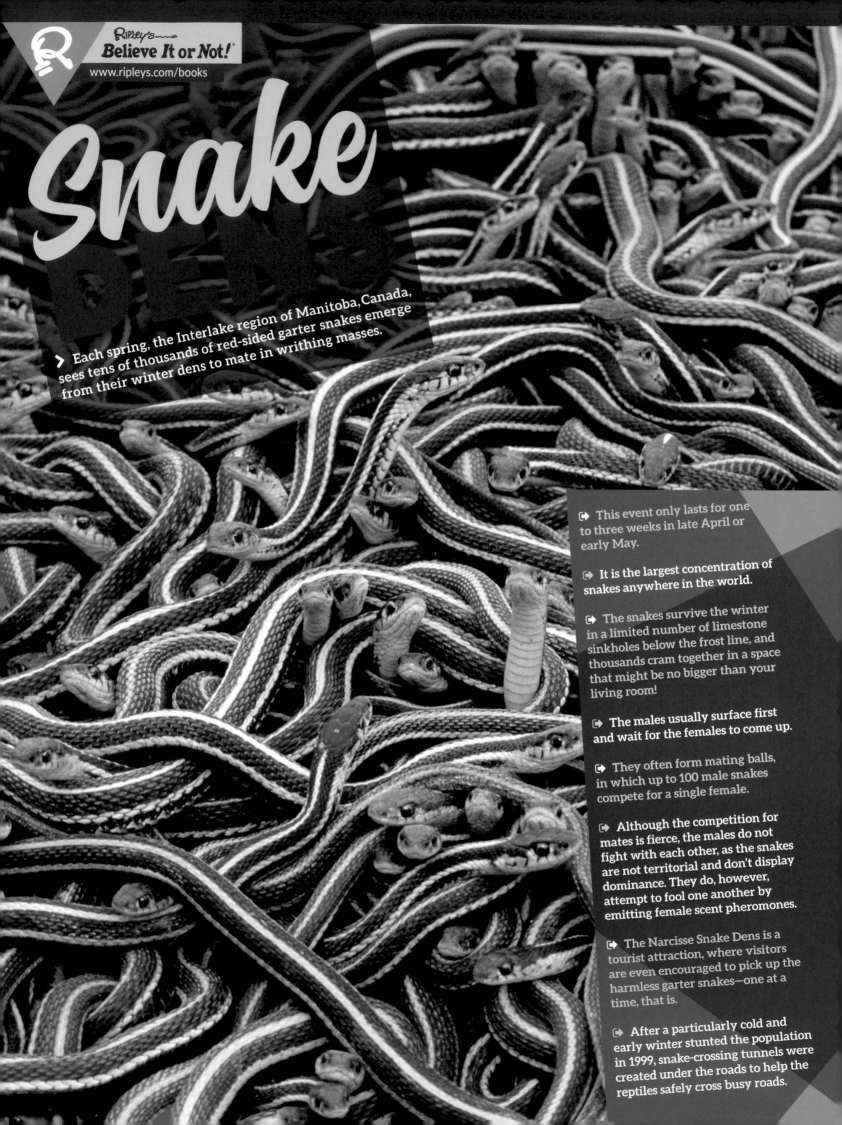

Snake
DENS

➤ Each spring, the Interlake region of Manitoba, Canada, sees tens of thousands of red-sided garter snakes emerge from their winter dens to mate in writhing masses.

➡ This event only lasts for one to three weeks in late April or early May.

➡ It is the largest concentration of snakes anywhere in the world.

➡ The snakes survive the winter in a limited number of limestone sinkholes below the frost line, and thousands cram together in a space that might be no bigger than your living room!

➡ The males usually surface first and wait for the females to come up.

➡ They often form mating balls, in which up to 100 male snakes compete for a single female.

➡ Although the competition for mates is fierce, the males do not fight with each other, as the snakes are not territorial and don't display dominance. They do, however, attempt to fool one another by emitting female scent pheromones.

➡ The Narcisse Snake Dens is a tourist attraction, where visitors are even encouraged to pick up the harmless garter snakes—one at a time, that is.

➡ After a particularly cold and early winter stunted the population in 1999, snake-crossing tunnels were created under the roads to help the reptiles safely cross busy roads.

SKIPPING TERRIER ▶ Together, Jessica the Jack Russell terrier and her owner Rachael Grylls, from Devon, England, performed 59 jumps over a skipping rope in one minute.

NOT EXTINCT ▶ Feared to have become extinct, the New Guinea highland wild dog was rediscovered in 2016—more than 50 years after the last confirmed sighting. An expedition to one of the world's most remote locations found evidence of at least 15 dogs living in the island's mountains.

DAILY WALK ▶ Bruno, a brown Chesapeake Bay-Labrador retriever mix owned by Larry and Debbie LaVallee, has been walking 4 mi (6.4 km) from his home to Longville, Minnesota, every day for over 12 years. He began by following Larry's garbage truck into Longville and has continued his daily trip to spend time with the townsfolk, who give him tasty treats. They have taken him to their hearts so much that he has become the town mascot with a wooden statue commissioned in his honor.

LIMB RETRIEVER ▶ Gertie, an 18-month-old German pointer owned by John Dooner, swam out to sea in Pembrokeshire, Wales, to retrieve a visitor's artificial leg. The woman's prosthetic leg had been swept out to sea by a freak wave.

GIANT WORM ▶ A rare living example of a giant shipworm was recently found by scientists in a shallow lagoon in the Philippines. The strange creature, which spends its life encased in a hard shell and submerged head-down in mud, can grow up to 5 ft (1.5 m) long.

GECKO TAIL!

DefiANT

» An unsuspecting baby gecko at King Rama IX Park in Bangkok, Thailand, struggled in a tug-of-war against a feisty fire ant. Photographer Wei Fu took the well-timed snap while searching for the right ant to shoot. The fire ant did not disappoint as it stood on its back legs trying to move the gecko, with the lizard's tail clamped in its mandibles.

ROCK SHRIMP ▶ A newly discovered species of pistol shrimp has been named *Synalpheus pinkfloydi* for Oxford University natural history scientist Dr. Sammy De Grave's favorite band, Pink Floyd. The shrimp, found off Panama's Pacific coast, uses a bright pink, enlarged claw to create a sound loud enough to kill a small fish.

MYSTERIOUS MILLIPEDE ▶ A newly discovered, millipede-like insect—*Illacme tobini*—found in a cave in California, has four penises, 414 legs, and 200 poison glands that spray a mysterious chemical.

SPEED MACHINES ▶ Cheetahs are able to reach great speeds partly because they run with their claws out. The extra traction they obtain on the ground operates on the same principle as the spikes on running shoes.

BEAR KEEPERS ▶ Visitors to the Wuhan Haichang Ocean Park in Hubei Province, China, can experience life as a polar bear keeper for three hours. For $145, they are given the chance to prepare food for the bears and to clean up their poop.

DOUBLE CAT ▶ In July 2017, an adorable kitten in Japan was spotted with a silhouette of a cat complete with pointy ears across its nose.

SIT. STAY. CONGA!

> The Pompeyo family of Sarasota, Florida, trained their 18 dogs to perform acrobatic tricks!

Former circus artists Jorge and Natalya and their daughters, Katerina and Isabella, travel the country performing choreographed shows with their talented dogs. Some of the tricks these clever canines can perform include skipping rope, leaping over hurdles, walking on their hind or front legs, pushing a toy car, jumping from great heights, and even dancing in a conga line!

SURFING RABBITS ▶ When heavy rain caused floods on Ferg Horne's farm near Dunedin, New Zealand, in July 2017, three wild rabbits escaped the rising water by hopping onto the backs of sheep and surfing to safety.

ANT TRAP ▶ *Allomerus decemarticulatus*, a species of ant that lives in the Amazon jungle, kills its prey by constructing trapdoors in the stems of plants. The ant lies in wait in a hidden, purpose-built hole in the stem that is slightly wider than its body, and when an insect stumbles over the trapdoor above, the ant grabs one of the victim's legs. The ant then wedges itself in place, a trick that allows it to hold on to prey more than 1,000 times heavier than itself.

CATERPILLAR INVASION ▶ Hundreds of thousands of crawling tent caterpillars infested the back of Tammi Hanowski's home near Saskatoon, Saskatchewan, Canada, in May 2017—there were so many that the floor appeared to be moving.

TARANTULA COLLECTOR ▶ Ming Cu shares her home in Bandung City, Indonesia, with 1,500 pet tarantulas. She has been collecting them since 2010, spending more than $55,000 on the spiders, which she keeps in a special room in her house. It takes her around 10 hours each day to feed them, make sure they have enough water, and check their health. She also breeds them, and at first she kept having to buy new males because the females would kill them and eat them after mating. She has been bitten 14 times and has been hospitalized by some of the most venomous species.

KITTEN WHEELCHAIR ▶ A team of eighth graders at Portsmouth Middle School, New Hampshire, created a 3-D-printed wheelchair for Ray, a blind kitten with a spinal condition that makes it difficult for him to walk.

HOUSE GUEST ▶ After his wife and son had heard strange sounds, Bob van der Herchen discovered that a 6-ft-long (1.8-m) boa constrictor had been living in the attic of his home in Englewood, Florida, for up to four years.

LIVE LOBSTER ▶ In 2017, security officers at Boston's Logan International Airport found a giant, 20-lb (9-kg) live lobster among a passenger's luggage. It was cleared and allowed through.

LIZARD REVIVED ▶ When Dale Hall returned to his home in Caloundra, Queensland, Australia, from walking his dog, he found a lifeless blue-tongue lizard lying at the bottom of his swimming pool, but he eventually managed to revive it after fishing it out and giving it CPR.

DOG WHISPERER ▶ Following complaints that his dog Dudley's barking was waking students at night, Brian Gertler, who lives in a dorm at Greenville University, Illinois, taught Dudley to bark in a whisper.

SNAKE RETURNS ▶ Cropan's boa, a snake native to Brazil's Atlantic Forest, was rediscovered in 2017 after a 64-year absence, with no previous specimen having been found alive since 1953.

TALL STORY ▶ Cody Hall proposed to his girlfriend at Dickerson Park Zoo in Springfield, Missouri, with the help of Mili the giraffe. Zookeepers attached his engagement ring to a lanyard and hung it around the giraffe's neck. She thought she was getting a private tour of the enclosure, but when she fed Mili with a tree branch, she saw the ring hanging down and Hall on one knee.

Tomas with his Argentine black and white tegu.

The most venomous animal he owns is this Vietnamese centipede.

Incredible Pet Collection

Tomas Pasiecznik of New Jersey has owned more than 100 different species of animals! The 18-year-old has a passion for invertebrates and reptiles, in particular, and shares videos of his pets with his 60,000+ YouTube subscribers. Included in his collection are a vinegaroon that sprays acid, a Barbados giant land crab, a cow killer wasp, an aggressive tokay gecko, a bright orange Honduran milksnake, a giant African millipede that can grow up to 12 in (30 cm) long, and an English bull terrier dog.

He's owned 110 tarantulas, including a rare Gooty Sapphire Ornamental tarantula.

Although scary, this tailless whip scorpion is harmless to humans!

LUCKY BEAK

» In May 2017, hikers heard a commotion in Cuyahoga Valley National Park, Ohio, and discovered a feisty American bullfrog half-swallowing the head of a red-winged blackbird. The frog's mouth was unable to expand around the bird's wings, which prevented the fowl feast from being eaten whole. They struggled for several moments before breaking free; the bird left shocked but unharmed.

HOME AQUARIUM ▶ The living room of Eli Fruchter's home in Israel contains a gigantic aquarium that holds 7,925 gal (30,000 l) of water and more than 150 tropical fish—and is so large he can dive into it and swim around inside to feed the fish by hand. To ensure that his fish live in perfect conditions, every week he drives a specially fitted golf cart to the nearby shores of the Mediterranean Sea and fills a tank with 260 gal (1,000 l) of fresh seawater for his aquarium.

MONKEY HELPERS ▶ Chilean tourist Maykool Coroseo Acuña was lost in the Amazon rain forest for nine days in February 2017—and said he only survived because a group of monkeys dropped him food and led him to shelter and water. He had been camping in Bolivia's Madidi National Park when he mysteriously wandered off, but claimed he was saved by the monkeys who left him a supply of fruit every day.

LOST BOOBY ▶ In 2016, a red-footed booby bird native to the tropical Caribbean somehow became lost and ended up 5,000 mi (8,000 km) away in southern England—the first recorded sighting of the species in the United Kingdom. Following a period of recovery from the effects of starvation and dehydration, the wayward bird, which was named Norman, was flown back to the Cayman Islands on a 12-hour British Airways flight with a veterinary escort.

ROOF, ROOF! ▶ Huckleberry, a golden retriever owned by Allie Burnitt and Justin Lindenmuth, climbs onto the roof of their house in Austin, Texas, every day and keeps watch on the property. Whenever he is let out in the backyard, he jumps across a 3-ft-wide (0.9-m) gap between a small hill and the roof.

PENGUIN DATING ▶ When Spruce, a one-year-old Humboldt penguin, was unable to find a mate among the 13 other penguins at his home in the Weymouth Sea Life Adventure Park in Dorset, England, his profile was put on an online dating site in the hope that it would attract the attention of other penguin keepers around the world who might have a suitable female. His profile listed him as a less-than-5-ft-tall (1.5-m) non-smoker, with interests including seafood and diving.

CROC WATCH ▶ Firefighters had to tackle a house blaze in Darwin, Australia, while being closely watched by a 13-ft (4-m) pet crocodile. The 70-year-old croc, named Albert, lives in a backyard enclosure and was unharmed by the fire that destroyed the two-story house.

SEAGULL SNATCH ▶ A tiny four-week-old kitten miraculously survived after being snatched from the ground near Rhyl, North Wales, by a marauding seagull. The kitten was attacked by a flock of gulls but was then dropped from the sky by one of the birds and landed scared but unhurt.

GATOR COLLISION ▶ An alligator was killed when it apparently tried to attack a plane that was landing at Orlando Executive Airport, Florida, in 2017. The 11-ft-long (3.4-m) reptile was crossing the runway when it seemed to jump up and lunge at the wing of a Piper PA-31 Navajo light airplane as it landed. The gator died instantly and the plane sustained wing damage.

FROG BAN ▶ It is illegal to keep amphibians—including newts, frogs, toads, and salamanders—as pets in Norway.

ONE HYENA LED ABBAS TO ITS DEN!

What a Mouthful

> Abbas Yusuf, known as "Hyena Man" in his city, feeds local hyenas raw meat—sometimes with his mouth—every night!

Decades ago, his father, Yusef Mume Salleh, started throwing food scraps to roaming hyenas to prevent attacks on his livestock in Harar, Ethiopia. Amazingly, he earned their trust, which was passed to his son after he retired. Livestock and people have remained virtually unharmed since the family first began, now attracting residents and tourists to the daring display.

HEDGEHOG BALLOON ▷ Zeppelin the hedgehog ballooned to twice his normal size after gas collected under his skin. The rare condition, called "balloon syndrome," can be caused by a traumatic event, such as an injury, which releases gas into the cavity under the hedgehog's skin and causes it to inflate like a beach ball. Luckily, the Scottish SPCA rescue team cured Zeppelin by deflating him.

HUGE HOUND ▶ Balthazar, a Great Dane owned by Vinnie Monte-Ervine, of Nottingham, England, measures 7 ft (2.1 m) long from nose to tail and weighs 217 lb (99 kg)—the same as a baby elephant.

COW SALIVA ▶ Cows produce more than three times as much saliva as milk. On average, they produce around 20 gal (75 l) of saliva every day, compared to 6 gal (22 l) of milk, but one study revealed a cow that created a whopping 66 gal (250 l) of saliva in a single day.

SHARP TONGUE ▶ The 10-ft-long (3-m) pirarucu fish (*Arapaima gigas*) of the Amazon is a ferocious predator that not only has teeth on the roof of its mouth, it even has them on its tongue.

SINGING VET ▶ If an animal patient appears anxious before surgery, Dr. Ross Henderson, a veterinarian at the Fox Hollow Animal Hospital in Colorado, serenades them by singing and playing the guitar to soothe their nerves.

DEADLY STRIKE ▶ A single lightning strike on April 29, 2017, killed 32 cows on Jared Blackwelder's farm near Cabool, Missouri.

CHICKEN SWEATERS ▶ Members of a knitting club at Fuller Village, a retirement home in Milton, Massachusetts, made sweaters for chickens to keep the birds warm through the New England winter.

JAGUAR VS. ANACONDA

» This kitty definitely likes the water. In September 2017, photographer Chris Brunskill captured a jaguar fighting a yellow anaconda along the Cuiabá River in western Brazil. Predator and prey battled for about 90 seconds, after which the jaguar came out victorious, hauling the stunned snake into the marshes. Jaguars will eat pretty much anything, including hefty yellow anacondas, which can grow up to 15 ft (4.6 m)!

CHUNKY MONKEY

> A wild macaque monkey, nicknamed Uncle Fat, became so obese after gorging himself on junk food left by tourists in Bangkok, Thailand, that his weight ballooned to about 60 lb (26 kg)—three times the weight of the average male macaque.

Uncle Fat reportedly had minion monkeys that brought him food up until wildlife officials corralled him and put him on a strict diet of lean protein, fruits, and vegetables. He's now on the way to a healthier, happier, diabetes- and heart-disease-free life.

SHARK BITE ▶ A nurse shark that bit Ervin McCarty in the stomach while he was spearfishing off the coast of Marathon, Florida, refused to let go for 30 minutes and eventually had to be cut away from his body with a knife.

ROLE REVERSAL ▶ While many frogs and lizards eat spiders, Florida's 1-in-long (2.5-cm) regal jumping spider (*Phidippus regius*) turns the tables by being able to feast on frogs and lizards three times its size.

TEAM EFFORT ▶ A gecko in Thailand survived after being swallowed whole by a snake thanks to two other lizards that began biting the snake's tail and body so that it eventually regurgitated the live gecko.

BRAINY BIRD ▶ The brain of a hummingbird accounts for 4.2 percent of its body weight, compared to only 0.013 percent in an ostrich. The hummingbird's relatively large brain helps it to stabilize its body while hovering and also to remember the exact location of flowers.

ADAPTABLE RAT ▶ The naked mole rat can survive for nearly 20 minutes without oxygen—by effectively turning itself into a plant. It is able to change its normal metabolism so that its body cells are powered by fructose (fruit sugar) rather than glucose, a process that requires no oxygen. The mole rat lives in underground African desert burrows, which can be 1.5 mi (24 km) long and have little air.

LOSING BEETLE!

Beetle BATTLES

> Every year at the beginning of their mating season, male rhinoceros beetles (*Xylotrupes gideon*) in northern Thailand are collected to fight in battle!

Adults and children alike will train their beetles for weeks by using a small noisemaker stick to teach the insects basic commands like left, right, attack, and caution. Prior to a fight, a female is placed inside a hole in a log which will serve as the dueling grounds. When it is time for battle, the female's pheromones drive the males into a frenzy and they attempt to throw each other off the log while listening to their trainer's commands. Rarely are the beetles injured, as the winner is decided when one retreats or is lifted off the log.

WIDE-EYED

» A video of researchers comparing this stubby squid (*Rossia pacifica*) to a child's toy and laughing at its big googly eyes reached nearly 5 million views on YouTube. Scientists aboard the research ship *Nautilus* were remotely operating a submersible camera about 3,000 ft (900 m) underwater off the coast of California when they found the adorable creature.

SKYDIVING BEAVERS ▶ In an attempt to deal with an overpopulation of beavers in the late 1940s, Idaho's Department of Fish and Game packed the animals into travel boxes, attached parachutes, and dropped them from an airplane into the 2.4 million-acre Frank Church-River of No Return Wilderness. All of the beavers survived their skydiving missions unharmed.

HOUSE FIRE ▶ A pet goat named Speedy saved 10-year-old Abigail Bruce and her family from a night fire that broke out at their house in Weiner, Arkansas. Speedy, who had been bought for Abigail just two days previously as an early birthday gift, woke her by hopping on her legs and chest and bleating loudly. Abigail ran to her parents' room, and when they realized that flames were engulfing the house, they all escaped safely through a bedroom window.

BEE SWARM ▶ Players in a 2017 spring training baseball game between the San Diego Padres and the Colorado Rockies at the Peoria Sports Complex in Arizona were forced to lie on the ground between pitches after a huge swarm of bees invaded the infield.

CONSTANT COMPANION ▶ To aid her recovery following a serious road accident in Milwaukee, Wisconsin, Carla Fitzgerald relies on a support animal: her pet duck named Daniel. She adopted Daniel when he was just two days old in 2012—a year before the accident—and now he is pretty much her constant companion, even flying aboard airplanes with her while dressed in little red shoes and a Captain America diaper.

PENGUIN SUIT ▶ Wonder Twin, a female Adelie penguin at SeaWorld, Orlando, Florida, was fitted with a wetsuit after she suddenly lost her feathers. She wore the custom-made suit for three months until her feathers grew back.

VAMPIRE SQUID ▶ The vampire squid (*Vampyroteuthis infernalis*) gets its name from its dark, webbed arms, which it can draw over itself like a sinister cloak. It lives in the dark ocean depths, and to capture as much light as possible, its eyes take up around one-sixth of its total body size.

CONFUSED CALF ▶ A baby wildebeest ran alongside a car for more than 4 mi (6.4 km) through Kgalagadi Transfrontier Park, which borders Botswana and South Africa, because it appeared to think the vehicle was its mother. The calf's natural instinct was to follow the biggest moving object closest to him, as he would do in the herd.

SHARK HOTSPOT ▶ According to scientific estimates, anyone who has swum in the ocean at New Smyrna Beach in Florida has been within 10 ft (3 m) of a shark.

TRAINING STICK!

Beetles are matched up by size and temperament before fighting.

Spectators place bets on their favorite beetles.

ANIMALS

CAN HOLD ITS BREATH UNDERWATER FOR 30 MINUTES!

SNAKE 'STACHE

» The tentacled snake (*Erpeton tentaculatum*) tricks its prey into swimming directly into its mouth! The aquatic snake anchors itself in the water and stays perfectly still, using its tentacles to determine where its fishy victims are located. When a potential meal gets close enough, the snake moves its body suddenly, initiating the fish's instinct to flee. The reptile takes advantage of this predictable movement and strikes toward the fish's escape route—sometimes even causing the fish to swim right into its mouth!

FREAK ACCIDENT ▶ Nearly 400 birds were found dead on the morning of May 4, 2017, next to a skyscraper in Galveston, Texas, after crashing into the building during a stormy migration flight. The 20 different species—mostly warblers and orioles—are thought to have flown toward the building's bright lights, which were left on at night, after mistaking them for the moon.

KITTEN STOWAWAYS ▶ Four kittens traveled 1,000 mi (1,600 km) from Poland to England inside a cardboard box after hitching a ride in the back of a delivery truck. Their three-day adventure began when the truck left a furniture factory in Zarow, and they traveled undetected through Germany, the Netherlands, Belgium, and France before arriving in England.

NEW SPIDERS ▶ In 2017, researchers visiting the remote Cape York peninsula in northern Queensland, Australia, discovered around 50 new species of spiders, including a venomous huntsman spider that is the size of a dinner plate.

KILLER ANTS ▶
Colonies of African driver ants can contain up to 50 million insects. When a column is on the march in search of food, the ants use their powerful jaws to kill and eat anything in their way—snakes, birds, small mammals, and even, occasionally, animals as big as zebras or cows.

TOXIC POLLUTION ▶ Killifish in the eastern United States have evolved to survive in highly polluted rivers with levels of toxins up to 8,000 times the lethal dose. Additionally, the mangrove killifish (*Kryptolebias marmoratus*) of Florida can live out of water for two months, altering its biological makeup to breathe air through its skin while hiding inside rotten branches and tree trunks.

HEAVY SLEEPERS ▶ A bear spent more than five hours trashing a house in Colorado Springs while Chris O'Dubhraic and his family slept inside. The bear entered through a window that had been left partly open, ripped off the kitchen door, ransacked rooms in search of food, and even peeked into the family's bedrooms while they were asleep.

ANGRY BIRDS ▶ In June 2017, Johnaton Pulain asked a priest to come and bless his house in Harbour Breton, Newfoundland, Canada, after a pair of vicious ravens laid siege to it for weeks. They damaged 10 panes of glass by repeatedly thrashing around his windows and scratching at the surrounding sills. At least one window sill was splashed with blood. He even placed three fake owls around the house to scare them off, but the ravens used them as resting posts. No other house in the area was attacked.

ORANGE CROCS ▶ The dwarf crocodiles that live in Gabon's Abanda caves are orange in color due to a chemical in bat excrement. They spend the dry season in the caves but emerge during the wet season to breed, and the water they have to swim through is turned into an alkaline sludge by thousands of bat droppings. The caustic urea in bat guano erodes the crocodiles' skin and gradually turns them orange.

CRAB IMPERSONATOR ▶ Pharaoh cuttlefish can mimic the appearance and arm movements of harmless hermit crabs so as to get closer to their prey without being detected and catch twice as many fish as a result. Imitating a crab also fools predators into thinking that the cuttlefish has a hard shell, making it less likely to be attacked.

FACELESS FISH ▶ A species of "faceless," gelatinous fish that was pulled up from 2.5 mi (4 km) below the ocean off the eastern coast of Australia in 2017 had only ever been seen once before—back in 1873 off Papua New Guinea. The mysterious creature has no eyes, and its mouth is located underneath its body, making it appear not to have a face.

CHEMICAL ALERT ▶ When an African Matabele ant is injured and needs help, it emits chemical substances to summon other members of the colony to rescue it and carry it back to the nest for treatment. Matabele ants are specialized termite hunters, but their attacks are often met with fierce resistance from the termites, resulting in numerous injuries.

FAMILY HERO ▶ Rescue dog Capone saved the lives of Angela Fullmer and her nine children after a fire broke out at their home in Des Moines, Iowa. In the early hours of the morning of March 15, 2017, with the whole family asleep, the microwave plug caught fire. The two-year-old miniature pinscher, Chihuahua, and whippet mix suddenly began barking furiously and running to the kitchen for at least two minutes before the smoke alarm went off. The flames quickly spread through the house, but, thanks to Capone's alertness, everyone got out safely.

INGESTED POISON ▶ When threatened, the tiger keelback snake (*Rhabdophis tigrinus*) of Southeast Asia releases the toxic irritant of poisonous toads that it has eaten. The snake itself is venomous, but its fangs are located at the rear of its jaws, making it difficult to inject its venom into larger objects. So it feeds on toads, not only being immune to their poison, but also being able to store it in its neck glands, ready for use. The snake prefers to save its own venom for hunting.

TRADITION GOES BACK CENTURIES

Sea
HORSES

> In a centuries-old tradition, horses are trained to wade chest-deep into the sea and pull 43-ft-long (13-m) nets along the seafloor to catch shrimp off the coast of Oostduinkerke, Belgium.

As the horses and fishermen walk parallel to the shore, a heavy chain ahead of the net vibrates the sandy bottom as it is pulled, making the shrimp leap up and into the trap. After 30 minutes, the fishermen take their horses back to shore for a rest while they empty the catch into their large baskets. Only practiced by about a dozen families currently, the unique technique requires high levels of trust between horse and rider.

❯ This parasitic *Phronima sedentaria* amphipod—a small crustacean related to sand fleas—has a transparent body and front claws that it uses to turn vulnerable zooplankton into a nest for its numerous offspring.

The tiny *Phronima amphipod* is found throughout the world's oceans, except the chillier waters of the Arctic and Antarctic. Its amazing camouflage, which also includes an anti-reflective coating, makes it nearly invisible underwater. Deep in the depths, it carves away the insides of barrel-shaped salps (zooplankton) and then settles into the remaining drum, roaming the open water safely with its young while feeding.

COULD THIS BE THE INSPIRATION BEHIND THE XENOMORPHS FROM THE ALIEN FILM SERIES?

IT LIVES INSIDE THE BODY OF ANOTHER ANIMAL WITH ITS BABIES!

NOW YOU SEE ME

FEATHERED DRUMMER ▶
The male palm cockatoo of Australia and New Guinea attracts a mate by playing the drums. It breaks off a small branch from a tree with its beak and then, holding the "drumstick" in his foot, beats the stick against a dead tree trunk. If a female is impressed by his drumming, she soon joins him. The drumming ritual may also serve to mark the bird's territory.

SWALLOWED TONGS ▶ When their pet snake Snickers swallowed a pair of barbecue tongs, two men in Adelaide, South Australia, saved the reptile's life by forcing it to regurgitate the metal implement. It took them an hour to massage the tongs back out of the snake's mouth, and it was left stunned but unharmed by the incident. It is believed the snake may have smelled food on the tongs and thought they were a snack.

CAT LADDER ▶ Şebnem Ilhan, of Tekirdag, Turkey, loves the stray cats in her neighborhood so much that to help them survive through the winter she installed a small metal ladder leading up to the window of her ground-floor apartment, allowing the cats to climb inside and escape from the cold. The ladder is only wide enough for small animals to climb, and the metal bars on the window keep out human intruders.

SWEPT AWAY ▶ In March 2017, a pregnant cow survived being carried almost 50 mi (80 km) down the flooded Richmond River in New South Wales, Australia, during Cyclone Debbie. The animal was swept away from a farm at Riverbank Road, Gundurimba, and finally managed to climb ashore three days later at Riverbank Road, Pimlico.

CLOSE ENCOUNTER ▶ A great white shark burst into an underwater observation cage where Chan Ming, a tourist from Shanghai, China, was watching it off the coast of Mexico. Bait was hanging outside the cage so that visitors could see the great whites close-up, but when the shark lunged at the food, it broke through the cage's metal rail. It then thrashed around in the cage before escaping, leaving Chan shocked but unhurt.

LONG NECK ▶ If the prehistoric dinosaur known as *Brachiosaurus* lived in our world, it could look into a window on the fifth floor of a building.

40 WINKS UNDER THE SEA

» Photographer Franco Banfi free-dived to a depth of around 50 ft (15.2 m) off the coast of the Caribbean island of Dominica to capture a pod of sperm whales napping together in a vertical position. The 40-ft-long (12.2-m) whales only spend 7 percent of their time sleeping in increments of 10 to 15 minutes, making them one of the world's least sleep-dependent animals. Interestingly, the giant marine mammals do not breathe or move at all during their dozes.

YOUR UPLOADS

Conjoined Bats

Marcelo Noqueira from the State University of Northern Rio de Janeiro provided Ripley's with photos of incredibly rare conjoined twin bats. In 2001, the pair of newborn male *Artibeus* bats were found already deceased on the forest floor under a mango tree in southeastern Brazil. Researchers believe the bats died at birth or were stillborn, since the placenta is still attached.

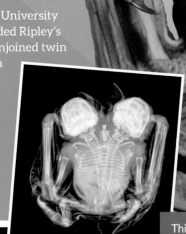

This X-ray shows two separate hearts and where their spines merged.

IT'S A JACK-o'-LANTERN!

PUMPKIN PYTHON

» Pumpkin the snake takes the cake for the most festive Halloween costume! The young royal python was born with orange and black patches that look just like jack-o'-lanterns.

MATING SEARCH ▶ Shortly after flying all the way from their wintering grounds in South America to their breeding sites in Alaska, male pectoral sandpipers will still fly up to 8,000 mi (12,800 km) in a single month in order to mate with as many females as possible.

FLUSHING FEVER ▶ Curt Coleman could never understand why his water bill was so high—until he found his cat Crazy Eyes standing on the toilet lid and using his front paws to operate the flush lever.

ELEPHANT ESCAPE ▶ An elephant named Kelly wandered through Baraboo, Wisconsin, for a couple of hours in June 2017 after her pachyderm partner, Isla, helped her escape from a circus by using her trunk to loosen bolts on their enclosure. Once free, Kelly walked across the shallow Baraboo River and into the backyard of a nearby home where she unlatched a gate and ate some flowers.

KANGAROO RACER ▶ On May 2, 2017, a kangaroo hopped onto a racetrack in Cessnock, New South Wales, Australia, during the last race of the day and briefly led the horses down the back straight before hopping off in another direction.

BALANCING DOG ▶ Pippa the border collie from Newcastle upon Tyne, England, can balance almost anything on her head—including two stacked mandarin oranges! Pippa is so calm she can also balance a cactus in a pot, a huge plastic box, or a single egg.

BIG CAT ▶ Omar, a Maine coon cat owned by Stephy Hirst, of Melbourne, Australia, weighs 31 lb (14 kg)—three times the size of an average cat—and measures nearly 4 ft (1.2 m) long. He eats raw kangaroo meat for dinner.

CHEWED WINDMILL ▶ A four-month-old Labrador puppy in Suffolk, England, swallowed a 1.5-ft-long (45-cm) metal pole after chewing off the end of an ornamental garden windmill. The pole was lodged in the pup's esophagus and stomach, but although he needed emergency surgery, he made a full recovery.

CLEVER COATI ▶ Sunny, a pet coati, is skilled at playing the game Connect 4. Sunny, who lives with his owner André in Berlin, Germany, uses his tiny paws to place the plastic pieces into the slots in the vertical grid. A member of the raccoon family, he has even been taught to wait his turn while playing the game.

MOSQUITO BITES ▶ The annual Russian Mosquito Festival in the town of Berezniki celebrates the presence of the blood-sucking insect—and even awards a prize to the person who has the most mosquito bites on their body. The 2016 winner of the "tastiest girl" category was nine-year-old Irina Ilyukhina who had 43 bites to show for going berry-picking in the forest with her mother.

CAT LOVER ▶ When New Yorker Ellen Frey-Wouter died at age 88, she left $300,000 in her will to her two cats, Troy and Tiger.

ANT ISLAND

❯ During the devastating Houston, Texas, flooding following Hurricane Harvey, a strange and alarming phenomenon was brought to the surface—fire ants forming a protective island to survive the deluge.

Photos and videos of the escaping ants flooded social media, highlighting how these ants, native to the floodplains of South America, escape extreme weather. The ants join forces as rising waters threaten the colony's mound, and they create a ball with the queen, eggs, larvae, and pupae tucked safely inside. The ants then slowly take turns being submerged in the water.

AMPHIBIOUS CENTIPEDE ▷ Unlike other centipedes, a newly discovered Southeast Asian species, *Scolopendra cataracta*, is equally at home in water as it is on land. An expert swimmer, it can run along the beds of streams and rivers in the same way that it does on dry land.

MILK MACHINE ▷ My Gold-ET, a four-year-old Holstein cow owned and bred by Tom and Gin Kestell of Waldo, Wisconsin, produced 77,480 lb (35,144 kg) of milk in 2016—more than three times the annual average for a Holstein.

DRAIN DRAMA ▷ A dog amazingly survived after being trapped down an uncovered storm drain in Nikopol, Ukraine, for three years. Local people had thrown it food during that time, but had been unable to rescue the dog because it kept hiding in a narrow central heating system until an animal handler finally managed to pull it out.

HAGFISH SLIME!

Slip'n SLIME

MARATHON COMPANION ▶ Australian ultramarathon runner Dion Leonard was accompanied for more than 80 mi (128 km) of the 156-mi (250-km) 2016 Gobi March by a stray dog. The small dog appeared on the second day of the seven-day marathon across Chinese mountain and desert terrain, and ran alongside Leonard for four of the six stages. At one point, he had to carry her in his arms across a wide river, even though it meant losing precious seconds in the race.

SUV RESCUE ▶ Guided by musher Neil Eklund, a team of nine Alaskan sled dogs pulled a tourist's stuck SUV out of the snow at the Chena River near Fairbanks, Alaska, on March 12, 2017.

SUPERHERO SNAIL ▶ Discovered for the first time in 2017—stuck to a shipwreck in the Florida Keys—the Spider-Man snail (*Thylacodes vandyensis*) catches prey such as tiny plankton and other organic material by shooting a mucus web. It reels in its catch and then recycles the slime to produce a new snare.

YOUNG HANDLER ▶ Four-year-old Jessica Allen, from Stafford, England, appeared as a dog handler in the main arena at the famous Crufts dog show in Birmingham in 2017, with her pet Australian terrier, Annie, who is older than she is!

WHISTLING DOGS ▶ Dholes, or Asiatic wild dogs, work together in packs to hunt prey, and plan their movements by whistling to each other.

SELECT SQUIRREL ▶ Southern California newspaper *Thousand Oaks Acorn* has featured a "squirrel of the month" every month since the mid-1990s.

> **A truck carrying 7,500 lb (3,402 kg) of slime eels overturned on a highway in Depoe Bay, Oregon!**

Slime eels, also known as hagfish, secrete large amounts of mucus when they are agitated, so when a truck hauling 13 containers full of them was involved in a four-vehicle pile-up, everything turned into a slippery mess. Luckily, no one was seriously injured, but it took workers more than three hours to clear the eels, at one point using a bulldozer to push them off the road!

OVER 3 TONS OF HAGFISH!

FAKE POOP ▸ The caterpillar of the giant swallowtail butterfly, *Papilio cresphontes*, mimics a lump of bird poop to make it unattractive to predators.

TANGLED TAILS ▸ Four baby squirrels were found on a sidewalk in Bangor, Maine, with their tails tangled together. The squirrels, which were all trying to run in opposite directions, were discovered by Andrew Day who then spent about 90 minutes patiently untangling them. The rare phenomenon is known as a "squirrel king" and is sometimes caused by tree sap dripping on to the baby squirrels' tails in their nest and fusing them together.

LARGE EYES ▸ A tawny owl's eye sockets make up 70 percent of its skull, while for humans, eye sockets make up just 5 percent.

MANTIS SHRIMP

» This colorful crustacean can pack a powerful punch! The mantis shrimp's spring-loaded clubs are so fast and strong they can crack aquarium glass. Scientists have recorded mantis shrimp punches at speeds of up to 50 mph (80 kmph)— 50 times faster than you can blink! It's so quick that it makes the water in front of it boil, creating flashes of light invisible to human eyes, and knocks its prey unconscious.

SPRING-LOADED CLUBS!

SILKY SMOOTH

» A hamster that was born with no hair due to a genetic mutation was able to keep warm after a staff member at the Oregon Humane Society crocheted it a tiny white sweater. The hamster, named Silky, has short, curly whiskers on her snout and lives in a heated environment.

CATERPILLAR VOMIT ▶ When attacked, caterpillars of the large white butterfly (*Pieris brassicae*) vomit a green fluid of semi-digested cabbage, which contains compounds that smell and taste unpleasant to predatory birds.

GUIDE CAMEL ▶ Dolly, a blind horse at the Pony X-Press Zoo in Winslow, Maine, has her own seeing eye camel. Caesar the camel acts as Dolly's guide, and she follows him around everywhere. She whinnies for him if he is not nearby and he bellows back at her.

FAKE RATTLERS ▶ North American burrowing owls have learned to mimic the hissing sound of an angry rattlesnake to remain undisturbed by predators in their underground homes.

TALKING COLLAR ▶ A London advertising agency has developed Catterbox, a smart collar that claims to translate a cat's meows into human speech. By analyzing different cat noises, the company has designed a digital sensor that detects meows and uses a special program to decipher their meaning.

GIANT COBWEB ▶ Spiders trying to flee flood waters in Tauranga, New Zealand, created a 100-ft (30-m) sheet of cobwebs in a field in April 2017.

TAKE IT TO-GO

» A raccoon hitched a 7-mi (11-km) ride on the back of a garbage truck in Rosslyn, Virginia. The masked critter had been scavenging through the trash for a tasty treat but ended up holding on to the rear ladder as the truck traveled through town.

SPLIT PERSONALITY ▶ A two-headed rat snake found by Wichita photographer Jason Talbott in a Kansas forest had heads that moved independently and possessed different personalities. One head was aggressive and kept biting, while the other head was much more passive.

POOP SNIFFING ▶ Mandrills sniff each other's poop to stay healthy. By detecting the odor of intestinal parasites in the feces of other members of the group, the African monkeys can identify who is ill and therefore avoid the risk of spreading the parasites by grooming.

DEADLY SERPENT ▶ One drop of the venom of the beaked sea snake, which lives in the Pacific and Indian Oceans, is potent enough to kill five adult men—and a full bite possesses sufficient venom to kill 53 people.

SNAKE TERROR ▶ On March 10, 2017, Monica Dorsett nearly crashed her car when a red rat snake slithered out of the vehicle's air conditioner vent just to the left of the steering wheel as she drove down a highway in Venice, Florida.

SHELL SHOCK ▷ The elephant bird of Madagascar, which became extinct in the 17th century, laid eggs so big you could make 50 omelets from a single egg. Its eggs were up to 13 in (32.5 cm) long and weighed 22 lb (10 kg), with a volume about 150 times greater than that of a chicken egg.

BLADE EATER

KNIFE ACTUAL SIZE!

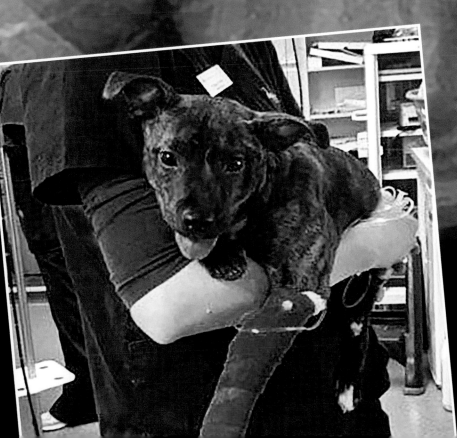

> Lexi the puppy swallowed an entire 8-in-long (20-cm), razor-sharp steak knife!

Thankfully, the Staffordshire bull terrier pup from Sydney, Australia, survived the scary incident. Veterinarians, who said Lexi was just millimeters from death, spent 45 minutes carefully inching the serrated blade back up her esophagus without damaging her vital organs.

123

ODD COUPLE ▶ A goat that was put into a Siberian tiger's den as lunch at Primorsky Safari Park in Shkotovsky, Russia, instead became the big cat's new best friend. Amur the tiger is normally fed two live animals a week, but seemed nonplussed when Timur the goat arrived and showed no sign of fear. The goat even began bullying the tiger, taking over Amur's bed and forcing him to sleep on the snow-covered shelter roof. The odd couple stayed together for more than two months until Timur was moved after they had a violent falling-out when the goat made the mistake of stepping on Amur while he was sleeping.

TRUCK ORDEAL ▶ Percy the cat survived a 406-mi (650-km), 40-hour journey through snow and rain while clinging precariously to the undercarriage of an 18-wheeler semitrailer truck. His owner—St. Paul, Minnesota, trucker Paul Robertson—thought he had lost his traveling companion for good when Percy jumped out of his vehicle at a rest stop in Ohio. After a long, fruitless search, Robertson had to leave to meet a delivery deadline, but when he finally reached Shoals, Indiana, he found that Percy had spent the remainder of the trip hiding under the truck.

FERRET PACEMAKER ▶ Zelda, a four-year-old ferret owned by Carl Hobi of Olathe, Kansas, was fitted with a pacemaker at Kansas State University. A heart blockage left her with a low heartbeat and a lack of energy, so surgeons fitted the device despite the ferret's small build, leaving them only millimeters of space to work in.

GREAT ESCAPE ▶ General, a 10-year-old Great Pyrenees dog, managed to escape from the Aquia-Garrisonville Animal Hospital in Stafford, Virginia, by opening three doors. Video of the escape shows him opening the latch to his kennel, using his mouth to pull down the handle on another door, and then pushing through a third door to make his way out into the hospital's parking lot. After going missing for seven hours, he was eventually discovered resting in the yard of a nearby home and was reunited with his owner Travis Campbell.

PUPPY SURGERY ▶ Thor, an 11-week-old Dogue de Bordeaux puppy, was rushed into surgery after swallowing 109 stones and a padlock in just 15 minutes. His owner, Damon Creevy, from Fife, Scotland, could feel the stones in the dog's stomach and could hear them rattle as he rolled him over.

GIRAFFE BIRTH ▶ More than 1.2 million people watched April the giraffe give birth on April 15, 2017, at the Animal Adventure Park in Harpursville, New York, after it was streamed live via webcam on YouTube. The zoo had begun livestreaming from April's enclosure two months earlier.

DEER DESTROYER ▶ The remains of three deer were discovered inside the body of a 16-ft-long (5-m) female Burmese python in Everglades National Park, Florida, in 2016. The snake had eaten two fawns and an adult doe within a period of 90 days, probably by hiding underwater and ambushing them as they drank.

RARE HYBRID ▶ A male sheep and a female goat mated to create a rare cross-breed called a geep on Mustafa Ace's farm in Belen, Turkey. The strange animal was born with the legs of a goat and the woolly coat of a sheep but was rejected by the mother goat because it didn't look like her other kids.

DOTING PARENTS ▶ An elderly couple in Haikou, China, have raised a 12-ft-long (3.7-m) python as their child for more than eight years. Shi Jimin adopted the young snake in 2009 to save it from certain death and has since watched it grow to weigh more than 120 lb (55 kg). Shi and his wife allow the snake, which they named Shi Nanwang, to slither freely around the house and sit on their laps while they watch TV. They even take him for walks around the neighborhood.

SUPER BUGS

The horned dung beetle *(Onthophagus taurus)* is the **STRONGEST INSECT**, able to pull up to 1,141 times its own weight.

Darwin's bark spider, of Madagascar, produces one of the strongest natural substances on Earth. Its web is **10 TIMES STRONGER THAN KEVLAR** (used in bulletproof vests) and 50 times **STRONGER THAN STEEL**.

A species of ant in the Amazon jungle *(Allomerus decemarticulatus)* **BUILDS TRAPS IN TREES** and latches onto prey before ganging up on it and ripping it to pieces.

While some ants live for weeks, the queens can live for up to **30 YEARS.**

Locusts can fly up to 50 mi (80 km) in one day **WITHOUT REQUIRING A REST.**

Fleas are capable of jumping **150 TIMES** their own height—the equivalent of a human jumping way past the length of the Golden Gate Bridge!

Trap-jaw ants *(Ondontomachus)* have such powerful muscles in their mandibles, they can use them to **LAUNCH THEMSELVES INTO THE AIR.**

⌃ YOUR UPLOADS

Ear-y Growth

Jane Fox from Newbury, England, contacted *Ripley's Believe It or Not!* to share photos of a Wiltshire horn sheep with a third horn growing from its ear! She added that the ewe "is not in any discomfort and is grazing happily in the field."

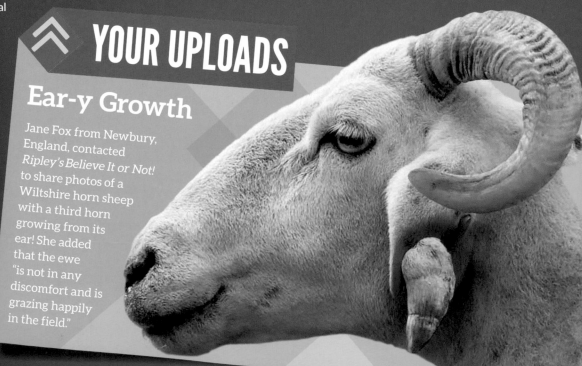

ONE MORE THING: THEY DON'T HAVE EYES

FACEHUGGER

> While working on a biodiversity survey in Mozambique's Gorongosa National Park, entomologist and photographer Piotr Naskrecki discovered a disturbing face-hugging bat fly that feeds on, you guessed it, bats.

Long-winged bats don't stand a chance against these wingless, spider-like flies from the family *Nycteribiidae*. Over time, their bodies have become flattened and hard, making it almost impossible for hosts to squash them, and their feet are equipped with large claws to hold them in place. True parasites, these bad bugs feed exclusively on blood, unable to survive for long outside of their host's body.

DEADLY SNACK ▶ A rooster at a village in Andhra Pradesh, India, pecked a deadly young cobra to death and then ate it.

EMERGENCY NEST ▶ In 2017, a pair of geese that regularly nest close to Lakeside Hospital in Omaha, Nebraska, laid six eggs in a flower pot outside the emergency room doors. The geese have nested near the hospital every spring since 2005.

PITBULL MAYOR ▶ In 2016, a pit bull named Brynneth Pawltro became the fourth dog mayor of Rabbit Hash, Kentucky. She polled more than 3,000 votes, defeating a cat, a donkey, and a chicken, among others.

GROWTH SPURT ▶ The female common mola, or ocean sunfish, can produce as many as 300 million eggs over a spawning season, more than any other known vertebrate. By adulthood the fish often grow to more than 60 million times bigger than their birth size.

HIDING PLACE ▶ A 4-ft-long (1.2-m) snake was pulled from a gas pump in Polk County, Georgia. Brandon Radke, who was buying gas at the station, wrapped his shirt around his hands for protection and used the pump nozzle to force the nonvenomous rat snake from its hiding place before managing to pull it out.

MONSTER MOTH ▣
This odd-looking moth lives in Southeast Asia and Australia and is famous for its massive furry tendrils protruding from its abdomen. The unsightly extensions on the *Creatonotos gangis* moth are actually scent organs called coremata (or hair-pencils), and they produce pheromones to attract mates during courtship.

EAR SELFIE ▶ Lucy, a rescue dog adopted by New York students Cassidy Troy and Zach Johnson, has a perfect self-portrait on her left ear. The black-and-white markings on her ear show two floppy ears, eyes, a nose, and a mouth.

COOKIE CALAMITY ▶ Buddy, a pug and Chihuahua crossbreed, had to be rescued by firefighters in Southampton, England, after getting his head stuck in his family's cookie jar.

BOY RATTLED ▶ On an early-morning visit to the bathroom, four-year-old Isaac McFadden was horrified to discover an adult western diamondback rattlesnake slithering up the toilet bowl of his family's home in Abilene, Texas. He called his mom, Cassie, and a snake removal company later found another 23 rattlesnakes hiding in the cellar and foundations of the house.

BLUE FUR ▶ In 2017, stray dogs going for a swim in the polluted Kasadi River in Navi Mumbai, India, often emerged with bright blue fur because of the industrial waste that had been pumped into the water.

COYOTE COLLISION ▶ A coyote survived an 18.6-mi (30-km) trip in a car grille after it was hit on the highway between Airdrie and Calgary in Alberta, Canada.

AUTO BIRTH ▶ A raccoon gave birth to two babies in the backseat of a convertible at an auto detailing shop in Manatee County, Florida. The mother had accessed the vehicle by crawling through a plastic cover on the car's window.

DOUBLE DUCKLINGS ▶ While hatching Pekin ducklings in an incubator at her home in Nova Scotia, Canada, Amber Brannen was amazed to see that one egg contained twin ducks connected by a single umbilical cord. Incredibly, the egg containing the twins, which she named "Nova" and "Scotia," was no bigger than the others.

ANGRY BIRDS

» Drones do not stand a chance against these birds of prey. In early 2016, police in the Netherlands began training eagles to take down illegal drones, and the program has been so successful there's now a fleet of raging raptors. The French have also hatched a program with golden eagles. With flight speeds up to 80 mph (128 kmph) and tough talons, there's no escape.

WHALE *Heart*

PRESERVED HEART!

> In 2014, a blue whale carcass washed up on the shores of Newfoundland, Canada, and its massive heart was removed, weighing 440 lb (200 kg)—the size of two elephant newborns!

The carcass making it to shore was surprising because when a blue whale dies, its 300,000-lb (136,078-kg) corpse usually sinks and acts as an underwater ecosystem for years after death. Since it was in exceptional condition, scientists were able to preserve the heart with a plastination technique. The four-step process keeps the organ from emitting any odors, prevents it from decaying, and helps it to retain properties of the original specimen.

WEDDING GUESTS ▶ Mountain Peaks Therapy Llamas and Alpacas, of Ridgefield, Washington, rents out smartly dressed llamas and alpacas to attend people's weddings. Copying the bride and groom, the animals wear veils and gowns or hats and bow ties.

CAT WALKER ▶ Each day, Masahiko Suga—the Cat Man of Kyushu—walks his nine pet cats on the streets of Japanese cities in an overcrowded baby stroller. He does it to encourage cat owners to take their pets out for walks in the same way as dogs. He also says it keeps his cats from becoming bored and destroying his furniture.

SNAKE HUNTERS ▶ A bite from a venomous sea snake can kill a person in as little as 20 minutes, but on Kudaka Island, Japan, elderly women wade into the water at night and, using a flashlight, catch the snakes for food with their bare hands.

KEBAB SNATCH ▶ Spotting an unattended kebab on a kitchen countertop, Howie, an eight-year-old chocolate Labrador owned by Sue Woodward, from Hampshire, England, devoured it in one gulp—but swallowed the metal skewer too. Veterinarians successfully removed the 15-in-long (37.5-cm) skewer, which stretched along his whole gullet and was lodged in his stomach.

LUCKY DOG ▶ In 2016, Chinese billionaire Wang Jianlin's son Wang Sicong paid more than $8,000 to buy eight newly released iPhone 7s for his pet dog Coco, an Alaskan Malamute.

HAPPY REUNION ▶ After falling overboard from a boat in Lake Michigan, Rylee, a 10-month-old Belgian Malinois dog, swam 6 mi (9.6 km) to shore and then walked 12 mi (19.3 km) through woods to be reunited with owners Ed and Kristin Casas.

BEE SQUAT ▶ To win a $600 wager, beekeeper Jamie Grainger from New Zealand sat butt naked on a beehive for 30 seconds, during which time he was stung repeatedly.

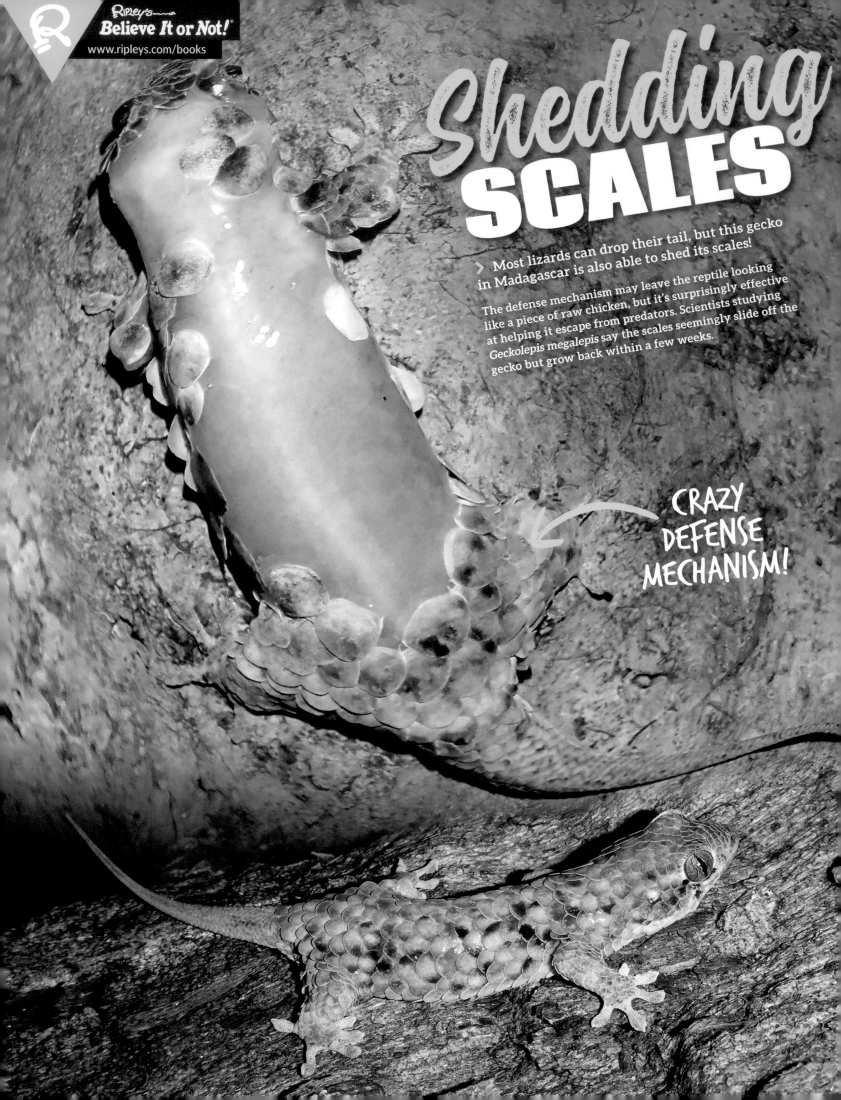

Shedding
SCALES

> Most lizards can drop their tail, but this gecko in Madagascar is also able to shed its scales!

The defense mechanism may leave the reptile looking like a piece of raw chicken, but it's surprisingly effective at helping it escape from predators. Scientists studying *Geckolepis megalepis* say the scales seemingly slide off the gecko but grow back within a few weeks.

CRAZY
DEFENSE
MECHANISM!

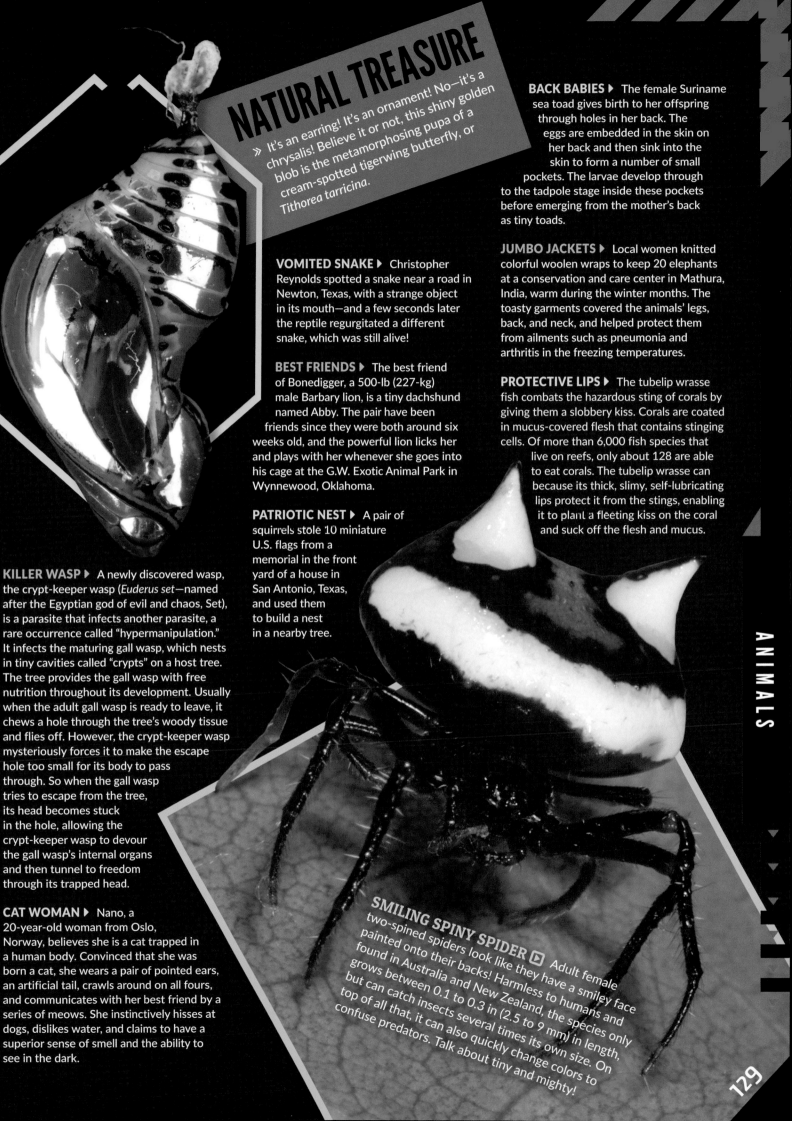

NATURAL TREASURE

» It's an earring! It's an ornament! No—it's a chrysalis! Believe it or not, this shiny golden blob is the metamorphosing pupa of a cream-spotted tigerwing butterfly, or *Tithorea tarricina*.

VOMITED SNAKE ▶ Christopher Reynolds spotted a snake near a road in Newton, Texas, with a strange object in its mouth—and a few seconds later the reptile regurgitated a different snake, which was still alive!

BEST FRIENDS ▶ The best friend of Bonedigger, a 500-lb (227-kg) male Barbary lion, is a tiny dachshund named Abby. The pair have been friends since they were both around six weeks old, and the powerful lion licks her and plays with her whenever she goes into his cage at the G.W. Exotic Animal Park in Wynnewood, Oklahoma.

PATRIOTIC NEST ▶ A pair of squirrels stole 10 miniature U.S. flags from a memorial in the front yard of a house in San Antonio, Texas, and used them to build a nest in a nearby tree.

KILLER WASP ▶ A newly discovered wasp, the crypt-keeper wasp (*Euderus set*—named after the Egyptian god of evil and chaos, Set), is a parasite that infects another parasite, a rare occurrence called "hypermanipulation." It infects the maturing gall wasp, which nests in tiny cavities called "crypts" on a host tree. The tree provides the gall wasp with free nutrition throughout its development. Usually when the adult gall wasp is ready to leave, it chews a hole through the tree's woody tissue and flies off. However, the crypt-keeper wasp mysteriously forces it to make the escape hole too small for its body to pass through. So when the gall wasp tries to escape from the tree, its head becomes stuck in the hole, allowing the crypt-keeper wasp to devour the gall wasp's internal organs and then tunnel to freedom through its trapped head.

CAT WOMAN ▶ Nano, a 20-year-old woman from Oslo, Norway, believes she is a cat trapped in a human body. Convinced that she was born a cat, she wears a pair of pointed ears, an artificial tail, crawls around on all fours, and communicates with her best friend by a series of meows. She instinctively hisses at dogs, dislikes water, and claims to have a superior sense of smell and the ability to see in the dark.

BACK BABIES ▶ The female Suriname sea toad gives birth to her offspring through holes in her back. The eggs are embedded in the skin on her back and then sink into the skin to form a number of small pockets. The larvae develop through to the tadpole stage inside these pockets before emerging from the mother's back as tiny toads.

JUMBO JACKETS ▶ Local women knitted colorful woolen wraps to keep 20 elephants at a conservation and care center in Mathura, India, warm during the winter months. The toasty garments covered the animals' legs, back, and neck, and helped protect them from ailments such as pneumonia and arthritis in the freezing temperatures.

PROTECTIVE LIPS ▶ The tubelip wrasse fish combats the hazardous sting of corals by giving them a slobbery kiss. Corals are coated in mucus-covered flesh that contains stinging cells. Of more than 6,000 fish species that live on reefs, only about 128 are able to eat corals. The tubelip wrasse can because its thick, slimy, self-lubricating lips protect it from the stings, enabling it to plant a fleeting kiss on the coral and suck off the flesh and mucus.

SMILING SPINY SPIDER ▶ Adult female two-spined spiders look like they have a smiley face painted onto their backs! Harmless to humans and found in Australia and New Zealand, the species only grows between 0.1 to 0.3 in (2.5 to 9 mm) in length, but can catch insects several times its own size. On top of all that, it can also quickly change colors to confuse predators. Talk about tiny and mighty!

ANIMALS

129

POP
CUL

MAGIC LETTER ▶ Before his writing career, *The Hobbit* and *The Lord of the Rings* author J. R. R. Tolkien worked for the Oxford English Dictionary company with a focus on Germanic words beginning with the letter "W."

ALIEN CHICKEN

» In November 2017, food blog *The NecroNomNomNomicon* graced us with a new creation: *Alien*-inspired facehugger feast roasted chicken. The recipe incredibly takes 24 hours and includes a full-sized roasting chicken, snow crab legs, and a homemade chicken sausage tail.

REDHEAD MAGAZINE ▶ Founded by Germany-based design student Tristan Rodgers, *MC1R* is a magazine aimed solely at people with red hair. It takes its title from the MC1R protein that regulates skin and hair color in mammals.

FAMOUS NAME ▶ American author Nathanael West's 1939 novel *The Day of the Locust* features a character called Homer Simpson.

DIET DEMAND ▶ Sir Paul McCartney agreed to play himself in a 1995 episode of *The Simpsons* on condition that the producers made Lisa a vegetarian.

FISH LOVER ▶ Before appearing at a festival in Northern Ireland, Eminem asked for a wooden pond to be constructed in his backstage area and filled with his favorite koi carp.

SAY CHEESE! ▶ Sculptor David Bradley recreated Beyoncé's famous photograph announcing her pregnancy with twins—in cheese. It took 28 hours and 44 lb (20 kg) of mild cheddar to construct the "Brie-oncé" model for the E20 Cheese Carving Championships in London, England.

SHARP ACTING ▶ For his role in the 1996 movie *Sling Blade*, Billy Bob Thornton put pieces of crushed glass into his shoes to make his walking gait appear more awkward.

LARGER HANDS ▶ The Sega Saturn controller was 10 percent larger in the United States than in Japan to account for Americans' larger hands.

KITTY COLLECTOR ▶ Masao Gunji, a retired police officer from Yotsukaido, Japan, has been collecting Hello Kitty memorabilia for more than 30 years, and now he has more than 10,000 items. To store them, he built a special pink Hello Kitty house and decorated the interior with Hello Kitty wallpaper.

SPACE ODDITY ▶ In 2016, former U.S. astronaut Buzz Aldrin was treated in a New Zealand hospital by Dr. David Bowie, namesake of the late English musician famous for his songs about space travel, including "Starman."

LUCKY BREAK ▶ Hawaiian ukulele player Clint Alama won the chance to perform for one night with reggae star Matisyahu at the Hollywood Palladium in Los Angeles after a judge allowed him to be temporarily released from jail. Matisyahu and his bassist Stu Brooks were at a Maui coffee shop when they heard Alama strumming the singer's hit "One Day." Matisyahu promptly sang along, but Alama had no idea who he was until he introduced himself. Matisyahu then invited Alama to perform the song with him in Hollywood, only for Alama to reveal that there was a warrant out for his arrest for an alleged probation violation.

TOILET BREAK ▶ The app RunPee advises users on the best time to take an urgent toilet break during a trip to a movie theater so that they do not miss a crucial moment. It picks out three-to-five-minute-long movie scenes that do not contain essential plot twists, exciting action, or laugh-out-loud moments.

ACTOR PHOTOS ▶ In 2016, the Huntley Hotel in Santa Monica, California, provided three framed photos of Hollywood star Jeff Goldblum in a guest's room. The guest, Seth Freedland, requested the pictures because he wanted to please his girlfriend who has had a big crush on the actor since she saw him in *Independence Day*.

Ripley's Exhibit
Cat. No. 172670

Chester Cheetah Sculpture

Made entirely from Cheetos and Cheeto packaging. Short-lived stay at the New York BION.

Snorlax from *Pokémon* made of 4,704 cans, feeding 1,225 people.

Rose from *Beauty and the Beast* made of 1,512 cans, feeding 1,564 people.

PAC-MAN made of 2,760 cans, feeding 2,209 people.

In the CANNED GOODS

> For the past 25 years, a unique charity art competition out of New York called Canstruction sees teams of volunteers use hundreds of thousands of unopened cans of food to create art.

Architects, engineers, and students spend weeks designing—but just one night assembling—their gravity-defying creations. Designs include Popeye, the throne from *Game of Thrones*, Pokémon, and even the rose from *Beauty and the Beast*. All cans are later donated to food shelters, soup kitchens, and food relief efforts in New York.

Mini Origami

Ripley's EXCLUSIVE

> David Kawai, of Ottawa, Ontario, Canada, uses just his fingers to make teeny tiny origami cranes that are about one-tenth the size of a thumbnail.

After a friend taught him how to do it, Kawai started making hundreds of paper cranes and then challenged himself to make the smallest one possible. Each fold in the paper has to be precise, down to a quarter of a millimeter.

Q Do you use tools other than your hands?

A Sometimes I use the table when creasing the paper with my fingernails, and before I even start folding, I have to use scissors to cut out a tiny square.

Q How many cranes have you made?

A By now I've made about 30 tiny ones. But I've made more bigger ones. Never counted.

Q Are they all cranes?

A Yes, I enjoy making cranes and have no motivation to make other animals.

Q Exactly how small do your mini cranes measure?

A The best way to measure them is probably based on the size of the initial unfolded square piece of paper, which usually has the same width and height of between 5 mm and 6 mm.

Q Have you tried or are you planning to try other patterns or animals?

A I have no plans to do other patterned paper or other origami animals. The paper I use handles the folds nicely. Anything thicker or thinner would either be hard to fold over at that scale, or just fall apart too much with each fold for the necessary structural integrity of the crane, the way I do it at least. But if the paper is the right weight, I'll gladly try. It's just not something I'm seeking out.

Q Do you keep them or give them away?

A I keep them, but I've given a couple away. I don't know yet what I want to do with them.

Q Would you ever make 1,000 mini origami cranes for someone?

A One day it would be nice to make 1,000 tiny ones. It would feel like a big accomplishment!

STUFFED PIGEONS ▶ *Turisti* (Tourists), an installation by Italian artist Maurizio Cattelan, featured 2,000 stuffed pigeons perched on top of the air conditioning pipes high in a Venice exhibition. Their presence was revealed to visitors below by the specks of fake bird poop that were deposited on the floor and on pieces created by other artists.

PHEASANT FEATHERS ▶ Clare Brownlow, from Kelso, Scotland, paints beautifully detailed pictures of pheasants using real pheasant tail feathers as her paintbrushes.

NOSTALGIA TRIP ▶ Before his old childhood home in Manhattan Beach, California, was finally demolished, Texas-based artist Gary Sweeney covered the outside walls of the house in 70 years' worth of family photos taken by his late father.

GRUESOME CURE ▶ German composer Robert Schumann (1810–1856) would often plunge his hands into the entrails of a slaughtered animal to heal the paralysis in his hands.

CARD VASES ▶ Zhang Kehua, from Qianjiang, China, creates realistic-looking, Chinese patterned porcelain vases out of thousands of folded playing cards. Some of his vases stand more than 6.5 ft (2 m) tall and contain more than 5,000 cards.

ELVIS COINCIDENCE ▶ In 1979, John Carpenter directed a made-for-TV biopic about Elvis Presley. Ten years earlier, Elvis had made his last acting appearance in a movie titled *Change of Habit*, playing a character called John Carpenter.

> **J. K. Rowling's seven Harry Potter books have sold more than 500 million copies worldwide—and if they were placed end to end, they would circle the planet six times.**

MARIO MAZE ▶ Tom Stoughton created an 8-acre *Super Mario Bros.* corn maze—featuring images of Mario, Luigi, Princess Peach, Toad, and Yoshi—in a field on his farm in Newark Valley, New York.

CHOCOLATE SHOES ▶ Master Japanese chocolatier Motohiro Okai has designed a range of life-size, realistic-looking chocolate shoes. The "Gentleman's Radiance" line look like normal shiny leather shoes in three different shades—light brown, dark brown, and red-brown—but instead every part, including the insole and laces, is made of chocolate. Each pair also comes with shoe care accessories, including a chocolate shoehorn and a jar of "shoe cream" that actually contains round disks of tempered chocolate.

BULLET SHELLS ▶ Federico Uribe, a Colombian artist based in Miami, Florida, creates cute animal sculptures and beautiful landscapes out of thousands of used bullet shells.

TV FAVORITES ▶ Alex Trebek and Johnny Gilbert have been host and announcer, respectively, on the TV game show *Jeopardy!* since 1984, notching up more than 7,500 episodes.

NEW STATUE ▶ Sculptor Carolyn D. Palmer was commissioned to create a new bronze statue of Lucille Ball in Celoron, New Jersey—the late comic actress' hometown—as a replacement for another artist's 2009 statue that many people thought bore so little resemblance to Ball that they dubbed it "Scary Lucy." It took Palmer nine months to make her statue, which is 6 ft (1.8 m) tall and weighs 800 lb (363 kg).

SPREADSHEET MISSION ▶ By keeping his finger permanently on the down arrow key, YouTuber Hunter Hobbs, of Norman, Oklahoma, discovered that it takes 9 hours 36 minutes 10 seconds to scroll to the bottom of a Microsoft Excel spreadsheet—a total of 1,048,576 rows. He passed the time by talking on the phone, listening to music, and playing games—all one-handed.

COLORFUL SOUNDS ▶ Artist Melissa McCracken, of Kansas City, Missouri, has a neurological condition called "synesthesia," which allows her to experience sounds, letters, and numbers as colors. She turns songs such as John Lennon's "Imagine" and Prince's "Joy in Repetition" into vibrant paintings.

Ripley's Exhibit
Cat. No. 173074

Shoes from Back to the Future II
Futuristic Nikes worn by Marty McFly
(actor Michael J. Fox).

The double buns, which actress Carrie Fischer famously disliked, took two hours to style every day!

Princess Leia
HAIR REBELution

> Believe it or not, Princess Leia's iconic hair-do did not come from a galaxy far, far away!

Star Wars heroine Princess Leia was fearless in battle, dedicated to taking down the Empire, and one of the Rebel Alliance's greatest leaders. All of these strong traits, down to the two buns coiled on the sides of her head, can be attributed to Mexico's female revolutionaries.

In 2002, *Star Wars* creator George Lucas stated that he looked to Mexico's female warriors, or *soldaderas*, for inspiration. Don't let their highly styled hair fool you. These women, who joined the revolution around the start of the 20th century, were tough and considered an important part of Mexico's rebel force!

Some historians note that the *soldaderas* were not the only ones to sport Leia's buns. The women of the Native American Hopi tribe may have also been intergalactic inspiration, but regardless of what culture Leia's hair originated from, it was inspired by strong women like Leia, and the woman who embodied her, Carrie Fisher.

ROGUE BUN

» Clara de la Rocha was a colonel in the Mexican Revolution (1910–1920), fighting against the longstanding dictatorship of Porfirio Díaz. It is thought that this photo of de la Rocha in particular, now archived at the Lucas Museum of Narrative Art, inspired Leia's famous coiled buns. Here, she is seen standing next to her father, General Herculano de la Rocha. Clara de la Rocha is known for a key 1911 battle in Sinaloa, northern Mexico, where she crossed a river on horseback and took out a power station in order to allow rebel forces to attack at night without being seen!

The "squash blossom" is the traditional hairstyle for unmarried girls in the Hopi tribe of Arizona and is created with the help of wooden disks.

LEIA BUNS ON A SOLDADERA!

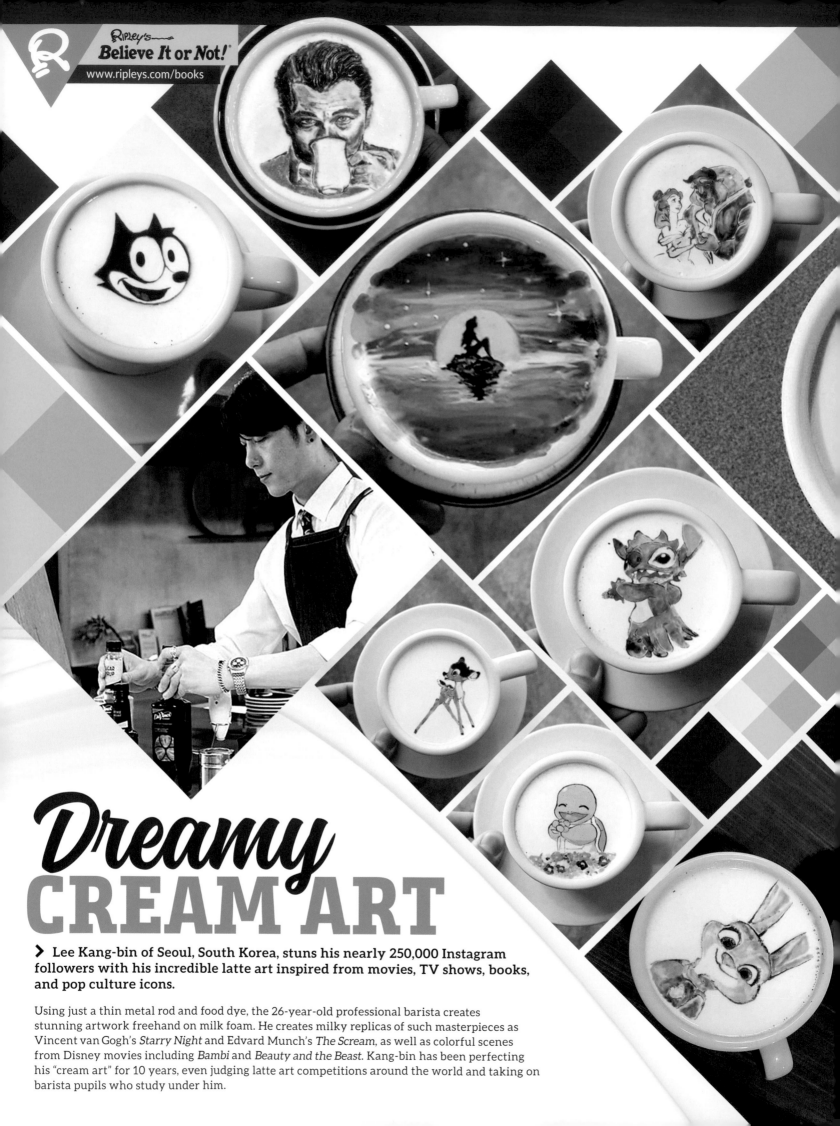

Dreamy
CREAM ART

> Lee Kang-bin of Seoul, South Korea, stuns his nearly 250,000 Instagram followers with his incredible latte art inspired from movies, TV shows, books, and pop culture icons.

Using just a thin metal rod and food dye, the 26-year-old professional barista creates stunning artwork freehand on milk foam. He creates milky replicas of such masterpieces as Vincent van Gogh's *Starry Night* and Edvard Munch's *The Scream*, as well as colorful scenes from Disney movies including *Bambi* and *Beauty and the Beast*. Kang-bin has been perfecting his "cream art" for 10 years, even judging latte art competitions around the world and taking on barista pupils who study under him.

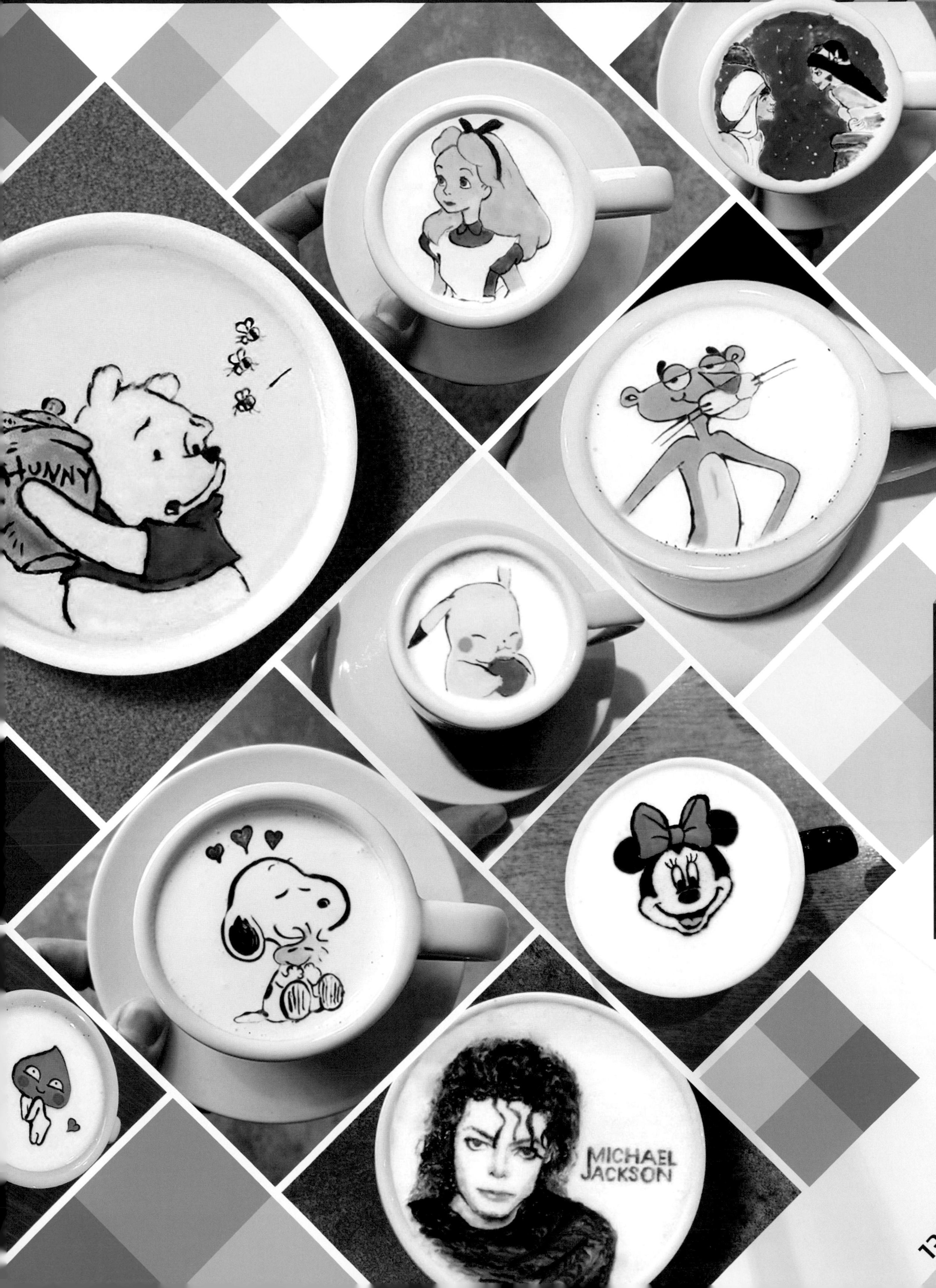
HUNNY
MICHAEL
JACKSON

HELLTHY JUNK FOOD

Ripley's
EXCLUSIVE

> Food junkies JP Lambiase and Julia Goolia of Orlando, Florida, are the architects behind Hellthy Junk Food—a website and YouTube channel featuring all sorts of unbelievably outrageous junk food creations that the couple make themselves!

In honor of our 100th anniversary, JP and Julia partnered with us to create something explosive—a grilled cheese volcano with tomato soup lava!

Q What inspired you to start making crazy food and posting to YouTube?

A We started the channel as a way of eating out less and still being able to enjoy our favorite restaurant foods at home. It was never our intention to make crazy food on YouTube, but it eventually turned into that when we realized our channel wasn't so much instructional as it was entertaining. It wasn't until we created the Pizza Cake over three years ago that the crazy food started to happen. Being a little odd or different in the food world evolved into what we are today.

Q What has been the most difficult thing to make?

A It would have to be the Junk Food House. We spent days drawing up blueprints, building, crafting, designing, etc. We wanted to show our junk food take on a gingerbread house for the holidays, making it out of our favorite savory junk foods.

Q *Do you eat everything?*

A No. We were both raised not to waste food, though, so every chance we get, when it's something unmanageable for the two of us to consume, we invite friends over to eat with us. The best example of this is when we invited two competitive eaters over to our house and together they both polished off over 8 lb (3.6 kg) of food. Mind you, that was just an appetizer for them. They got a 32-in (0.8-m) pizza after that.

Q *What was your most disgusting creation?*

A JP has created a lot of disgusting dishes, such as the Giant KFC Drumstick made out of a dog bone, frequently cross-contaminating various proteins and stuffing random food inside other food. But our most disgusting creation of all time has to be the ketchup and mayonnaise ice cream.

Q *Are there any creations that turned out so bad they were never released as an episode?*

A The only creation that we can recall that never made it as an episode was the Churro Fries; it just never panned out. We'll show our fails on camera because at the end of the day it's all about being 100 percent transparent with our audience. Nobody's perfect. It's okay to fail, and if you can learn from it, it's that much better.

Q *Are there any foods that act in unexpected ways when scaled up?*

A Anything chocolate, or chicken, when scaled up has a less desirable effect. Thick chocolate is hard to consume, and large copious amounts of chicken provide an unbalanced flavor distribution. However, on camera they look incredible. Mostly everything else giant we create acts like a giant pie that you can slice up and share with friends and family.

Q *What are some tips for anyone wanting to create giant, crazy foods?*

A The whole essence behind creating giant, crazy foods is to share it with people. Share the experience. Share the WOW, Believe It or Not! Our tip is to start with something that you have the tools and capability for because it can be pricy. We recommend the Giant Crunchwrap because it's sharable, simple, and absolutely delicious!

141

A RECIPE FOR DISASTER

❯ The volcano is built out of grilled-to-perfection grilled cheese sandwiches over top of a fondue machine filled with "magma"—that is, classic tomato soup. At the point of eruption, the "magma" turns into "lava," and when the fondue machine is turned on, it becomes one beautiful disaster.

PREP TIME: 2 hours
COOK TIME: 15 minutes
TOTAL TIME: 2 hours 15 minutes

INGREDIENTS:

Tomato Soup Fondue
· 4 Campbell's Family Size Tomato Soup, 22.6 oz
· Milk
· Water

Grilled Cheese
· 6 Giant Bread Loaves (180 slices)
· 6 Package American Cheese Slices (24 count)
· 1 Jar Mayonnaise (as spread, butter as substitute)

THINGS YOU'LL NEED:
· Fondue Fountain: Small OR Giant
· Electric Griddle
· Parchment Paper
· Stock/Soup Pot

INSTRUCTIONS:

1. Assemble fondue fountain per manufacturer's instructions.

2. Make your soup by opening up the cans and pouring the tomato base into a pot. For 4 family-size tomato soups, we used 1 can water and 1 can milk. Add your liquid, either water or milk, or both (up to you). Make sure to test the tomato soup's consistency before pouring it into your fondue fountain's base. If it is too thick, it won't flow through the machine. If it is too thin, it will splatter.

3. Pour the soup into your fondue machine base. Wrap your machine with parchment paper and secure at the top tier and set aside.

4. Preheat a griddle or a sauté pan to medium-high heat. Spread mayonnaise or butter onto your bread. We find that mayonnaise is perfect for grilled cheese because it's easier to spread and provides bolder color, texture, and flavor. Place cheese in between your bread and grill until golden brown. Repeat until all of your grilled cheese sandwiches are cooked.

5. Start your build. For a smaller fondue machine, cut small triangles out of the grilled cheeses and stack them up the side of the machine, using toothpicks when needed to secure in place. For the giant volcano, cut the grilled cheese into large triangles and built around, in the same fashion. This is the part that you can have fun with. Make your own design!

6. Once built, preheat the fondue machine for 5–10 minutes before turning on.

7. Finally, turn the fondue machine on, feast your eyes on the beautiful disaster, and dig in!

HELLTHY NUTRITIONAL INFORMATION:
Serving size: 1 · Calories: 10,950 · Fat: 500g · Saturated fat:15g
Unsaturated fat: 0g · Trans fat: 0g · Carbohydrates: 1,170g · Sugar: 490g
Sodium: 6,500mg · Fiber: 20g · Protein: 390g · Cholesterol: 50mg

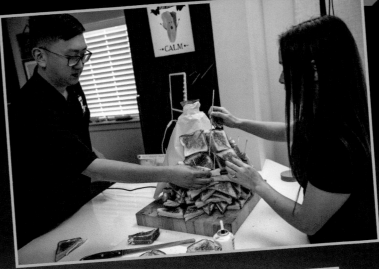

RIPPED *From* HISTORY

"I WANT TO BUY A VOLCANO"!

Ripley

VOLCANIC CORNFIELD

Working in his fields in 1943, a Mexican farmer saw a hole open in the ground, from which smoke and dust emerged, as well as sulfurous materials. Slowly, a volcanic cone took form. Now called Parícutin, the volcano had reached a height of 1,391 ft (424 m) by the time it became dormant in 1952. Robert Ripley tried to buy this volcano!

Ripley in Mexico standing with a volcano in the background (c. 1940).

143

TARDIS LIBRARY

» Dan Zemke, of Detroit, Michigan, built and installed a free library inside of a life-size TARDIS replica from the classic BBC show *Doctor Who*. Zemke wanted to liven up an empty lot across from his home by combining his love for the show and reading. The structure stands 10 ft (3 m) tall, weighs nearly a ton, and holds 140 books hidden behind painted panels.

FAKE NAMES ▶ A 75-year-old woman from Kingston, Ontario, Canada, was unable to sell her Chevrolet SUV for nine months after learning that fictional characters Fred and Pebbles Flintstone had placed a lien—a debt order—on the vehicle. The fake names were used to test vehicle identification numbers in the government's computer system, but because they had never been removed, the lien remained on the SUV until the error was finally corrected.

PROPHETIC POSTER ▶ During the assassination attempt on Don Vito Corleone in the 1972 movie *The Godfather*, a poster seen in the background promotes a boxing match featuring American professional boxer Jake LaMotta. Over the next nine years, actor Robert De Niro won two Academy Awards. . . for playing Vito Corleone in *The Godfather: Part II* and Jake LaMotta in *Raging Bull*.

DEATH WISH ▶ When she was 14, Angelina Jolie wanted to be a funeral director and even did a mail-order degree in the subject. She considered choosing it as a career path after being disappointed with the way her grandfather's funeral was conducted.

TV PHOBIA ▶ Icelandic singer Björk was once afraid of televisions. A poet convinced her that they made her susceptible to hypnosis.

HOME SOIL ▶ When Polish composer Frederic Chopin died in Paris, France, in 1849, he was buried with a small urn of authentic Polish soil that he had kept since 1830.

HOT SCENE ▶ A spectacular battle sequence for season seven of Game of Thrones featured an incredible 73 fire burns, while 20 stuntmen were set on fire simultaneously.

CHOCOLATE SCULPTURES ▶ French chocolate artist Nikolai Popov creates paintings and sculptures from chocolate, including a model of the Eiffel Tower, China's Terracotta Army, miniature dinosaurs, a chess board, and a grand piano. A 2016 exhibition in China of 700 of his works used a total of 3,300 lb (1,500 kg) of chocolate—equivalent to more than 30,000 chocolate bars.

REBEL ROCKER ▶ Steve Coupe, of Auckland, New Zealand, created a rocking X-wing starfighter from Star Wars completely out of solid wood. It was made and auctioned off for charity and took Coupe about 60 hours to construct without any plans. The rocker is 3.75 ft (1.1 m) long, 4 ft (1.2 m) wide, and comes with a removable wooden R2-D2, rotating head and all.

VIEW FROM THE BACK! ➔

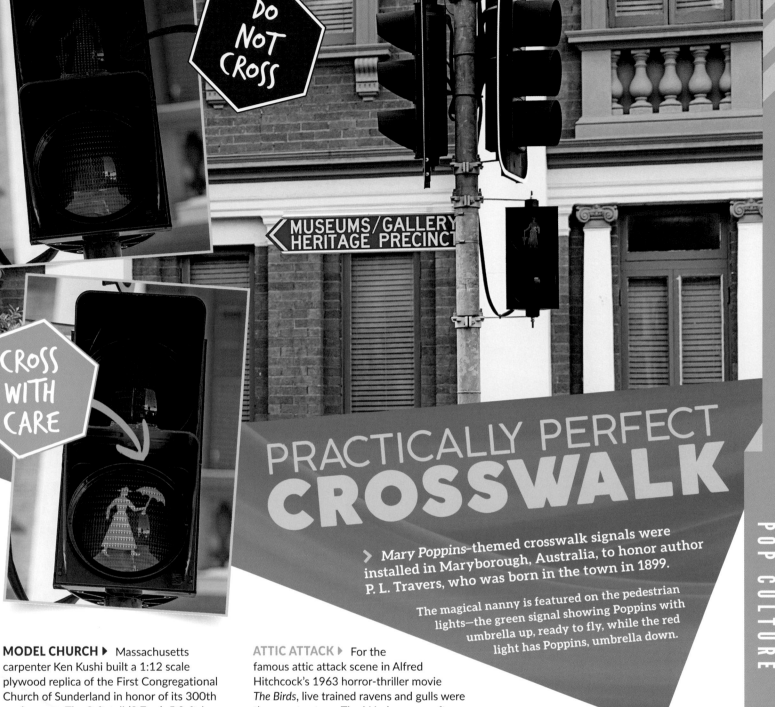

DO NOT CROSS

CROSS WITH CARE

MUSEUMS/GALLERY HERITAGE PRECINCT

PRACTICALLY PERFECT
CROSSWALK

> Mary Poppins–themed crosswalk signals were installed in Maryborough, Australia, to honor author P. L. Travers, who was born in the town in 1899.

The magical nanny is featured on the pedestrian lights—the green signal showing Poppins with umbrella up, ready to fly, while the red light has Poppins, umbrella down.

MODEL CHURCH ▶ Massachusetts carpenter Ken Kushi built a 1:12 scale plywood replica of the First Congregational Church of Sunderland in honor of its 300th anniversary. The 9-ft-tall (2.7-m), 5.8-ft-long (1.8-m) model took around 200 working hours, has real copper roofing, a papier-mâché stained glass window, and is detailed down to a small steel bell that hangs in the bell tower.

BEAN COUNTER ▶ German composer and pianist Ludwig van Beethoven (1770–1827) was so meticulous that he would count out exactly 60 coffee beans each time he made a cup of coffee.

EARLY START ▶ While still in elementary school, George R. R. Martin—author of the books behind *Game of Thrones*—used to write and sell monster stories for pennies to other children in his home neighborhood of Bayonne, New Jersey.

ATTIC ATTACK ▶ For the famous attic attack scene in Alfred Hitchcock's 1963 horror-thriller movie *The Birds*, live trained ravens and gulls were thrown at actress Tippi Hedren, one after another, for a week. Some of the birds were tied to her clothes with nylon threads to stop them from flying away. Filming would be halted every few minutes so that her clothing could be torn and fake blood painted on her skin. On the last day of shooting, one of the birds actually clawed Hedren's eye.

TINY CHESSBOARD ▶ Ahona Mukherjee, from Bangalore, India, used polymer clay to make a tiny chessboard, measuring 0.35 × 0.35 in (0.9 × 0.9 cm), complete with 32 pieces, some just 0.08 in (0.2 cm) tall.

LITERARY NEIGHBORS ▶ Harriet Beecher Stowe (1811–1896), author of *Uncle Tom's Cabin*, lived next door to Mark Twain in Hartford, Connecticut.

BLINDFOLD GAMER ▶ On May 24, 2017, gamer katun24 completed *Super Mario World* in only 13 minutes 31 seconds—all while blindfolded.

MANY TALENTS ▶ Massachusetts-born William Moulton Marston (1893–1947), the creator of Wonder Woman, also invented the polygraph machine.

NO MORE! ▶ In 2017, a thrift store in Swansea, Wales, asked people to stop sending them copies of Dan Brown's mystery-detective novel *The Da Vinci Code* because they were receiving a copy of the book almost every week.

POKÉMON MURAL ▶ Efren Andaluz, aka Andaluz the Artist, became so captivated by the *Pokémon Go* craze that he used 125 cans of spray paint to create a giant mural featuring all 151 first-generation Pokémon on a 50-ft-long (15-m) wall on the outside of his studio in Huntington, New York. It took him 10 days to complete the mural, and he needed a mechanical lift to reach the top of the 25-ft-tall (8-m) wall.

EXPLOSIVE MAP ▶ Cartographer Matt Dooley created a map of the Mississippi River and its tributaries from Minneapolis, Minnesota, to St. Louis, Missouri, by igniting gunpowder. After making a paper stencil of the river's outline, he sandwiched the stencil between two sheets of paper and two plywood pieces, and then placed a small amount of gunpowder on top of the stencil. He then weighed the sandwich down with bricks, lit the fuse, stood back, and the gunpowder marked the sheet of paper beneath the stencil.

STRANGE THING ▶ Shortly after the release of the second season of Netflix's *Stranger Things* in 2017, a strange thing hit the market: an Eleven-shaped candle holder that "bleeds" candle wax. The ceramic ornament, which comes with two red candles, nicely complements a feast of Eggos. Note: psychokinetic powers not included.

BLOOD PORTRAIT ▶ Artist Lee Wagstaff, of London, England, created *Shroud*, a self-portrait that was screen printed on linen in his own blood. He made the screen from a negative photograph of his whole body and then drew 1 pint (0.6 l) of his own blood—enough to print two life-size images.

MARSHMALLOW TRUMP ▶ Wisconsin artist Cynthia Lund Torroll made a portrait President Donald Trump entirely out of marshmallow Peeps. It took her about six hours to create, during which time she kept her fingers dipped in warm, soapy water so that the Peeps were easier to work with.

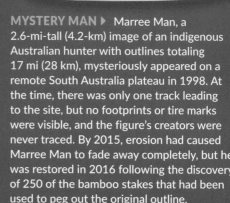

MYSTERY MAN ▶ Marree Man, a 2.6-mi-tall (4.2-km) image of an indigenous Australian hunter with outlines totaling 17 mi (28 km), mysteriously appeared on a remote South Australia plateau in 1998. At the time, there was only one track leading to the site, but no footprints or tire marks were visible, and the figure's creators were never traced. By 2015, erosion had caused Marree Man to fade away completely, but he was restored in 2016 following the discovery of 250 of the bamboo stakes that had been used to peg out the original outline.

GUARDIANS OF GEEK

› Located in France, the Chapel of Bethlehem is a 15th-century medieval building guarded by gargoyles that look like modern-day monsters! The sculptures, which feature a Xenomorph from the *Alien* franchise, and Gizmo, a cuddly creature from the 1984 film *Gremlins*, pictured, are perched on the chapel's ancient corners.

SUMMON THE DRAGON ▶ Street artists Blesea and Baby K turned an abandoned beach blockhouse in Réville, France, into Shenron, the dragon from the popular anime *Dragon Ball*. According to the series, Shenron is the massive dragon summoned to fulfill a wish when all seven Dragon Balls are reunited.

HEARTBEAT RING ▶ A new hi-tech ring allows the wearer to feel a loved one's heartbeat in real time even though he or she may be thousands of miles away. Wearers of the Touch HB "heartbeat sharing" rings download a companion smartphone app, pair it with the ring, and add their loved one's profile in the app. Then whenever the rings are tapped, the wearers will be able to feel the other person's heart rhythm on their finger. Each ring has more than 100 components, including a battery, sensors, and a physical feedback motor.

SAND IMAGES ▶ Tim Bengel, an artist from Stuttgart, Germany, uses different shades of sand on a sticky board to create lifelike images of people and places. After covering a blank canvas board with slow-drying adhesive, he sprinkles on black and gold sand in the shape of the design, adding the fine detail with a scalpel. When the design is finished, he spreads white sand over the entire canvas before shaking off the excess to reveal the artwork underneath. A sand image of the Palace of Versailles in France took him 300 hours to complete.

TV DRUMS ▶ The Braun Tube Jazz Band, founded by Japanese artist Ei Wada, uses old cathode-ray tube TV sets as electric percussion instruments. Wada teams multiple TV sets with PC-controlled video decks at different pitches. By connecting guitar amps to his feet, when he touches the TV screens, they produce a buzzing noise and sound like electric drums, enabling the band to play thumping dance numbers. He also incorporates into his music the sounds made by old reel-to-reel tape recorders and discarded ventilator fans.

VETERAN PIANIST ▶ New York City pianist Irving Fields still played seven gigs a week at age 100. He started playing music when he was eight and has recorded nearly 100 albums.

KNITTED MASTERPIECE ▶ Using a primitive circular loom, Greek artist Petros Vrellis hand-knitted 1.25 mi (2 km) of continuous black thread as 4,000 straight lines winding around a series of pegs on the circumference to create a stunning replica of a portrait by 16th-century Renaissance painter El Greco. He broke the El Greco masterpiece down into pixels and then used a specially designed computer algorithm to formulate the exact pattern required for his loom artwork.

MOUSE PARK ▶ Art collective Anonymouse constructed a tiny, mouse-sized and mouse-themed amusement park in Malmo, Sweden. The model, called Tjoffsan's Tivoli, after a rodent character created by children's author Astrid Lindgren, featured a scary cat-shaped ride, a Lucky Cheese stall, and a fortune teller called Madame Raclette. The group previously created a 25 × 12 in (62 × 30 cm) restaurant for mice.

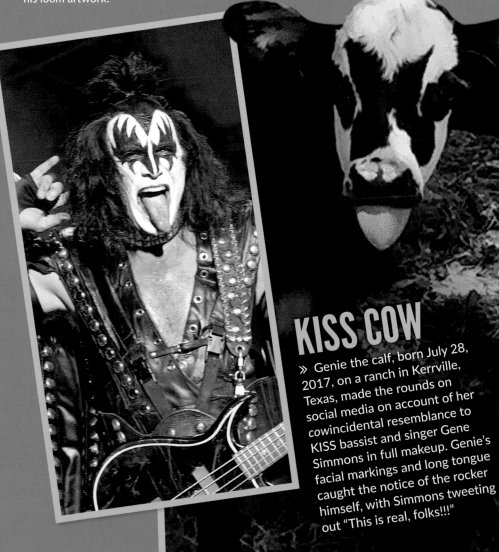

KISS COW

» Genie the calf, born July 28, 2017, on a ranch in Kerrville, Texas, made the rounds on social media on account of her coincidental resemblance to KISS bassist and singer Gene Simmons in full makeup. Genie's facial markings and long tongue caught the notice of the rocker himself, with Simmons tweeting out "This is real, folks!!!"

STRANGE Sushi

GIMME A BREAK ▶

A KIT KAT Chocolatory shop in Japan offered a sweet twist to traditional sushi to celebrate the opening of their new location. The candy sushi was originally introduced as an April Fool's Day joke, but after so much positive feedback, it was decided to make them a reality for a limited time. KIT KAT flavors such as raspberry, Hokkaido melon with mascarpone cheese, and pumpkin pudding were layered on top of white chocolate-covered puffed rice treats dusted with wasabi powder and then wrapped in seaweed.

ON A ROLL

» Keiko Yamamoto, aka "Sushi Queen," from London made sushi rolls using items she found at her local Greggs bakery. Some of her creations include jam doughnut rolls, cheese and onion onigirazu, and a sausage roll dragon roll topped with thinly sliced avocado. She also produced a video series so others can learn how to make their own Gregg's sushi.

BUGGIN' OUT!

> To celebrate the end of winter, a restaurant in Japan served up bug-filled sushi rolls!

Tokyo restaurant Kome to Sakasu, or "Rice and Circus," offered a creepy crawly version of a traditional ehomaki roll alongside their regular menu of scorpions, beetles, kangaroo, crocodile, and more! Ehomaki, or "lucky direction," sushi rolls are eaten for good luck during Setsubun celebrations, while facing the new year's lucky direction and in total silence. They always have seven ingredients and are never sliced, but they usually don't contain insects!

GRASSHOPPERS, SILKWORMS, AND BEE LARVAE INSIDE!

UNBROKEN RUN ▶ Pink Floyd's 1973 album *The Dark Side of the Moon* spent a staggering 14 years straight in the Billboard Top 200, finally exiting in July 1988, 736 weeks after it debuted on the album chart.

EARLY GPS ▶ In the 1984 Eddie Murphy movie *Beverly Hills Cop*, the LAPD used a made-up technology called a satellite tracking system—11 years before the U.S. government's first real GPS system became fully operational.

FAMILY TIES ▶ Researchers have discovered that *Sherlock* star Benedict Cumberbatch and Sherlock Holmes creator Arthur Conan Doyle are 16th cousins twice removed.

MELTED MAKEUP ▶ To remove his makeup for the role of Drax in *Guardians of the Galaxy Vol. 2*, American actor Dave Bautista had to sit in a sauna for over 45 minutes at the end of each day. Prosthetics were stuck to his skin for the movie, so he had to stay in the hot sauna until the makeup melted off his body.

SUBLIMINAL MESSAGE ▶ When the demonic boss Diablo is released in the final level of video game *Diablo 1*, he says something unintelligible. When played in reverse, the voice can be heard to say, "Eat your vegetables and brush after every meal."

FINGER SCAR ▶ While playing the scene in the movie *Home Alone* where Harry bites Kevin's finger, Joe Pesci actually bit nine-year-old Macaulay Culkin, leaving a small permanent scar.

GROHL ALLEY ▶ A run-down alley in Warren, Ohio, was renamed Dave Grohl Alley after the Foo Fighters frontman, who was born in the city. Grohl even showed up at the dedication, along with his family, and played a song on guitar.

LOST ACCENT ▶ At one point in his career, actor Gary Oldman had played so many American characters in movies that he lost his British accent and had to go to a speech therapist to get it back.

BIG SELLER ▶ In the week it was released in November 2015, Adele's *25* accounted for 41 percent of total album sales in the United States.

GHOSTLY APP ▶ Spirit Story Box, an iPhone app launched by Roger Pingelton and Jill Beitz, of Greenwood, Indiana, claims to let the user know what nearby ghosts are thinking.

HOCKEY MEMENTO ▶ In a rider to the contract for his 2007 concert tour, Canadian singer Michael Bublé asked for a local team hockey puck as a memento of every place he visited.

All Dressed Up

> **Emma Jayne Cake Design created a gorgeous replica of a couture wedding gown completely made out of cake!**

Baker Emma Jayne spent three weeks recreating designer Mak Tumang's Angela wedding gown down to the last detail, incorporating opal and Preciosa crystals, along with colored sugar paste. The confounding confection was showcased at the Cake International trade show in London, where many people were unable to tell it was not a real wedding dress.

SQUADRON SUPREME

MARVEL COMICS

Believe it or not, the cremated ashes of legendary American comic book writer Mark Gruenwald, who died in 1996, were mixed into the first print run of his compilation of Marvel's *Squadron Supreme*.

CHARACTER BUILDING ▶ In order to get in character for his role as a prisoner in the 1993 film *In the Name of the Father*, English actor Daniel Day-Lewis lived on prison rations to lose 30 lb (14 kg), went without sleep for two days, spent nights in the cold jail cell on the set, was interrogated for three days by real police officers, and asked that the crew hurl abuse and cold water at him.

CHANCE DISCOVERY ▶
Nick Jonas of the Jonas Brothers was discovered singing in a barbershop at age six while his mother was getting her hair cut—and within a year, he was performing on Broadway.

NIGHT RESCUE ▶ A 62-year-old man playing *Pokémon Go* at night in the woods behind his home in Coeymans, New York, had to be rescued after he became stuck in waist-deep mud.

DIRTY JEANS ▶ Fashion retailer Nordstrom sells jeans caked in fake mud—for $425 a pair. The jeans are designed to embody rugged, Americana workwear.

DRUMROLL ▶ Allister Brown, of Lisburn, Northern Ireland, played a drumroll nonstop for 22 hours, playing the last three hours with severe cramping in his arms.

CAT WALK ▶ Italian composer Domenico Scarlatti (1685–1757) wrote his "Cat Fugue" after his cat Pulcinella walked across the keyboard of his piano.

MYSTERY MOVIE ▶ *100 Years: The Movie You Will Never See*, starring John Malkovich, was completed in 2015 and immediately enclosed in a bulletproof safe that will not unlock until November 18, 2115.

EARLY REJECTION ▶ Dr. Seuss's first children's book, *And to Think That I Saw It on Mulberry Street*, was rejected by 27 publishers, but his books have gone on to sell more than 600 million copies worldwide.

THAT'S A WRAP!

» A new form of therapy sees adults become babies. Otonamaki, or "adult wrapping," has taken Japan by storm; the method is claimed to alleviate posture problems and stiffness. Taken from the practice of Ohinamaki, when babies are wrapped up to help with their physical development, sessions of adult wrapping last around 20 minutes and include wrapping the body in a large piece of breathable cloth that mimics the comfortable feel of a mother's womb.

JEDI TRAINING

> A chain of gyms in England held *Star Wars*–themed workouts so members could train like a Jedi!

David Lloyd Clubs© offered the classes on *Star Wars* Day—May the Fourth—and allowed aspiring Jedi to wear robes and yield lightsabers while participating in exercises inspired by the popular films, like Jedi swipes and leaps.

FITNESS COACH

Ripley's Exhibit
Cat. No. 171861

Matchstick Millennium Falcon
Created by artist Patrick Acton with 910,000 matchsticks!
Origin: Iowa, United States

BELIEVE IT OR NOT, THIS REPLICA OF THE MILLENNIUM FALCON IS 15 FT (4.5 M) LONG!

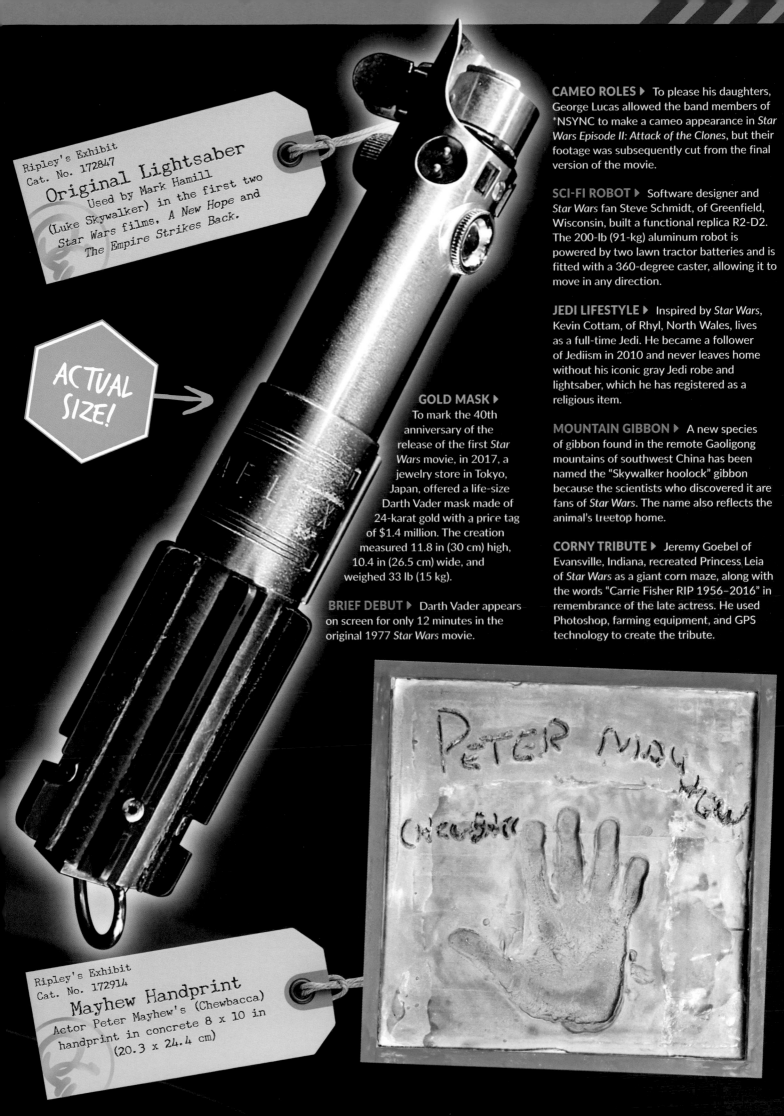

ACTUAL SIZE! →

CAMEO ROLES ▶ To please his daughters, George Lucas allowed the band members of *NSYNC to make a cameo appearance in *Star Wars Episode II: Attack of the Clones*, but their footage was subsequently cut from the final version of the movie.

SCI-FI ROBOT ▶ Software designer and *Star Wars* fan Steve Schmidt, of Greenfield, Wisconsin, built a functional replica R2-D2. The 200-lb (91-kg) aluminum robot is powered by two lawn tractor batteries and is fitted with a 360-degree caster, allowing it to move in any direction.

JEDI LIFESTYLE ▶ Inspired by *Star Wars*, Kevin Cottam, of Rhyl, North Wales, lives as a full-time Jedi. He became a follower of Jediism in 2010 and never leaves home without his iconic gray Jedi robe and lightsaber, which he has registered as a religious item.

GOLD MASK ▶ To mark the 40th anniversary of the release of the first *Star Wars* movie, in 2017, a jewelry store in Tokyo, Japan, offered a life-size Darth Vader mask made of 24-karat gold with a price tag of $1.4 million. The creation measured 11.8 in (30 cm) high, 10.4 in (26.5 cm) wide, and weighed 33 lb (15 kg).

MOUNTAIN GIBBON ▶ A new species of gibbon found in the remote Gaoligong mountains of southwest China has been named the "Skywalker hoolock" gibbon because the scientists who discovered it are fans of *Star Wars*. The name also reflects the animal's treetop home.

CORNY TRIBUTE ▶ Jeremy Goebel of Evansville, Indiana, recreated Princess Leia of *Star Wars* as a giant corn maze, along with the words "Carrie Fisher RIP 1956–2016" in remembrance of the late actress. He used Photoshop, farming equipment, and GPS technology to create the tribute.

BRIEF DEBUT ▶ Darth Vader appears on screen for only 12 minutes in the original 1977 *Star Wars* movie.

POP CULTURE

153

OTHER BROTHER ▶ When Pete Townshend of the rock band The Who appeared in a season 12 episode of *The Simpsons*, his character was voiced by his brother, Paul Townshend, because Pete was unavailable.

NINE LIVES ▶ Before reaching age 13, Mark Twain nearly drowned nine times in the Mississippi River and the dangerous Bear Creek in Hannibal, Missouri. He enjoyed playing in water, but friends and family were frequently called upon to rescue him before he eventually learned to swim.

WRITER'S BLOCK ▶ In the seven years that William Wordsworth was the United Kingdom's poet laureate, from 1843 to 1850, he did not write a single line of poetry.

SLOW SONG ▶ A slow-motion sound effect used in the 2012 science fiction movie *Dredd* was based on a Justin Bieber song that had been slowed down 800 percent.

SEVEN YEARS ▶ Thomas Gray's 1751 poem "Elegy Written in a Country Churchyard"—one of the best-loved English poems—is 128 lines long and took him seven years to write.

POOP FASHION ▶ Jalila Essaïdi, a designer from Eindhoven, the Netherlands, uses scientific techniques to turn cow poop into fashionable clothing—that doesn't stink!

PIRATES AHOY!
» In May 2017, ghostly art installations were revealed at low tide, surprising beachgoers at three different British coastline locations. The 6.5-ft-high (2-m) pirate sculptures portray characters from the fifth *Pirates of the Caribbean* film. A team of sculptors took six weeks to build the salty statues before they were installed overnight.

LIVING DOLLS

> Made by Spanish company Babyclon, these unsettling silicone dolls look, move, and feel like an alien baby from the film *Avatar*, and you are hereby forgiven for thinking they were real.

The company also produces animatronic human babies costing upward of $5,000, with motors inside that make them appear to breathe, crawl, or laugh. As if that's not enough, Babyclon also makes baby chimpanzees, tiny mermaids, and even babies with elf ears.

SLOW CONNECTION ▶ Only 1 percent of the population of the African country of Eritrea uses the internet, compared to 100 percent in Iceland.

LION TAMER ▶ As a 16-year-old boy, Hollywood actor Christopher Walken worked one summer as a lion tamer in a touring circus owned by Terrell Jacobs. Walken said the elderly lion, a female named Sheba, was very sweet, like a dog.

HOMER'S HOME ▶ The Fox Broadcasting Company owns the rights to *The Simpsons* until 2082—95 years after they were created.

POE'S BEST ▶ During his lifetime, Edgar Allan Poe's best-selling book was *The Conchologist's First Book*, a textbook about seashells.

HOGWARTS HOUSES ▶ J. K. Rowling thought up the names for the houses at Hogwarts in *Harry Potter* while she was on an airplane. She jotted them down on a sickness bag.

YOUNG DJ ▶ Itsuki Morita played an hour-long public set as a DJ at a restaurant and bar in Osaka, Japan, at age six.

E.T. HONEY BUN ▶ In November 2016, a Twitter post by Danielle York of Manchester, New Hampshire, threw the internet into a frenzy with just a simple photo of a Walmart honey bun that looked eerily like E.T. the extraterrestrial. Eager Photoshoppers made the most of the sweet viral sensation—E.T. scone home.

Block BUSTED

> Lights, camera, action! Movies based on real life events have been dazzling the silver screen ever since the invention of the motion picture camera in the 1890s. Here's a plot twist—although a movie can be based on a true story, not everything you see is true. Check out some of your favorite films to see how they are blockBUSTED!

The Sound of Music (1965)

Georg von Trapp (portrayed by Christopher Plummer) is a stern Navy officer who rules his house with an iron fist—and without music. Maria von Trapp (portrayed by Julie Andrews) is a beloved stepmother who brings love and music back into the family's lives.

But actually...

Georg was a gentle and affectionate father who encouraged the children in their musical activities long before Maria.

While she was a caring and loving person, Maria was prone to angry outbursts—yelling, throwing things, and slamming doors.

Jaws (1975)

Based on the novel by Peter Benchley, a giant great white shark goes on a killing spree, terrorizing a small New England town.

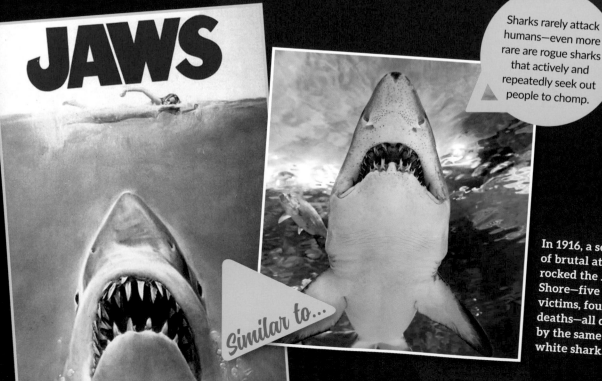

Similar to...

Sharks rarely attack humans—even more rare are rogue sharks that actively and repeatedly seek out people to chomp.

In 1916, a series of brutal attacks rocked the Jersey Shore—five victims, four deaths—all done by the same great white shark.

Braveheart (1995)

Scottish rebel William Wallace (portrayed by Mel Gibson) fights to reclaim freedom from the hellish English—all while sporting some fiendish blue war paint and a kilt.

But actually...

Scotsmen during that time period did not wear belted plaid kilts.

Pocahontas (1995)

Playful and headstrong Pocahontas tries to avoid a war between her tribe and the Jamestown settlement, as well as keep her love interest, John Smith, alive.

In reality...

Pocahontas's real name was Amonute, and she was about 10 years old when she met then 27-year-old John Smith. Contrary to the Disney film, no romance just around this riverbend.

Anastasia (1997)

After the Russian Revolution, the lost Grand Duchess Anastasia of Russia tries to find out who she is and where her family is after some unfortunate memory loss.

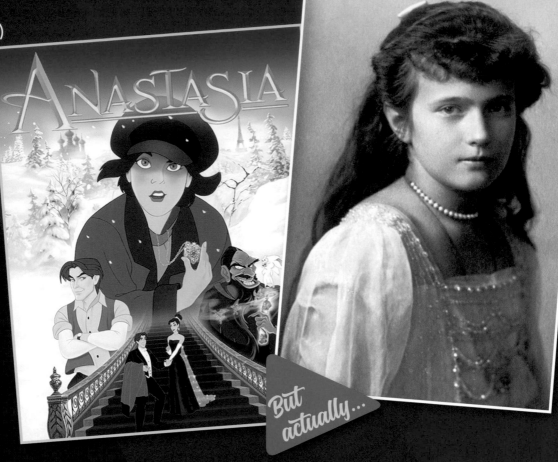

Anastasia was executed along with the rest of her family—although the theory did persist that she somehow survived, which spawned many imposters.

But actually...

Gladiator (2000)

Maximus the war general (portrayed by Russell Crowe) becomes a gladiator and kills the evil Emperor Commodus in the Colosseum as revenge for killing his family.

In reality...

Emperor Commodus did exist and engaged in show combat in the Colosseum, but he was not killed in the arena—he was strangled in his bath. Are you not entertained?

300 (2007)

With nothing but red capes, sharp swords, and bare chests, 300 fierce Spartan warriors fight (and die) in the Battle of Thermopylae.

But actually...

Spartans totally wore body armor to protect them and their rippling abs.

The Revenant (2015)

In the dead of winter, rugged frontiersman Hugh Glass gets mauled by a grizzly bear, his son gets murdered, and then he is left for dead and crawls his way back to civilization for some sweet revenge.

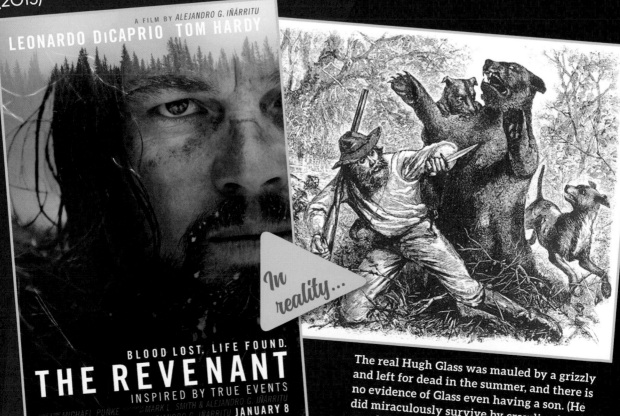

In reality...

The real Hugh Glass was mauled by a grizzly and left for dead in the summer, and there is no evidence of Glass even having a son. (He did miraculously survive by crawling his way back hundreds of miles.)

NACHO AVERAGE
Wedding Dress

> Bride-to-be Diane Nguyen created a wedding dress made of Taco Bell burrito wrappers all to win a free wedding inside the Tex-Mex chain's Las Vegas Cantina flagship restaurant.

Her cheesiness took the Internet by storm, but while she and fiancé Nick Ward were ready to "guac and roll," they unfortunately didn't win the contest. Nguyen took it well—her dress was torched with the help of a flamethrower. Taco 'bout spicing it up.

BASEBALL TANK ▶ Taylor Swift has a fish tank filled with vintage baseballs in the living room of her New York City apartment.

BED SCENE ▶ The first couple shown in bed together on prime time U.S. TV were Fred and Wilma Flintstone when the cartoon series first aired on ABC between 1960 and 1966.

ARTISTIC CRAWL ▶ For a show in New York City, Chinese-Canadian performance artist Terence Koh crawled on his knees around an 8-ft-tall (2.4-m) mound of rock salt for 25 days, eight hours a day.

LONDON'S BURNING ▶ To commemorate the 350th anniversary of the 1666 Great Fire of London, a 394-ft-long (120-m) wooden replica of 17th-century London was set alight on the River Thames in 2016. The model was designed by American artist David Best and built by unemployed Londoners over a period of several months.

ARTWORK IS COMPLETLY FLAT AGAINST THE WALL AND FLOOR!

3-D GRAFFITI
» Artist Sergio Odeith from Portugal creates anamorphic art, painting optical illusions on different surfaces, including 90° corners. He takes his street art all over the world, leaving eye-popping insects, "floating" objects, and 3-D letters in his wake.

TIRE SCULPTURES ▶ Every week, Cheryl Quinlivan makes a new roadside sculpture from old tires to amuse motorists in Logan, Queensland, Australia. Her creations have included a Christmas tree, an Olympics-themed exhibit, and one based on *Game of Thrones*.

ROBOT ACTOR ▶ *Spillikin*, a 2017 U.K. stage play put on by the Cornwall-based Pipeline Theater, starred actress Judy Norman opposite a humanoid robot. The robot could talk, display facial expressions, blink, move its hands, and turn its head. It was controlled by laptop prompts offstage, and writer/director Jon Welch had it preprogrammed so that, on receiving a certain cue, it would say the same thing and react the same way in every performance.

PYROTECHNIC ART ▶ Instead of a paintbrush, Marcus Dove, of Leicester, England, creates spectacular artworks using flares, fireworks, blowtorches, colored smoke, and even a homemade missile launcher. He uses the missile launcher to fire paint at a large canvas hanging on a wall about 15 ft (4.6 m) away.

SOCCER NAMES ▶ British thriller author Lee Child—creator of the Jack Reacher novels—has woven into his books the names of more than 20 players from his favorite soccer team, Aston Villa.

HAPPY ENDING ▶ Ernest Hemingway wrote 47 different endings to his semi-autobiographical 1929 novel *A Farewell to Arms* before he was finally satisfied.

SCIENCE ADVICE ▶ Writers of the TV show *The Big Bang Theory* often use actress Mayim Bialik's help with science facts for the show, because she has a PhD in neuroscience.

BOTTLE MOSAIC ▶ More than 500 employees from Coca-Cola Bulgaria constructed a 2,691-sq-ft (250 sq m) mosaic in the shape of a giant Coke bottle from 72,933 empty glass bottles.

Ripley's Exhibit
Cat. No. 172115
Bowie Record Portrait
David Bowie as Ziggy Stardust made from broken records, by Ed Chapman.
Origin: Manchester, United Kingdom

WASTELAND WEEKEND

> Every September, the Mojave Desert hosts the annual *Mad Max*-themed Wasteland Weekend—a five-day festival just bursting with post-apocalyptic chaos.

Those brave enough to attend must don costumes and are not allowed to break character. Even talking about other "universes," such as *Star Wars* or *Harry Potter*, is strictly forbidden. Some Wastelanders bring decorated vehicles, while others participate in thrilling fights at the Thunderdome. Visitors beware, it's a world of fire and blood!

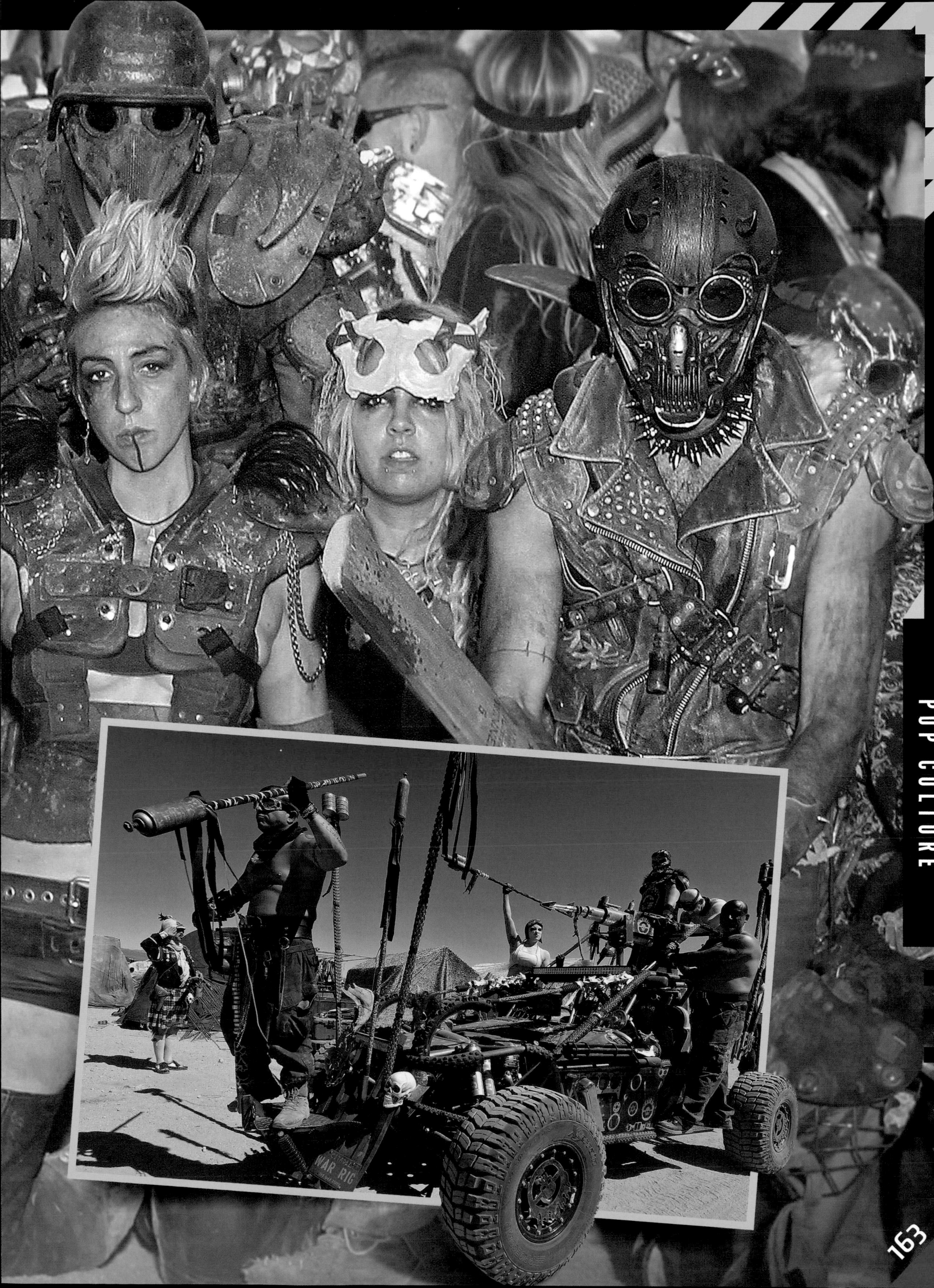
WAR RIG

BOOKMARKED

 Ernest Vincent Wright's 1939 novel, **GADSBY**, was written entirely without the use of the **LETTER "E"**!

A 1977 comic book featuring the rock band **KISS** was printed with red ink that had been mixed with the **BAND MEMBERS' BLOOD!**

ANTHROPODERMIC BIBLIOPEGY is the practice of binding books in human skin.

The longest work of fiction, at 4,061,129 words, is **THE SUBSPACE EMISSARY'S WORLDS CONQUEST**—Internet fan fiction based on a **NINTENDO** game.

In 1931, the book **ALICE IN WONDERLAND** was banned in China because there is no scientific basis for **TALKING ANIMALS.**

 Researchers at University College London developed the **"HISTORIC BOOK ODOUR WHEEL"** to categorize the smell of old library books!

Just **1,000 WORDS** make up **90 PERCENT** of all writing.

BAND REUNION ▶ When Edward Hardy, a 95-year-old jazz pianist from England posted an online ad for musicians to jam with, three of those who replied were his former bandmates whom he had not seen in more than 35 years.

BART INVASION ▶ As part of an art project by Elissa Patel titled BartOnBART, 15 people wearing Bart Simpson masks rode San Francisco's BART (Bay Area Rapid Transit) system on August 9, 2016.

GAME BOY ▶ Belgian student Ilhan Ünal built a giant working Game Boy that measures 40 in (100 cm) tall, 24 in (60 cm) wide, and 8 in (20 cm) thick. It is so big that it would need its own seat on an airplane.

RINGO SONG ▶ Under the name Bonnie Jo Mason, the singer who would later be known as Cher recorded an unsuccessful 1964 novelty song "Ringo, I Love You" about the drummer of the Beatles.

BUSY DAY ▶ Over a period of 24 hours from August 8 to 9, 2017, four local jazz musicians—Leonard Patton, Mackenzie Leighton, Matthew Smith, and Ed Kornhauser—played 70 shows in 70 different venues around San Diego, California.

MONSTER BIKE ▶ Frank Dose, from Schleswig-Holstein, Germany, built a rideable bicycle weighing a colossal 2,419 lb (1,098 kg). The monster bike was made from scrap metal and features 5-ft-diameter (1.53-m) tires from an industrial fertilizer spreader.

SILENT SCHOOL ▶ The school in the video game Silent Hill was based on the school from the Arnold Schwarzenegger movie Kindergarten Cop.

TINY MODEL ▶ Gattem Venkatesh, from Chinadoddigallu, India, carved a model of the Empire State Building into a 0.7-in-long (18-mm) toothpick.

VALUABLE VASE ▶ In 2017, a Chinese vase sold for 450 times its guide price at an auction in Birmingham, England, after what was thought to be a copy turned out to be a valuable 500-year-old antique. The auction house had priced it at just $2,500, but when bidders spotted that the vase dated back to the Ming dynasty, it eventually sold for over $1 million.

CAB LICENSE ▶ While shooting the 1976 movie Taxi Driver, Robert De Niro obtained a cab driver's license and picked up fares during breaks from filming.

MINIATURE KITCHEN ▶ Cook Kate Murdoch, from Surrey, England, presents a series of YouTube videos called "Tiny Kitchen," where she prepares doll-size meals using a frying pan the size of a thumbnail, a miniature stove heated by a candle, and cutlery that is no bigger than a needle.

FROM MEMORY ▶ At the 2017 BBC Promenade concerts in London, England, the Aurora Orchestra played Ludwig van Beethoven's 45-minute long "Eroica" Symphony entirely from memory.

HAIR PORTRAITS ▶ Rather than sweeping his customers' cut hair off the floor of his hair salon, Wang Xiaojiu, a barber from Jilin City, China, carefully arranges it to create detailed works of art that look like charcoal drawings. He uses just a hairbrush and a plastic card to design portraits of mythological heroes and popular comic book characters such as Iron Man, Wolverine, and Spider-Man.

MISSING FEET ▶ Leonardo da Vinci's famous painting The Last Supper, which hangs in a convent in Milan, Italy, originally featured Jesus's feet. But in 1652, builders sent to install a doorway in the refectory where the painting is on view decided that it was necessary to cut into the bottom-center of the mural, thereby chopping off Christ's feet.

BOOK TEMPLE

> For an art festival in Kassel, Germany, Argentine artist Marta Minujín built a full-size replica of the classical Greek temple the Parthenon using 100,000 books that have been banned at one time in history.

Constructed with a steel framework, *The Parthenon of Books* was built on a Nazi book-burning site, and all books were donated by the public from a short list of more than 170 titles, including Dan Brown's *The Da Vinci Code*, Mark Twain's *The Adventures of Tom Sawyer*, and J.D. Salinger's *The Catcher in the Rye*.

Ripley's Exhibit
Cat. No. 171878

Cassette Tape Prince
Created by artist
Erika Iris Simmons.
Origin: Illinois, United States

RETRO THEATER ▶ Bus driver Anderson Jones spent four years and $100,000 building a retro movie theater in the back yard of his home in Stoke-on-Trent, England, complete with a 17 × 7 ft (5.2 × 2.1 m) screen, red curtains, and 34 red seats. It has its own projection room and even a foyer with a concession stand offering popcorn and candies. All the interior fittings—from door handles to exit signs—were reclaimed from old theaters.

SOAP SCULPTOR ▶ Italian artist Daniele Barresi uses a sculpting knife to carve beautiful models of birds, fish, and flowers out of ordinary bars of soap. He began sculpting fruits and vegetables when he was just seven years old but has recently moved on to working with soap.

VULTURE QUARTET ▶ The Beatles nearly had roles in a Disney movie. The producers of *The Jungle Book* wanted them to voice the four "mop top" singing vultures in the 1967 animated movie, but John Lennon declined the offer because they were too busy.

TINY NIGHTCLUB ▶ Designed by Gerard Jenkins-Omar and Stephen Robson, Club 28 is a mobile nightclub in Rotherham, England, that measures just 6.5 ft (2 m) high, 3 ft (0.9 m) wide, and 5 ft (1.5 m) deep. Its tiny dance floor can accommodate six partygoers and a DJ.

TOOTHPICK TRIBUTE ▶ Tang Jialu, from Chongqing, China, spent two and a half months creating a 3-D portrait of Michelangelo's *David* from 87,000 toothpicks.

TWO SKULLS ▶ There are two skulls in the tomb of Austrian composer Joseph Haydn (1732–1809). After his death, his head was stolen by phrenologists, and a replacement skull was put in his tomb. Then in 1954, the real skull was restored, but the substitute was not removed.

SAME NAME ▶ Bruce, the "vegetarian" great white shark in *Finding Nemo*, was named for the mechanical shark used in *Jaws*, which itself had been named for director Steven Spielberg's lawyer.

FISH WALL

≫ The Flying Fish restaurant in Little Rock, Arkansas, is home to the world's first Billy Bass adoption center—a wall decorated with more than 300 animatronic, singing Big Mouth Billy Bass novelty fish that customers leave in exchange for a basket of catfish.

MONTH-LONG MOVIE ▶ When completed around 2020, *Ambiancé*, a movie by Swedish director Anders Weberg, will last for 720 hours—that's 30 days. He has filmed more than 400 hours to date, and in 2016, he released a seven-hour trailer for the movie.

FAKE ROARS ▶ Not a single genuine lion roar can be heard in the Disney movie *The Lion King*. The filmmakers found that a lion's roar was not impressive enough, so they used tiger roars for some general lion sounds, and when more specific roars were required, they were provided by voice actor Frank Welker snarling into a trashcan.

CORNY TRIBUTE ▶ An 8-acre (3.2-hectare) corn maze was carved into a field in Sterling, Massachusetts, in 2016, depicting the likeness of retiring Boston Red Sox baseball player David Ortiz. The maze featured a cornstalk image of Ortiz's trademark home run pose of pointing two fingers to the sky.

OBITUARY COLLECTOR ▶
Ernest Hemingway once read his own obituary in a newspaper. After being badly injured in two separate plane crashes in two days while vacationing in Africa in 1954, he saw his death notice in an American newspaper a few days later in a café in Venice, Italy. He kept a scrapbook of all the obituaries of him that appeared in the U.S. press at that time and enjoyed reading them after breakfast every morning while drinking champagne.

PREMATURE PLUNGE ▶ For a stunt in the 1988 movie *Die Hard*, English actor Alan Rickman was deliberately dropped two seconds early to capture the true reaction of his character, the villainous Hans Gruber, falling to his death from the Nakatomi Plaza. Rickman had agreed to fall backward onto an airbag 25 ft (8 m) below on the count of "three," but director John McTiernan thought he would get a better reaction if they secretly dropped him on the count of "one."

DOLLAR COLLAGES ▶ Artist Mark Wagner, from Brooklyn, New York, makes collages of landmarks, fantastical garden scenes, and political figures such as Barack Obama, Abraham Lincoln, and Donald Trump out of dollar bills. Each collage is created using small pieces of deconstructed bills, which are carefully glued into place with a brush. He uses every single part of the bill in his artworks, and his 17-ft-tall (5.2-m) collage of the Statue of Liberty used 81,895 individual scraps from 1,121 one-dollar bills.

HOBBYHORSING

▶ The Finnish sport of competitive hobbyhorsing is the same as conventional show jumping, except that the riders jump fences while straddling a stuffed toy horse on a wooden stick, complete with glued-on eyes and mane.

They tackle obstacles as high as 3 ft (0.9 m), and there are also dressage competitions where the riders demonstrate style, elegance, and nimble footwork. Some riders become so attached to their stick horses that in addition to giving them names, they groom them and place covers on them at night as they "sleep."

167

RECRE**AT-ACT**ION

Hiding behind an unassuming house in England is a massive, 18-ft-tall (5.5-m) recreation of an AT-ACT walker from *Rogue One: A Star Wars Story*. Inventor and plumber Colin Furze built it for his friend's son, Harvey Dunnett, using materials such as wooden panels and Chinese woks! The head can move and a ladder drops from inside, revealing a playroom full of *Star Wars*–themed gadgets and toys.

HI-TECH UMBRELLA ▶ A French company has designed the Oombrella—an umbrella that links to a smartphone app and alerts the user 30 minutes before rain is due.

TOAST ARTWORKS ▶ For a 2016 exhibition in London, England, electrical manufacturer Tefal recreated famous artworks on toast, using different foods for the colors. The toast masterpieces included versions of Claude Monet's *Water Lilies*, Sandro Botticelli's *The Birth of Venus*, and Vincent Van Gogh's *The Bedroom*.

WITCH TRIALS ▶ Science fiction writer Ray Bradbury (1920–2012), author of *Fahrenheit 451*, was a descendant of one of the women convicted for being a witch at the infamous Salem witch trials in 17th-century Massachusetts. Mary Perkins Bradbury was sentenced to be hanged in 1692 but managed to escape before she could be executed.

TAXIDERMY HEADS ▶ Louise Walker, of London, England, makes more than $70,000 a year by knitting faux animal taxidermy heads, including woolen foxes, badgers, deer, and cattle.

GPS IMAGES ▶ Stephen Lund, from Victoria, British Columbia, Canada, has created more than 60 doodles—including a dinosaur, a giraffe, Darth Vader, and Michelangelo's *David*—on maps of the city's streets by using his bicycle and a GPS tracking app. He sketches an outline of the required shape on a map, and as he cycles the route, the GPS device records his travels to create the image. He averages 44 mi (70 km) per sketch.

PUZZLED VISITOR ▶ A 91-year-old woman filled in a crossword puzzle at a German art museum, only to discover that the crossword was a modern artwork worth $100,000. *Reading-work-piece* was created in 1965 by avant-garde artist Arthur Koepcke and takes the form of an empty crossword puzzle. The woman, on a 2016 visit to Nuremberg's Neues Museum, wrongly thought that it was an interactive display and filled in some of the blank spaces with a ballpoint pen.

PAPER POT ▶ Neelu Gunvantbhai Patel, from Ahmedabad, India, made a 16-ft-high (5-m), 6 ft (1.8 m) in diameter pot from 24,000 pages of old newspaper and 5,950 rolled paper sticks. The sticks provide the scaffolding to hold the pot together, but, even though she has worked with waste paper for 20 years, the act of rolling 600 sticks a day caused the skin to peel off from her fingers.

BRICK BURGER ▶
While stepping barefoot on a LEGO is undeniably painful, biting down on this bun is sure to be a much more pleasant (and tastier) experience. Founded by Jergs Correa, you can grab one of these playful meals at the Brick Burger restaurant in Pasig City, the Philippines, in one of four different colors!

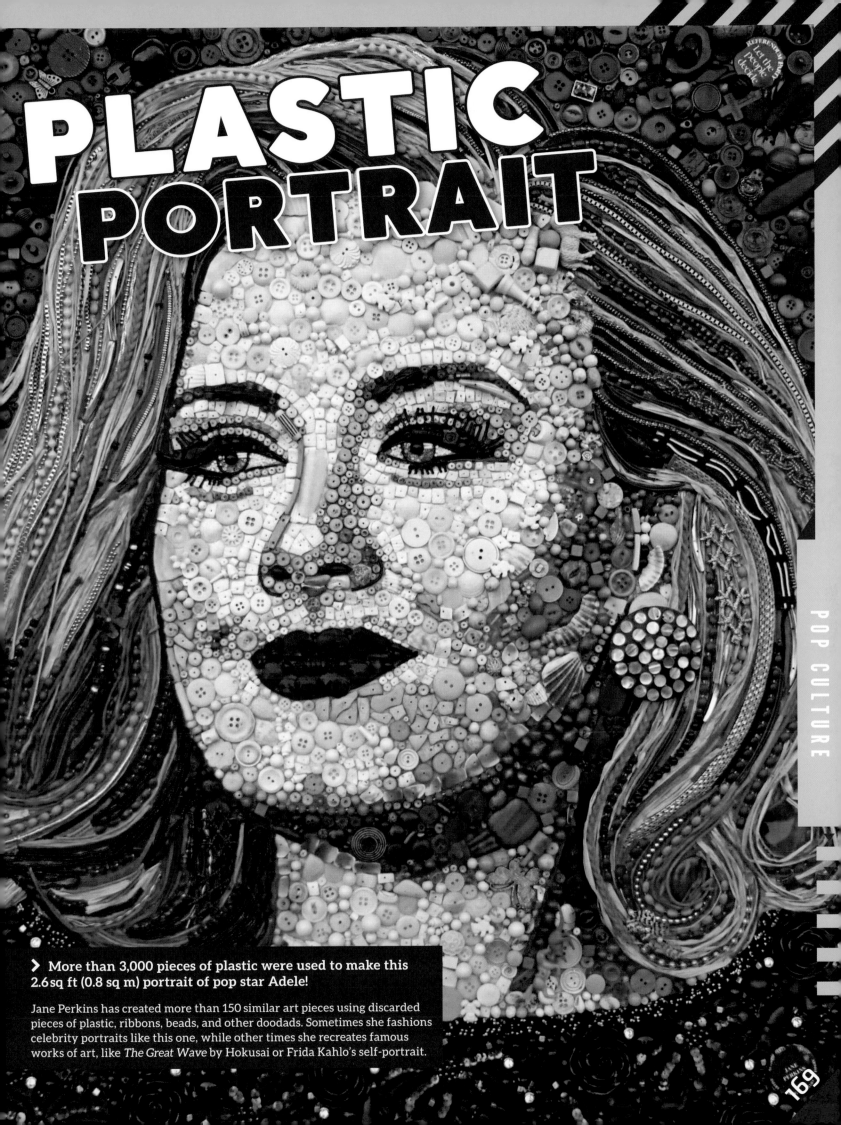

PLASTIC PORTRAIT

> **More than 3,000 pieces of plastic were used to make this 2.6 sq ft (0.8 sq m) portrait of pop star Adele!**

Jane Perkins has created more than 150 similar art pieces using discarded pieces of plastic, ribbons, beads, and other doodads. Sometimes she fashions celebrity portraits like this one, while other times she recreates famous works of art, like *The Great Wave* by Hokusai or Frida Kahlo's self-portrait.

BOARD GAMERS ▶ Friends David Deuis and Leigh Ryan played Australian sheep-farming board game Squatter for 72 hours in Wagga Wagga, New South Wales, in August 2016. During that time, they rolled the dice an estimated 4,220 times—about once every minute.

GIANT BOARD ▶ Students at Wageningen University in the Netherlands constructed a Monopoly board that was made from 804 printed panels and covered a total area of 9,690 sq ft (900 sq m)—twice the size of a basketball court.

TILE BREAKER ▶ Lisa Dennis, from Kent, England, can break over 923 roof tiles in 1 minute with her bare hands. The tae kwon do expert often smashes two 10-tile stacks at a time, one with each hand.

FRONT FLIP ▶ New Jersey's Lee O'Donnell performed the world's first successful monster truck front flip at the Monster Jam World Finals in Las Vegas, Nevada, on March 25, 2017. Accelerating on only his back wheels, he drove his truck "The Mad Scientist" up a ramp, somersaulted spectacularly through the air and landed on all four wheels on the other side.

32 PUNCTURES ▶ Devanshu Shivnani, from New Delhi, India, cycled 3,750 mi (6,000 km) around his home country in less than 20 days, averaging about 200 mi (320 km) every day. He rode through 36 cities in 13 states and would have been faster but had to stop to repair the 32 tire punctures that he suffered en route.

LONG CUE ▶ French pool player Florian "Venom" Kohler constructed a 17.6-ft-long (5.4-m) pool cue and then played an entire game with it.

ENDURANCE RIDE ▶ On February 26, 2017, endurance rider Carl Reese, from Los Angeles, California, rode 2,119 mi (3,390 km) on a motorcycle in 24 hours around a track in Uvalde, Texas, at an average speed of 88 mph (140 kmph). His top speed on the BMW K1600GT was 141 mph (225 kmph). In August 2015, he had ridden 2,829 mi (4,526 km) from Los Angeles to New York City in just 38 hours 49 minutes.

HUMAN FOUNTAIN ▶ After consuming several bottles of water, Kirubel Yilma, a 21-year-old student from Ethiopia, can spray a continuous fountain of water out of his mouth for almost a minute. By practicing breathing techniques for months, he has learned the skill of regurgitating water from his stomach.

GLOW ROW

> Lighting sets the mood—even for a night-time paddle down river rapids and waterfalls!

Brothers Brendan and Todd Wells suited up with flashing LEDs as they kayaked their way down Washington State's White Salmon River in the dark, taking on class-five rapids and waterfalls up to 70 ft (21.3m) tall! Although treacherous, they called it, "a very psychedelic experience!"

WORMY VISITORS

» In January 2017, doctors in India removed 150 live worms, some measuring 10 in (25 cm) long, from 22-year-old Neha Begum's stomach during a five-hour operation. She had been suffering from excruciating stomach pain and vomiting for months, and several doctors were unable to diagnose her symptoms—that is, until they found a mysterious obstruction in her intestines and decided to open her up.

MODEL BOAT ▶ A miniature boat built for a science project by 9- and 10-year-old students at St. Andrew's School of Math and Science in Charleston, South Carolina, sailed 3,900 mi (6,240 km)—all the way across the Atlantic Ocean. The 5-ft-long (1.5-m) fiberglass Carolina Dreamer, which was fitted with a GPS tracker so that the children could monitor its journey, was launched from the United States in May 2015 and washed ashore nine months later in West Wales, United Kingdom, despite losing its sail in the course of its voyage.

GREAT ESCAPE ▶ Alone and having dislocated his shoulder in a fall, mountaineer and scientist John All, from Bellingham, Washington, managed to pull himself out of a 70-ft-deep (21-m) icy crevasse in the Himalayas by using his only functioning arm. He had broken 15 bones in the fall, suffered internal bleeding, and it took him four hours to crawl back out of the crevasse.

BRICK FLAG ▶ John Lang, of Omaha, Nebraska, built a U.S. flag with 680,000 red, white, and blue interlocking plastic toy bricks. The finished flag, which was two years in the planning, measured 60 × 30 ft (18 × 9 m) and was assembled with the help of 200 volunteers in a parking lot.

SEISMIC SENSOR ▶ Spanish cyborg artist Moon Ribas can sense every earthquake that takes place anywhere in the world thanks to a tiny seismic sensor that she has had implanted under her skin near her elbow. The chip is connected to an iPhone app that collects seismic data, and whenever there is an earthquake, her implant vibrates. The strength of the vibrations depends on the power of the quake. During the devastating 7.8 quake in Nepal in 2015, Ribas woke in the middle of the night with potent vibrations coursing through her arm even though she was nearly 5,000 mi (8,000 km) away from the epicenter.

WHAT'S INSIDE

A British gastroenterologist treated a 76-year-old woman for stomach pains, removing a pen that had been inside her for **25 YEARS**—and the **PEN STILL WORKED!**

In 2010, doctors in Shanghai, China, removed a **CHOPSTICK** from the stomach of a 50-year-old man when he came in complaining of stomach pains **28 YEARS** after he swallowed it!

BLIND CLIMBER ▶ Justin Salas, of Tulsa, Oklahoma, is a professional photographer and rock climber— even though he is legally blind. He climbs steep 50-ft-high (15-m) rock faces by relying on feel and memory and tackles rocks that are considered extreme challenges even for advanced climbers with perfect vision. With the help of a "seeing-eye" friend, he has also performed bike stunts, mastering the spectacular 540 Cab trick, which involves a 360-degree midair spin and a backward landing.

The Missouri Glore Psychiatric Museum boasts a **MOSAIC OF 1,446 OBJECTS** removed from the stomach of a patient with a compulsive swallowing disorder.

Doctors operated on Ove Sohlberg of Lycksele, Sweden, and removed a **SHARP WOODEN STICK** that had been lodged in his abdomen, causing stomach pain, for **25 YEARS!**

Doctors in India removed **263 COINS, 100 NAILS, SHAVING BLADES, GLASS SHARDS, STONES,** and a 6-in (15-cm) piece of **RUSTED IRON SHACKLE** from the stomach of one man!

After compulsively **PULLING HER HAIR OUT AND EATING IT** for more than six years, Saddie Grace England had a 4½-lb (2.4-kg) **HAIRBALL** removed from her stomach.

In 2017, after being constipated for years, a 22-year-old man in China was operated on, and doctors removed a tract of his bowels that contained 28 lb (12.7 kg) of **FECES!**

In 1997, Silvio Jimenez, age 67, of Bogotá, Colombia, had **SURGICAL TWEEZERS** removed from his stomach—that had been left there **47 YEARS EARLIER!**

Doctors removed **78 PIECES OF CUTLERY** from the stomach of Margaret Daalman in Rotterdam, Netherlands!

In 2008-2009, Nguyen Thi Manh of Vietnam had a startling **119 CORRODED NAILS** removed from her **STOMACH!**

ALL EARSSS

> In January 2017, Ashley Glawe, of Portland, Oregon, had to take a trip to the ER to remove her pet snake from her gauged earlobe!

Glawe was playing with her ball python named Bart when the curious critter slithered through her stretched earlobe and promptly became stuck. The ER doctors had to numb her ear and then stretch it even more so Bart could wiggle free.

PEOPLE

COLOSSAL CUCUMBER ▶ Butch Taulton, a 72-year-old farmer from Knoxville, Maryland, grew a 43-in-long (107-cm) cucumber in his garden. Grown from a packet of seeds, it reached that size in just three months.

ELDERLY SIBLINGS ▶ Thirteen brothers and sisters of the Donnelly family in County Armagh, Northern Ireland, had a combined age of 1,073 years in March 2017—Sean (93), Maureen (92), Eileen (90), Peter (87), Mairead (86), Rose (85), Tony (83), Terry (81), Seamus (80), Brian (76), Kathleen (75), Colm (73), and Leo (72).

ONE WHEEL ▶ Dutch motorcycle wheelie king Egbert van Popta reached a speed of 213.3 mph (343 kmph) riding his Suzuki Hayabusa for 0.6 mi (1 km) on just its back wheel at Elvington Airfield, Yorkshire, England, in August 2016.

PINBALL WIZARD ▶ In October 2016, hospital worker Wayne Johns, from Staffordshire, England, played pinball for more than 30 hours straight.

HUGE AFRO ▶ At age 13, Tyler Wright, of Maryland Heights, Missouri, had an Afro hairstyle that measured a whopping 10 in (25.4 cm) high, 9.2 in (22.9 cm) wide and 71 in (177 cm) in circumference.

FAST HOLE ▶ Playing as a relay team, four French professional golfers—Romain Wattel, Alex Levy, Gregory Havret, and Raphael Jacquelin—completed a 500-yard hole at Spain's Valderrama Golf Club in just 34.8 seconds.

FREE CLIMB ▶ On June 3, 2017, Californian climber Alex Honnold became the first person to scale the 3,000-ft-tall (900-m) El Capitan Mountain in Yosemite National Park solo and without a rope or any other safety equipment. The free-solo ascent took him nearly four hours, and in places he had to dangle from the rock face by his fingertips. Until recent years, it took climbers weeks to reach the summit of El Capitan, even with the help of a partner and climbing gear.

LEECHES USED TODAY ARE FARMED, RATHER THAN COLLECTED!

Doctor LEECH

> Leeches have been used in medicine for centuries, but believe it or not, leeches are still used in medicine today!

In 2004, the FDA approved leeches as medical devices, used to remove blood from congested wounds. They are also essential to the bizarre beauty trend of leech facials!

While filming a Ripley's "Cool Stuff Strange Things" episode for YouTube, Ripley's Researcher Sabrina Sieck experienced a leech facial performed by Dr. Nidia Diaz from St. Petersburg, Florida—one of only five private practitioners in the United States to use leeches medicinally (called hirudotherapy).

THE LEECH'S MOUTH

LEECH SWEAT POSSIBLY URINE!

Dr. Diaz then used Sabrina's own leech-extracted blood (mixed with the leech's saliva) to finish up with a vampire facial.

RUBIK'S RIDER ▶ On June 4, 2017, 17-year-old P. K. Arumugam, of Chennai, India, solved 1,010 Rubik's Cubes in 6 hours 7 minutes while riding a bicycle. He had been training for the feat for six months, practicing for three hours every day.

SENIOR SPRINTER ▶ Man Kaur, from Chandigarh, India, won the 100 meters, 200 meters, and the javelin throw at the 2017 World Masters Games in Auckland, New Zealand—at age 101. She has won 19 gold medals since taking up sprinting at age 93 and is usually the only one competing in her age category.

PRINTED SHOES ▶ Tall teen Broc Brown, of Michigan Center, Michigan, finally found a pair of shoes to fit his size-28 feet, thanks to a 3-D printer. The 7.7-ft-tall (2.3-m) Brown has Sotos syndrome, or cerebral gigantism, and could never find affordable shoes in his size until California-based company Feetz stepped in. They used an app to convert photos of the 19-year-old's feet into 3-D models, which were then turned into a pair of custom-fit shoes by a 3-D printer. The black and red shoes are the colors of his favorite basketball team, the Chicago Bulls.

ECLIPSE CHASER ▶ Iranian Babak Tafreshi has traveled thousands of miles around the world to witness total solar eclipses that last for only a few minutes at a time. He saw his first eclipse in 1995 when, as a 17-year-old, he traveled more than 1,000 mi (1,600 km) to the Afghanistan border to watch 14 seconds of totality. He has subsequently experienced eclipses in such diverse locations as Zambia, Antarctica, Panama, Spain, Siberia, and Indonesia. A total eclipse occurs somewhere on Earth about every 18 months, but a specific location will only experience one every 375 years.

FLASHING EYELASHES ▶ Swedish designer Tien Pham has invented F. Lashes, a range of colored flashing LED eyelashes that are connected to a tiny battery at the back of the user's head. They stick to the eyelids with regular eyelash glue and come in a variety of bright colors and lighting modes—for example, "follow," where the lights follow the movement of the head; "sparkle," where they light up individually; and "dance" mode, where they blink at short intervals.

DRONE DIVER ▶ Latvian daredevil Ingus Augstkalns completed a skydive from a drone. After being lifted 1,082 ft (330 m) into the air by a giant, 28-propeller drone, he was dropped and then parachuted safely down to the ground. The 34-sq ft (3.2-sq m) drone weighs 154 lb (70 kg) and can carry a weight of 440 lb (200 kg).

CRAZY CARS ▶ Eccentric car designer Kanyaboyina Sudhakar, founder of the Sudha Cars Museum in Hyderabad, India, built a replica of a 1922 Ford Tourer car that is 26 ft (7.9 m) tall, 50 ft (15 m) long, and 19 ft (5.8 m) wide. It took him three years to create the two-story car, which has handmade metal wheels with a diameter of 9 ft (2.7 m) and a giant chessboard on the roof. Sudhakar can be seen driving the streets in many of his 700 crazy contraptions, including cars in the shape of a camera, a computer, a book, a handbag, a suitcase, and a coffee mug.

PARAPLEGIC FLIP ▶ Only a year after damaging his spinal cord in a crash while attempting to do the world's first double front flip on a dirt bike—an accident that left him permanently paralyzed in a wheelchair—Bruce Cook, from Kelowna, British Columbia, Canada, was back on the bike performing a sensational paraplegic back flip in a circus show. Since he no longer has the use of his legs, he has to be strapped to the bike to pull off the stunt, which means if the bike crashes, he crashes, too.

TOOTH COLLECTOR ▶ For 13 years, Abu Dhabi–based, Indian-born dentist Dr. Nizar Abdul Rahman has collected almost every tooth that he has extracted from his patients—and he now has more than 10,200 teeth. After pulling them, he cleans them with disinfectant and preserves them in hydrogen peroxide. He can even tell someone's likely profession by the state of their extracted teeth. For example, electricians will often have a V-shaped groove from their habit of using their teeth to open the insulated covers of electric cables, while tailors may have a minor abrasion in the center from their tendency to hold a needle in their mouth while working.

SPORTS STATE ▶ Basketball and volleyball were both invented in Massachusetts in the 1890s. Basketball was devised by Dr. James Naismith in Springfield in 1891, and volleyball was invented by William G. Morgan in Holyoke in 1895.

ANIMALS IN MEDICINE

AFRICA'S DRIVER ANTS have bites strong enough to stitch a wound shut! Once in place, the ant can be decapitated, and its jaws will stay clasped together.

Venom from the **BRAZILIAN ARROWHEAD VIPER** was used to create hypertension and congestive heart failure treatment drugs.

In 2005, the FDA approved a diabetes drug derived from **GILA MONSTER** venom.

HORSESHOE CRAB BLOOD is used to make a test for bacterial contamination in medicine.

Some U.S. states allow **KANGAROOS** as therapy animals.

In the early 20th century, **MAGGOTS** were often used to clean wounds, feasting on diseased and dying flesh.

Ripley's EXCLUSIVE

BICYCLE *Ballerina*

> Lea Schäepe of Potsdam, Germany, can ride a bike while standing on the handlebars!

Actually, she can ride a bike in many unconventional ways, thanks to her years of practice in artistic cycling. It's most popular in Germany and usually performed on an indoor court where people watch from stands. Having won a dozen national competitions in Germany, Lea's taking her bike to the streets and hoping to bring the impressive sport to the United States.

Q How were you introduced to artistic cycling?

A Every autumn we have a celebration, in a small town near Potsdam, where we welcome the change of the season. One year, when I was a young girl visiting, I happened upon a spectacle that forever changed my life. I witnessed artists performing what seemed to be impossible acrobatics on their bicycles. Being so impressed by what I saw and unable to get the images out of my mind, I soon asked my parents to register me in a sports club for artistic cycling.

Q What do you love most about artistic cycling?

A Everyone can ride a bike, but not everybody can stand on the handlebars of a bike. Artistic cycling is so special to me. It keeps me grounded and frees me at the same time. It is a discipline that no one will ever master because there is always something new to try and attempt.

Q *How do people in the United States react to your artistic cycling?*

A Everywhere I went people seemed fascinated with my art and wondered where I learned my discipline and why they had never seen anything like it before. (Interestingly, what many people do not know is that artistic cycling began in the United States more than 120 years ago.) These interactions, conversations, and genuine feelings of interest from people make me believe the United States is ready for artistic cycling again. I am hoping to be a part of that!

Q *What kind of bike is used in artistic cycling?*

A We use a modified form of fixed gear bicycles. Looking at the machine from a distance, you may think it is a traditional bike. However a closer in inspection will reveal great differences. If you are looking for the brakes, you will not find them on this style of bicycle.

80 ANTHEMS ▶ Eleven-year-old Capri Everitt, from Vancouver, British Columbia, Canada, sang 80 national anthems in 80 countries in nine months, performing each anthem in its own language—a total of 41 different languages. Starting in Canada on November 20, 2015, and finishing in Washington, D.C., on August 12, 2016, where she sang before a huge crowd at a Washington Nationals baseball game, she traveled the world with her parents, singing in countries such as Sweden, Greece, Germany, Poland, India, China, the Philippines, and Australia.

BIRD LOVER ▶ Lawrence Cobbold has a collection of more than 21,000 bird-related items that completely fills his house, three sheds, and a garage in Plymouth, England. He started the collection 30 years ago and now has more than 15,000 bird ornaments, 4,800 thimbles, 1,000 fridge magnets, 300 plates, 300 pictures, 150 mugs, and 100 jigsaw puzzles. They take up so much space that, even after moving to a bigger house, he has to cook and do his laundry at his parents' home. He used to sleep there, too, but has finally managed to find space for a bed in his own house.

Without using any safety equipment, Russian daredevil Oleg Sherstyachenko (aka Oleg Cricket) completed a series of acrobatic stunts on the narrow rooftop ledge of a Hong Kong skyscraper, just centimeters from an unguarded drop to the street hundreds of feet below. After riding a hoverboard along the ledge, he performed backflips and somersaults before doing pull-ups on the building's steel support beams. His previous stunts have included a front flip over the top of a car that was speeding toward him at 60 mph (96.5 kmph).

GIANT FEET ▶ Twenty-year-old Jeison Orlando Rodríguez Hernandez, from Maracay, Venezuela, has feet that are nearly 16 in (40 cm) long and wears specially made U.S. size 26 shoes. He stands 7.25 ft (2.2 m) tall, but his body grew at a normal rate until he was 10, when he had a dramatic growth spurt, doubling his shoe size in a year. From age 14, he has had shoes made out of cloth, but these never last longer than three weeks, and he is frequently forced to go around barefoot.

Pakistani martial arts master Muhammad Rashid can crush nearly 80 full drink cans in a minute using only his elbow. He is also able to crack open 35 coconuts in one minute with his head.

HEAVY LOAD ▶ Ben Blowes, from England, completed the 2017 London Marathon in 5 hours 58 minutes 37 seconds while running with a 55-lb (25-kg) clothes dryer on his back.

DEVOTED DAD ▶ Mark Evans, from Wrexham, Wales, has had his daughter Lucy's name tattooed on his back 267 times.

TASTY TOWER ▶ At a festival in Forno Di Zoldo, Italy, Dimitri Panciera managed to balance 121 scoops of ice cream on a single cone.

HUMAN DOMINOES ▶ A total of 1,200 people—arranged in 34 rows—formed a human mattress domino chain that was successfully toppled in 13 minutes 38 seconds in Fort Washington, Maryland, on March 22, 2016.

TEEN PILOT ▶ Although 17-year-old Oliver O'Halloran, from Hobart, Tasmania, Australia, was still too young to drive a car legally on the road, in 2017 he flew a single-engine airplane solo and unassisted around Australia—a 20-day flight covering 9,320 mi (15,000 km).

AMAZING FEAT ▶ Born without arms, Mexico's Adriana Irene Macias Hernández can light 11 candles in one minute using her feet. She also uses her feet to write, cook, hold a cell phone, and apply her makeup.

NEWS DRIVER ▶ In a 57-year career, Mel Rulison delivered more than five million newspapers. He retired in 2017 at age 87 from his job as a driver for *The Leader-Herald*, a daily afternoon paper published in Gloversville, New York.

LONG NAILS ▶ Luu Cong Huyen, from Vietnam's Nam Dinh province, has not trimmed his fingernails for more than 35 years. His longest nail measures over 22 in (55 cm), and he is so worried about them breaking, especially when wet, that he covers his hands with plastic bags if venturing outside in the rain. For the same reason, he rarely bathes, always sleeps alone, and often asks his wife to feed him with a spoon.

CHAMPION'S PHOBIA ▶ As a small boy, Adam Peaty, from Staffordshire, England, had an irrational fear of water and would throw a tantrum at bath time, refusing to sit in the tub—but at the 2016 Olympic Games, he won gold in the men's 100-meter breaststroke swimming event in a world record time. It took him years to overcome his hydrophobia, and even when he was 14—just seven years before his gold medal—he was still laboring in the "slow lane" of his local pool.

KUNG FU GRANDMA ▶ Zhang Hexian, the "Kung Fu Grandma," still teaches martial arts classes in Zhejiang Province, China, at age 94. She has been practicing martial arts for 90 years, learning kung fu when she was just four years old.

43,000-MILE RIDE ▶ Leigh Timmis, of Derby, England, cycled 43,000 mi (69,000 km) around the world between 2010 and 2017, spending an average of just $7 a day. On his travels, he encountered a bear in Canada, and temperatures of 129°F (54°C) in the Australian outback and -40°F (-40°C) in Tibet.

ROBOTIC HAND ▶ Using 3-D-printing technology, 14-year-old Leonardo Viscarra, from Cochabamba, Bolivia, made his own prosthetic hand for $100. He was born with an undeveloped left hand and could not find an artificial one that fit him properly, so he studied online videos and designed a robotic hand made primarily of thermoplastic. It allows him to hold a range of objects that he could not grip before.

AX STYLIST ▶ Instead of scissors, Russian hairstylist Daniil Istomin uses a razor-sharp ax to cut his customers' hair—by placing their heads on a chopping block. He had always wanted to try something different, so after experimenting with cutting hair while blindfolded and wielding two pairs of scissors simultaneously, he eventually landed on the ax, initially perfecting his technique on mannequins. He says the ax is easier to use because with one stroke he can cut as much hair as with 10 scissors strokes.

TALL BONFIRE ▶ For their annual midsummer festival, the residents of Ålesund, Norway, build a bonfire of wooden pallets, which in 2016, piled on top of each other, reached 155 ft (47 m) tall—about the same height as the Arc de Triomphe in Paris.

MODERN TWIST

» The Daasanach tribe of Africa reuses discarded objects such as bottle caps, watches, and SIM cards to make fashion accessories. Spread out across Kenya, Ethiopia, and Sudan, the tribe spends months collecting material, which is repurposed into unique headgear or jewelry. The colorful items are worn by all members of the tribe.

KNIFELINE

> **Using a yoga pose, 14-year-old Anamika Kothari of India puts on eyeliner with knives!**

The bendy young teen holds the sharp objects with the back of her knees after dipping them in black kajal—a type of eyeliner. While she balances on her shoulders, she slowly lowers her legs and gently drags the knife blades across her skin, creating an edgy look.

LONG HAIR DON'T CARE

> In the late 1800s, seven sisters from upstate New York wowed crowds with their long locks, touring the world at dime museums, P. T. Barnum's circus sideshows, and even world's fairs.

The Sutherland sisters—Sarah, Victoria, Isabella, Grace, Naomi, Dora, and Mary—were billed as the "7 Wonders of the World! 7 Accomplished musicians! 7 Ladies with 49 feet of hair! 7 Feet of hair each!" But the long-haired ladies—who actually had 37 ft (11.3 m) of hair between them—had humble beginnings on their family's turkey farm, where their mother concocted a smelly lotion to make their hair grow. . . and grow it did.

While they were talented singers and musicians, people didn't flock to see their skill so much as to see them let loose their luscious locks—a spectacle, since proper women of the time would only let down their hair in private. With the Victorian era's emphasis on women having long hair, they capitalized on the patent medicine trend and sold "hair fertilizer," which was a made-up mixture, as their mother had died and taken the hair growth recipe with her to the grave. Despite this, it made them rich: they netted $90,000 in sales the first year, which is about $2.25 million today.

The girls eventually built a mansion on their family's turkey farm, living out the rest of their eccentric lives together for the most part.

Miss Grace Sutherland (shown here) calmly, but proudly, poses with her 5-ft-long (1.5-m) mane.

DESPITE MARKETING 49 FT (15 M) OF HAIR, THEY ACTUALLY HAD 37 FT (11.3 M) BETWEEN THEM!

RIPPED *From* HISTORY

THE SEVEN SUTHERLAND SISTERS of New York MADE WEALTHY IN THE EARLY 1900s BY THEIR HAIR AND SCALP TONIC, HAD A COMBINED HAIR LENGTH OF **37** FEET

In 1981, the Ripley's Believe It or Not! cartoon featured the Sutherland sisters on the June 7 panel.

CRASH DIET Juan Pedro Franco, from Aguascalientes, Mexico, lost 385 lb (175 kg)—more than the weight of two average-sized men—in three months so that he could undergo life-saving gastric bypass surgery aimed at reducing his weight by 50 percent. Franco, who once weighed 1,311 lb (595 kg), was so obese that he spent nearly seven years confined to his bed.

SUPER SOAKER ▶ Former NASA engineer Mark Rober, of Orange County, California, has built a 7-ft-long (2.1-m) water gun that is pressurized at 2,400 lb (1,090 kg) per square inch, making it eight times more powerful than a fire truck hose. Producing a jet of water traveling at more than 270 mph (435 kmph), it can slice watermelons, bananas, and hot dogs in half; split open a soda can; and shatter a line of wine glasses.

PIZZA FESTIVAL ▶ More than 40 chefs in Puglia, Italy, baked 5,836 pizzas in less than 12 hours at the town's pizza-themed festival in September 2016.

FEAST TABLE ▶ To welcome their New Year, on December 1, 2016, the ethnic Dong people of southern China joined together 1,730 tables to form one enormous 2.3-mi-long (3.7-km) table on the highway in Jiasuo village for a feast that was attended by more than 10,000 people.

13-HOUR WHEELIE ▶ Japanese motorbike rider Masaru Abe performed a wheelie on a Yamaha Jog scooter for an incredible 310 mi (500 km) at a race track in Saitama on May 1, 2017. He rode on one wheel for more than 13 hours despite experiencing back pain just two hours into the stunt; he spent most of the last hour screaming in agony.

MOURINHO TATTOOS ▶ Vivien Bodycote, a grandmother from Leicestershire, England, has 35 tattoos of Manchester United's Portuguese manager Jose Mourinho on her body.

ENORMOUS NEEDLES ▶ Art and design student Betsy Bond, from Wiltshire, England, created a pair of enormous knitting needles that are 14.4 ft (4.4 m) long and have a diameter of 3.6 in (9 cm).

POST OFFICES ▶ For more than 35 years, Steve Powell, of Brisbane, Australia, has been traveling thousands of miles back and forth across the country taking photographs of more than 800 Australian post office buildings.

CENTENARIAN SKYDIVER ▶ On May 14, 2017, at age 101, Verdun Hayes, of Somerset, England, made a tandem skydive from a height of 15,000 ft (4,572 m). The great-grandfather completed the jump with 10 other people, including three generations of his family and the doctor who gave the go-ahead for the stunt.

CANINE TOOTH ▶ On February 3, 2017, Dr. Jaimin Patel, a dentist from Vadodara, India, extracted a canine tooth from 18-year-old college student Urvil Patel that measured an amazing 1.5 in (3.7 cm) long—nearly twice the length of the average human tooth.

BALL SPINNING ▶ On April 8, 2017, Sandeep Singh, of Punjab, India, spun a basketball for 53 seconds on a toothbrush held in his mouth. He has been spinning balls since he was 10, starting with volleyballs before progressing to basketballs.

HUMAN WASHING LINE

» Acrobats and daredevils flock to a suspended net and tightropes dangling precariously over a 400 ft (121 m) canyon in Utah. Created by thrill seeker Andy Lewis in 2015, the Mothership Space Net Penthouse contains a central hole for base and bungee jumping enthusiasts. Talk about falling through the cracks!

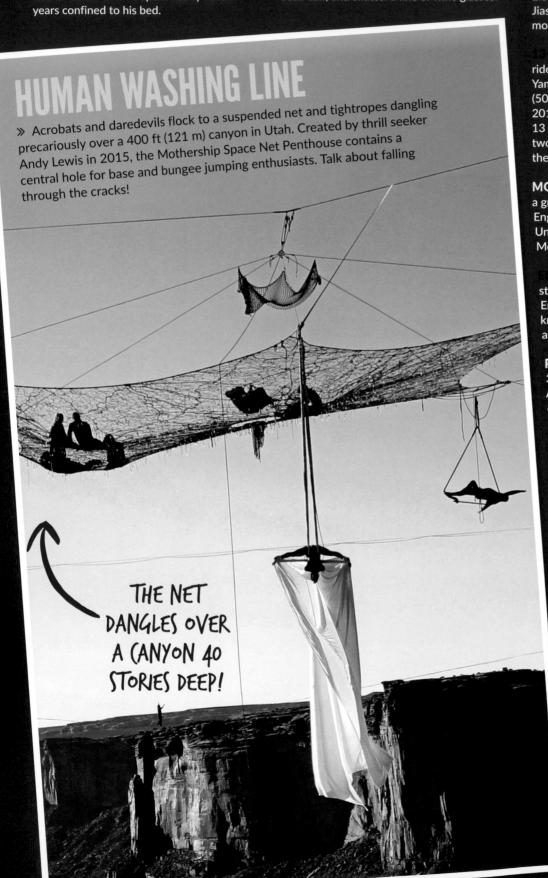

THE NET DANGLES OVER A CANYON 40 STORIES DEEP!

Sunscribes

> Using mirrors and magnifying glasses as his paintbrushes, artist Michael Papadakis from Colorado harnesses the power of the sun to burn drawings onto wooden canvases.

The glass allows him to refract the sun's rays onto a specific area of the wooden surface. This art form is called "heliography," and the images he creates range from romantic scenes on fence posts to landscapes of city skylines.

Q *What inspired you to use this medium?*

A My inspiration started while I was traveling the world in 2012 and was looking to travel light and still create art. This idea of painting with the sun presented itself almost naturally to me, as no one ever showed me, nor had I ever seen someone do it before. This tool became my "traveler's paintbrush," as I used it for 14 months traveling by foot from South Korea all the way to Greece making artwork with the local sunshine along the way!

Q *What is "heliography," and how does it relate to your art?*

A I believe heliography is the language of the sun. If the sun could talk, I believe this art form is how the sun would draw its stories. I am simply holding and redirecting the sun's power to create beautiful, meaningful art.

Q *Can you briefly explain your artistic process?*

A I usually start early at the crack of dawn to find a beautiful or meaningful location to catch some of first rays of light. Typically, I sketch my images out first to speed up my process. I work at all hours of the day. Sun painting is all about angles, and when the sun is at more of a 90° angle from the horizon, like in the evening, that is the most optimal. This process works year-round. In fact, my favorite time to paint is in the winter when it's 30°F (−1°C) out and the sun is low on the horizon. I feel the middle of winter is the sun's most powerful time.

Q *What materials do you use?*

A I use a combination of lenses and mirrors. Some lenses have very long focal lengths, which allow me to "paint" from 15 ft (4.6 m) away! I always, I repeat, always wear welding shades! Sunglasses are not enough. If I am painting in a public setting, I always bring extra welding shades for onlookers. Maybe the most important tool is water; I always have a spray bottle or bucket of water on hand for safety.

MAD FOR MARMITE

» Shelly McClellan, from Hemel Hempstead, Hertfordshire, England, loves Marmite yeast extract so much that she has collected more than 200 vintage jars of the savory spread and eats it at every meal. She has eaten thousands of jars of Marmite in her lifetime and always has one in her handbag. Her kitchen has a shrine to the product, while her lounge features a 3-ft-tall (0.9-m) Marmite shop display.

ROYAL DUTIES ▶ From the time his wife became Queen Elizabeth II in 1952 to his retirement from public duties in 2017, Prince Philip, Duke of Edinburgh, fulfilled more than 22,219 solo engagements, made 637 solo overseas visits, and gave more than 5,490 speeches.

TOUGH GUY ▶ Strongman Amandeep Singh, from Haryana in northern India, has a repertoire of more than 2,500 stunts. He can lift a man off the ground with his teeth, break stones with his bare hands, lift a heavy motorbike above his head with ease, and withstand being run over by a car.

HEAVY CUBE ▶ Mechanical engineering students at the University of Michigan created a 1,500-lb (681-kg) hand-solvable Rubik's Cube. The cubelets in the giant puzzle, which took three years to design and build, can be easily moved by an individual due to an internal arrangement of rollers and transfer bearings.

PUT IT IN PARKOUR ▶ Abdullah Omar Al Ali of Dubai, United Arab Emirates, can do a handstand on top of a moving truck—while the truck is balancing on two wheels! The 21-year-old daredevil had only been practicing parkour for a year when he pulled off the impressive stunt.

YOUNG CHAMPION ▶ At Aspen, Colorado, in 2016, 13-year-old Estonian freeskier Kelly Sildaru became the youngest-ever Winter X Games gold medalist when she won the women's ski slopestyle competition.

FIRE EXTINGUISHER ▶ Ashrita Furman of New York City can extinguish 37 lit matches with his tongue in one minute.

FOUR-HOMER ▶ On June 6, 2017, the Cincinnati Reds' Scooter Gennett became only the 17th player in Major League Baseball history—and the first Red—to hit four home runs in a game. Before enjoying a field day against the St. Louis Cardinals, Gennett had hit just 38 career home runs in five seasons—a total of 1,637 at bats.

BOOT RUNNER ▶ Damian Thacker, from Sheffield, England, ran the 26.2-mi (42-km) 2017 London Marathon in 3 hours 21 minutes 27 seconds while wearing rain boots.

TUMOR TUMMY

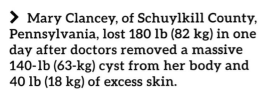

> Mary Clancey, of Schuylkill County, Pennsylvania, lost 180 lb (82 kg) in one day after doctors removed a massive 140-lb (63-kg) cyst from her body and 40 lb (18 kg) of excess skin.

Over the course of around 15 years, the 71-year-old grandmother thought she was simply gaining weight as she got older, until one day she found herself unable to get out of bed. One trip to the hospital and a CT scan later soon revealed that Clancey actually had an ovarian cyst that made up almost half of her body weight! The surgery to remove the mass required two operating tables—Clancey on one and the tumor on the other. When she was opened up, the tumor rolled onto the table, and a nurse was able to wheel it out of the room.

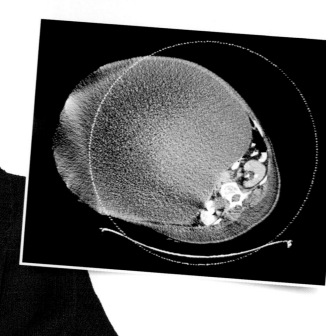

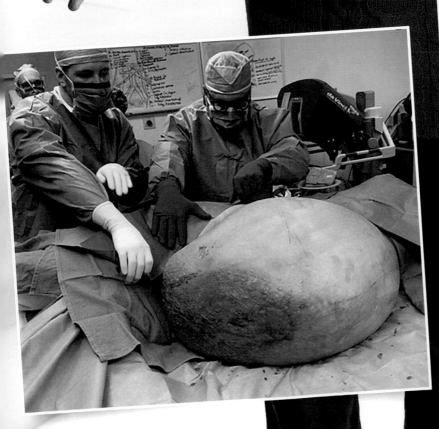

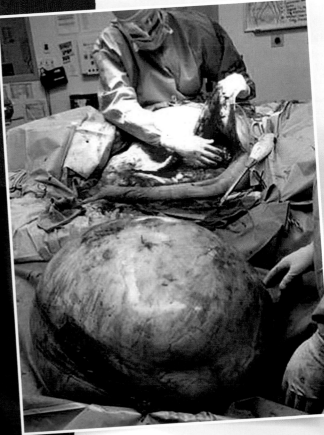

FAMILY PHOTO

» More than 500 members of one family gathered for a photo in Shishe village, Zhejiang Province, China. They met up to celebrate the completion of the Ren family tree, which had not been updated for 80 years. The family, which originates from the village, can be traced back more than 850 years, and in total it has at least 2,000 living relatives, spanning seven generations.

ONE-ARMED RIDER ▶ Despite being born with no lower left arm, Jack Dumper, from Bristol, England, can perform amazing BMX stunts by tying the sleeve of his hooded sweatshirt to the bike's handlebars and using his left shoulder and upper back to steer. He practices BMX tricks for 60 hours a week and, with one arm, is able to pull off daring spins and jumps with such skill that he competes against the world's top professional riders.

SEVEN WONDERS ▶ In just 13 days, Megan Sullivan, from San Francisco, California, visited the New Seven Wonders of the World—Chichen Itza (Mexico), Machu Picchu (Peru), the statue of Christ the Redeemer (Brazil), the Colosseum (Italy), Petra (Jordan), the Taj Mahal (India), and the Great Wall of China. She traveled 28,211 mi (45,140 km) across 12 countries, taking 15 flights.

CAN HEAD ▶ Jamie Keeton, of Chicago, Illinois, has a rare skin condition that allows him to stick cans, bottles, and other objects to the sides of his head. The condition makes his skin pores act like suction cups, and he uses this unusual ability to promote products, earning up to $8,000 in a weekend from companies who stick their branded product to his head. Known as "Can Head," he can stick as many as eight cans to his face and head simultaneously.

POOP COLLECTOR ▶ George Frandsen, of Jacksonville, Florida, has collected more than 5,000 pieces of fossilized poop, called coprolites, from 15 states in the United States and eight other countries. They range in size from a tiny termite poop to a 4-lb (0.5-kg) specimen, and they range in age from 10,000 to 400 million years old. His biggest and most cherished coprolite is "Precious," produced in South Carolina some 20 million years ago, probably by a species of ancient crocodile.

FAMILY ADVENTURE ▶ With their children Woody and Zephyr and Jack Russell terrier Zero in tow, Patrick Jones and Meg Ulman set off from their home in Daylesford, Victoria, Australia, and cycled 3,750 mi (6,000 km) around the country for more than 14 months, surviving by eating plants, fish, and foraged roadkill.

TALENTED TOT ▶ Arat Hosseini, from Babol, Iran, could perform a backflip while swinging from a horizontal bar at seven months old, do consecutive backflips at 13 months, and do splits while balanced on his hands on top of a TV set before his second birthday. His astonishing strength and agility have earned him more than 1 million followers on Instagram.

Healing TONGUE

> An 80-year-old spiritual healer in Bosnia and Herzegovina claims to be able to cure people with impaired vision by licking their eyeballs!

Hava Celebic says her healing tongue, which she sterilizes with alcohol before licking, has cured around 5,000 people. Her tongue is so revered that she believes locals will cut it out when she dies so that they can continue to use its powers.

YOUNG CHAMPION ▶ Competing at the Rio Olympics, 16-year-old Canadian swimmer Penny Oleksiak became the first athlete born in the 21st century to win an Olympic gold medal in an individual event. She was born on June 13, 2000, in Scarborough, Ontario, and tied for first place with Simone Manuel of the United States in the women's 100-meter freestyle final on August 11, 2016.

BOTTLE SHIPS ▶ Danish sailor Peter Jacobsen (1873–1960) built more than 1,700 miniature ships in bottles in his lifetime, earning the nickname "Bottle Peter."

FINGER SNAPPER ▶ Japanese student Satoyuki Fujimura can snap his fingers nearly 300 times a minute. That works out to five times per second—in comparison, a blink of an eye takes one-third of a second. So Fujimura, who learned the secret of rapid-fire snapping from his mother, can snap his fingers faster than the blink of an eye!

GAZA SAMSON ▶ Despite being just 20 years old and weighing 143 lb (65 kg), Mohamed Baraka, a young Palestinian known as the "Samson of Gaza," can pull an 18-ton truck with his teeth for a distance of 330 ft (100 m).

PENGUIN SUITS ▶ Rachel Rauwerda and Stacey Collie, from Thunder Bay, Ontario, Canada, ran the 2016 Antarctic Marathon wearing penguin suits. Despite facing 60 mph (96 kmph) winds and driving snow, which made their suits wet and heavy, Rauwerda completed the full 26.2 mi (42 km), while a knee injury forced Collie to drop down to the half-marathon distance.

PARK RANGER ▶ At age 95, Betty Reid Soskin is the oldest serving U.S. national park ranger. She's worked at the Rosie the Riveter WWII Home Front National Historical Park in California for more than 10 years. Even after being attacked by a burglar in June 2016, she was back at work about three weeks later.

189

SHOWER
Strands

Ripley's
EXCLUSIVE

> Lucy Gafford, a multimedia artist from Mobile, Alabama, creates artworks with her own shower hair.

Instead of letting the loose strands wash down the drain after she has washed her hair, she collects the wet hair, spreads it on the bathroom wall, and uses her fingers to arrange it into identifiable shapes. Her first creation was a squirrel in 2014, and she has since made more than 400 shower hair drawings, including Princess Leia from *Star Wars*, Santa Claus, and Picasso's *Self Portrait*. She posts a new artwork on social media at least once a week.

Q *How did you begin to dabble in this medium?*

Every time I shower, my hands get covered in hair, which I wipe on the wall to prevent it from clogging the drain. After showering one night in 2014, my mass of wet hair resembled a squirrel. I tweaked it around, took a picture, and posted it on Twitter. Initially it was intended to be funny, but I kept doing it—soon becoming obsessed with seeing how complicated I could get using my hair to create images. I have transitioned from pushing the hair around and creating a loose, messy image, to using the individual hairs to create detailed contour drawings as if each hair were a pen stroke.

Q *Do you only use your own hair?*

I only use my own hair. There's a chance that my husband has had a hair or two in some of my drawings because it's hard to tell our hair apart—he grows his as long as mine occasionally.

Q *What reactions do you get from your art?*

I've seen disgust, amazement, and amusement. Most people find it funny and relatable, since everyone loses hair and has probably lived with someone who leaves theirs on the shower wall.

Q *Do you trim your hairs to size or work with what the shower gods give you?*

I cut the hairs with my teeth by biting them to make the sizes I need for each piece. Sometimes I have to cut pieces smaller than an eyelash. I've gotten really good at it over the years but still occasionally lose them in my mouth.

DOUBLE FLIP ▶ FMX biker Greg Duffy executed the world's first double front flip in a professional competition at the 2016 Nitro Games in Salt Lake City, Utah.

FRIENDLY BEES ▶ Charles Wieand, from Columbus, Ohio, stood naked among a colony of bees for 45 minutes without getting stung once. He performed the stunt at his father's beehives in Eau Claire, Michigan, remaining perfectly still as the bees swarmed all around him.

CARD TRICK ▶ Zhou Chaofeng, a kung fu artist from Mianyang, China, can slice open a full can of beer by throwing a playing card at it.

BACKFLIP CATCH ▶ Professional wakeboarder Dante Digangi caught a football in midair while performing a backflip on his wakeboard on a lake in Groveland, Florida.

UNBEATEN ROWERS ▶ When New Zealand rowers Eric Murray and Hamish Bond won the gold medal in the men's coxless pairs at the 2016 Olympics, it was their 69th consecutive victory, a winning streak spanning seven years.

HOTTEST PEPPERS ▶ Seasoned competitive eater Wayne Algenio, of New York City, ate 22 Carolina Reaper chili peppers in 60 seconds on April 24, 2016—without drinking any liquids, not even water. The peppers measure over 1.5 million on the Scoville heat unit scale, making them the hottest peppers in the world. Afterward, he had to stand for an additional minute without taking in any liquids or vomiting before he was finally able to drink milk to soothe his burning throat.

MUSCLE MAN ▶ Arm wrestler Jeff Dabe, from Stacy, Minnesota, is known as "Popeye" because his huge forearms measure 19 in (49 cm) in circumference and his hands are so large he can hold a basketball in each one. Born with oversized limbs, he competed in arm wrestling contests with his right arm until he injured it and eventually switched to his left arm.

CROSSING AUSTRALIA ▶ Setting off on March 3, 2017, 13-year-old Si-am Juntakereket, from Cornwall, England, cycled across Australia—a distance of 2,768 mi (4,454 km)—in just 29 days. He did so despite facing temperatures of 104°F (40°C), suffering seven tire punctures in one day, and being forced to spend a day in the hospital after being treated for insect bites.

STANDING RIDE ▶ Stuntman Ravinder Singh (aka Ravi Patiala), from Patiala, India, rode a Royal Enfield motorcycle nonstop for 17.5 mi (28 km) along a road in Punjab state while standing on the seat without any support. His standing ride took him 22 minutes 25 seconds at an average speed of 45 mph (72 kmph).

FAST FOOD ▶ Ricardo "Rix Terabite" Francisco, from the Philippines, ate five 3.7-oz (107-g) hamburgers in a single minute at a competitive eating contest in Manila.

HELICOPTER HERO ▶ With the help of a harness and ropes tied around his waist, Belarusian powerlifter Kirill Shimko pulled the world's largest helicopter—weighing nearly 35 tons—for a distance of 66 ft (20 m) along an airfield in Minsk.

SEVEN LANGUAGES ▶ Although she is only four years old, Bella Devyatkina, from Moscow, Russia, can speak seven different languages. Her parents started teaching her English when she was just two, and she showed such a flair for it that they hired native tutors to teach her other languages. She can now communicate in Russian, English, French, Spanish, German, Chinese, and Arabic, and spends six hours a day studying foreign languages.

TANDEM MARATHON ▶ Dominic Irvine and Charlie Mitchell rode a tandem bicycle the length of the United Kingdom—842 mi (1,355 km) from Land's End, Cornwall, England, to John O'Groats, Scotland—in just over 45 hours. They averaged 18.7 mph (30 kmph) and completed 225,000 bike pedal revolutions.

HEAD-TO-HEAD

» Vietnamese circus brothers Giang Quoc Nghiep and Giang Quoc Co climbed up 90 steps outside St. Mary's Cathedral in Girona, Spain, while balanced head-to-head. One walked up the steps while the other balanced upside-down on top of his head, yet they achieved the climb in only 52 seconds. Born into a circus family, they have been perfecting the stunt for 15 years.

PICKLED EARLOBES

» German circus performer and professional sword swallower Hannibal Hellmurto had his earlobes cut off after dangerously over-stretching them to a length of 2.4 in (6 cm). He then pickled the amputated earlobes and sold them at a horror-themed auction in Warwickshire, England, for more than $500.

KING CUCUMBER ▶ In 2015, Daniel Tomelin, of Kelowna, British Columbia, Canada, grew a cucumber that measured a whopping 44.5 in (112 cm) long.

SIX-ARMED ROBOT ▶ The Sub1 robot, developed by German engineer Albert Beer, can solve a Rubik's Cube in only 0.637 seconds—faster than it takes to find "Rubik's Cube" through an online search engine. A microcontroller board operates the robot's six mechanical arms, which spin the columns and allow it to complete the puzzle in just 21 moves.

60-FOOT SWING ▶ Chris Cruze built a porch swing in Moss Bluff, Louisiana, that is 60 ft (18 m) long, weighs 548 lb (249 kg), and seats 40 people.

SHACKLED SWIM ▶ On March 2, 2017, S. Sabarinathan, a 20-year-old college student from Nagapattinam, India, swam 3.1 mi (5 km) in the Bay of Bengal with his hands and legs bound with iron chains. He had practiced swimming with his hands and legs cuffed for six months and completed the swim in 2 hours 20 minutes 48 seconds.

ORGAN CHALLENGE ▶ In July 2016, Welshman John Richards, despite never having had a formal organ lesson in his life, finally completed his 20-year quest to play all 94 cathedral organs in Britain.

YAKETY YAK ▶ In June 2017, a yak yogurt drinking contest was held in a theme park in Sichuan Province, China. Tourists participated in the event, which saw contestants drink yogurt without their hands. The winner won by drinking two large bowls of yak yogurt in just five minutes.

GOAL RUSH ▶ Croatian soccer striker Stjepan Lucijanic scored a hat-trick (three goals) in five consecutive games for NK Dracice Dakovo in 2016.

BODY TWISTER ▶ Contortionist Claudia Hughes, from London, England, can fold her 5.4-ft-tall (1.6-m) body into a 20 × 12 × 12-in (50 × 30 × 30-cm) cupboard and can wash dishes with her feet flipped over her head while balancing on her arms.

100 MARATHONS ▶ Ryan Holmes, from Whitstable, Kent, England, completed his 100th marathon at the age of just 21 years and 172 days. Often running two races a week, he has covered over 2,600 mi (4,184 km), greater than the distance from London, England, to Newfoundland, Canada.

CORN CHOMPER ▶ On April 24, 2016, Yasir Salem, from New York City, ate 47 ears of sweet corn in 12 minutes at the 2016 Sweet Corn Fiesta in West Palm Beach, Florida.

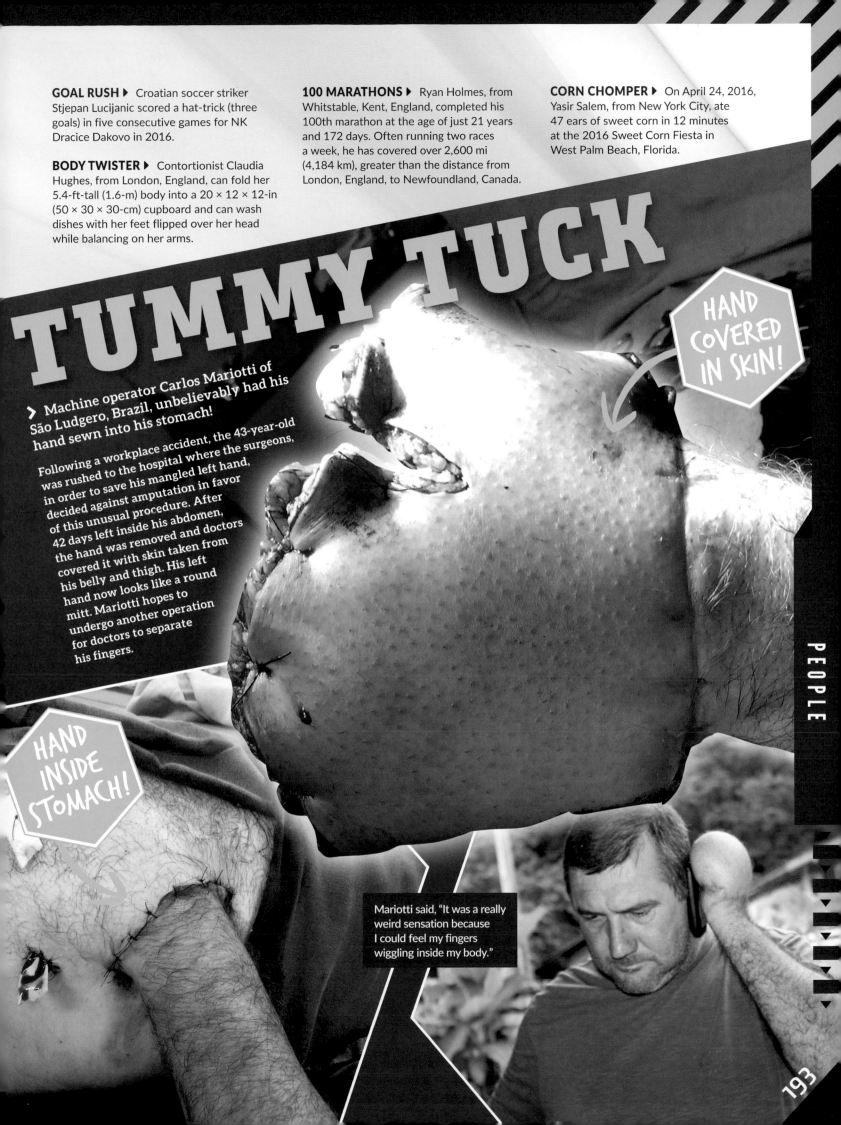

TUMMY TUCK

HAND COVERED IN SKIN!

HAND INSIDE STOMACH!

▶ Machine operator Carlos Mariotti of São Ludgero, Brazil, unbelievably had his hand sewn into his stomach!

Following a workplace accident, the 43-year-old was rushed to the hospital where the surgeons, in order to save his mangled left hand, decided against amputation in favor of this unusual procedure. After 42 days left inside his abdomen, the hand was removed and doctors covered it with skin taken from his belly and thigh. His left hand now looks like a round mitt. Mariotti hopes to undergo another operation for doctors to separate his fingers.

Mariotti said, "It was a really weird sensation because I could feel my fingers wiggling inside my body."

PEOPLE

193

UNDERWATER FLIPS ▶ Wearing scuba diving gear, Dan Bowman, from Orem, Utah, performed 308 consecutive front flips underwater in an hour at a pool in American Fork on August 8, 2016.

BOTTLE CAPS ▶ In just five years, Hans Heiland, from Ybbs, Austria, built up a collection of 10 million beer bottle caps. The collection weighed 18 tons, and in 2016, he sold it to a metal collector for $1,700, delivering the caps in three large trucks.

BODY STRENGTH ▶ Although she stands just 5.3 ft (1.6 m) tall and weighs only 134 lb (61 kg), petite Daniella Means from Hong Kong can flip a 704-lb (320-kg) tire and deadlift more than double her body weight.

ONE JOB ▶ Monica Evans has worked in the accounts department of a components firm in Warwickshire, England, for more than 70 years. She started as a 19-year-old in 1947, and in that time, she has barely had a sick day and has made only one mistake—in 1959—when she failed to account for a missing two pence.

TREE PLANTER ▶ Abdul Samad Sheikh, a rickshaw driver from Faridpur, Bangladesh, planted at least one tree every day for nearly 50 years. He began as a 12-year-old and planted more than 17,500 trees before his death in 2017.

BMX MOM ▶ Bored with just watching while her son Axel went BMX racing, Jaqueline Taheny, from Darwin, Australia, decided to take up the sport herself, and within eight years the 43-year-old was representing her country at the world championships.

RECORD ROOST

❯ On May 31, 1949, Cleveland Indians fan Charley Lupica climbed onto a wooden platform attached to the top of a pole and remained there for 117 days.

The frenzied fan vowed to stay until the Indians reached first place. While on the perch, Charley was given toilet facilities, a radio, a television, and meals. His stunt ended after Indians owner Bill Veeck Jr. transported him to the Municipal Stadium, where he was greeted by family and gifted a new car!

THE POLE WAS 16 FT (4.8 M) TALL!

Only a canvas shielded Charley from the elements!

THIS ISN'T MESSI!

MESSI LOOKALIKE ▶ Iranian student Reza Parastesh looks so much like Barcelona's Argentine soccer star Lionel Messi that in May 2017 police officers in Hamedan, Iran, had to impound his car to stop people from causing traffic chaos by taking selfies with him.

On June 10, 2017, 1,336 runners competed in a 0.6 mi (1 km) race in Cary, North Carolina, wearing flip-flops.

NIAGARA STUNT ▶ On June 15, 2017, aerialist Erendira Wallenda hung by her teeth from a helicopter 300 ft (90 m) above Niagara Falls. She was tethered to a hoop suspended from the helicopter, and after performing a few acrobatic moves, she dangled by her teeth with the help of a mouth guard. She pulled off the daring stunt five years to the day after her husband Nik had walked a tightrope across the Falls.

British strongman Thomas Inch (1881–1963) used to offer $300 to anyone who could lift the "Inch dumbbell," a 172-lb (78-kg) weight that he had designed with extra thick handles, which made it extremely difficult to lift. Few managed it, apart from Inch himself, even when he was 72.

NOVELTY CROCS ▶ Self-proclaimed "crocoholic" Andrew Gray, from Northamptonshire, England, has a collection of nearly 7,000 novelty crocodiles. His love of ornamental crocodiles began around 2000 when, seeking furniture for his new house, he instead bought a 3-ft-long (0.9-m) wooden crocodile.

In 12 months—from February 11, 2015, to February 11, 2016—65-year-old Danny McDonald, of Tignish, Prince Edward Island, Canada, did 200,000 push-ups. He started off doing 200 a day, eventually working up to an incredible 1,400.

SPEED SKATER ▶ On August 29, 2016, Kyle Wester, from Denver, Colorado, rode a skateboard downhill at a speed of 89.4 mph (143 kmph).

RIB FEAST ▶ Competitive eater Matt "The Megatoad" Stonie, from San Jose, California, ate 71 pork ribs in five minutes in Homestead, Florida, on November 22, 2015.

On September 9, 2016, 12-year-old Shristi Sharma, from Nagpur, India, limbo skated on ice for a distance of 33 ft (10 m) under 11 bars placed 3.3 ft (1 m) apart at a height of just 13 in (33 cm) above the ground.

BRIDGE JUMPS ▶ Mike Heard, of Auckland, New Zealand, performed 430 bungee jumps off the Auckland Harbour Bridge in 24 hours, averaging one jump every three minutes.

FAST CUT ▶ In December 2016, Sheetal Shah, a beautician from Surat, India, cut the hair of 571 people in 24 hours, averaging just over two minutes for each haircut.

SERVE'S UP

» In July 2017, Australian Christiaan Hart and his girlfriend, Catherine, hit a few tennis volleys while wakeboarding in Hong Kong. The pair each took turns tossing a tennis ball from the boat while the other rode in the water!

FEET FIRST

Ripley's EXCLUSIVE

Q How heavy are the tables you juggle?

A The table I juggle is 30 lb (13.6 kg) with metal reinforced edges that can really do some damage if you drop it!

Emma Phillips of Whangarei, New Zealand, is the only performer in the world that can juggle both umbrellas and tables with her feet!

After seeing a Cirque du Soleil show at 16 years old, she knew that was the world in which she belonged. Four years later, she began training at prestigious performance schools in China. She was discouraged from trying to juggle both tables and umbrellas, as they use opposing muscles and techniques. However, her hard work and perseverance paid off, and she now travels the world performing her one-of-a-kind juggling act.

Q What's harder to juggle—tables or umbrellas?

A Juggling umbrellas takes the smallest adjustments of balance, so small that even when it looks like I'm holding it still you can see up close that there are still tiny adjustments happening to keep it balanced. Table juggling takes extreme focus, determination, and power. And a very high pain threshold! It took me months to adjust my balance with umbrellas after I began using the table.

Q What else can you juggle with your feet?

A I also studied carpet spinning contortion in China, so I would twist my body and balance, all while spinning a small carpet on my feet. It's also fun sometimes to just play with random objects with my feet to test out my balance and challenge myself!

EMMA IS ALSO SKILLED IN CONTORTION AND AERIAL ACROBATICS.

Q *What's your favorite stunt to perform?*

A My favorite stunt to perform is probably juggling the table—the reaction and energy I feel from the audience is incredible and unlike the reaction to juggling the umbrellas or performing aerial hoop, which is more an appreciation of watching something beautiful and artistic. But when I start spinning the table so fast it's a blur, I can actually hear the audience react and it gives me so much adrenaline and power!

Q *Where's the most interesting place you've performed?*

A I was touring with a magic show when we visited a small town in Finland 93 mi (150 km) past the Arctic Circle that had never had a show visit before. The entire town came to watch and presented us with gifts afterward. Outside there was more than 3 ft (1 m) of snow, and it honestly looked like we were inside a snow globe.

SPINNING CARPETS WHILE JUGGLING A TABLE!

EXTENDED CHRISTMAS ▶ By flying almost 20,000 mi (32,000 km) across the world and passing through different time zones from east to west, Scotsman Fraser Watt managed to enjoy a 47-hour Christmas Day. He set off at midnight on Christmas Eve 2016 from Auckland, New Zealand, and traveled via Hong Kong, London, and Los Angeles to arrive at Honolulu, Hawaii, at 11:38 p.m. local time, still on Christmas Day.

DREAM DEBUT ▶ On November 19, 2016, Joe Thomas Sr., of Blackville, South Carolina, finally achieved his dream of playing college football—at age 55. Appearing as a running back for South Carolina State, for whom his son, Joe Jr., played from 2010 to 2013, Thomas made one carry and three hand-offs against Savannah State. At the end of South Carolina's 32-0 victory, he was carried off the field by his teammates.

PATIENCE PAYS ▶ At the 2016 U.S. PGA Championship at Baltusrol Golf Club in Springfield, New Jersey, Australian John Senden waited for 22 seconds for his putt to drop into the hole. Facing a 15-ft (4.6-m) putt on the 16th, he left the ball teetering agonizingly on the edge of the cup, but he waited patiently until it finally dropped in.

EXTREME GALLBLADDER

» In 2016, a gallbladder removed from Suman Rao, a 46-year-old woman from Churu, India, measured 11.8 in (29 cm) long—more than four times the length of a normal one!

DOMINOES TOPPLED ▶ In Westland, Michigan, the Incredible Science Machine team toppled a circle bomb of 76,017 dominoes. It took 18 domino artists 10 days to construct the elaborate formation, which fell from the center of the circle to its outer edge in just seconds.

GORILLA COSTUME ▶ Police officer Tom Harrison, from London, England, completed the 26 mi (42 km) course of the 2017 London Marathon by crawling on all fours while dressed in a gorilla costume. "Mr. Gorilla," as he is known, eventually finished the course in six-and-a-half days.

HOT SHOT ▶ On November 15, 1993, 71-year-old retired podiatrist Dr. Tom Amberry, from Long Beach, California, shot and made 2,750 consecutive free throws on the basketball court. He only stopped after 12 hours when the gym janitors told him to.

EXPERIENCED SCIENTIST ▶ Dr. David Goodall is still working as a scientist at Edith Cowan University in Perth, Western Australia, at age 102. He attends campus up to four days a week to conduct research, review academic papers, and supervise PhD students.

GRAVEYARD MEDITATION ▶ Liu Taijie, a 30-year-old divorcee from Chongqing, China, helps other women overcome the pain of depression and divorce by running graveyard meditation classes in which they simulate being dead. The women lie down in shallow holes lined with plastic foil, with their eyes closed and their hands resting on their chest. The idea is to show that life goes on even after hardships.

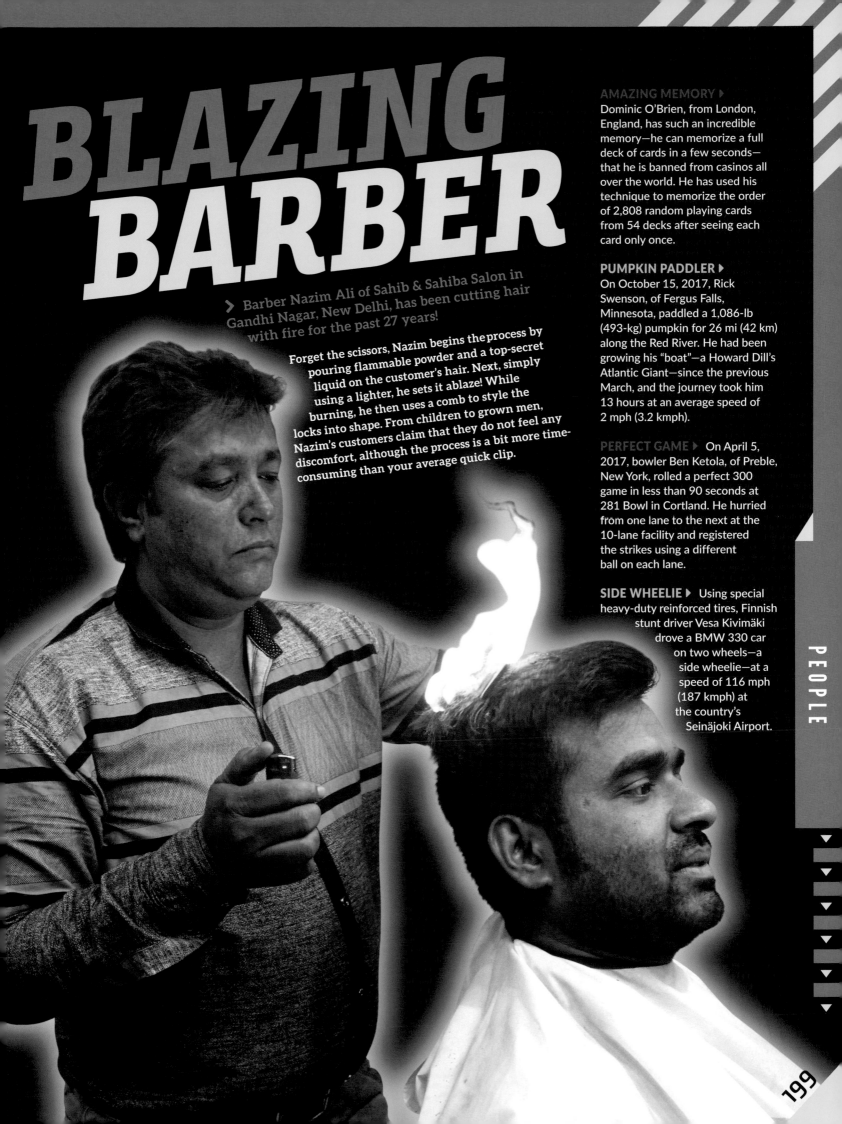

BLAZING BARBER

> Barber Nazim Ali of Sahib & Sahiba Salon in Gandhi Nagar, New Delhi, has been cutting hair with fire for the past 27 years!

Forget the scissors, Nazim begins the process by pouring flammable powder and a top-secret liquid on the customer's hair. Next, simply using a lighter, he sets it ablaze! While burning, he then uses a comb to style the locks into shape. From children to grown men, Nazim's customers claim that they do not feel any discomfort, although the process is a bit more time-consuming than your average quick clip.

AMAZING MEMORY ▶
Dominic O'Brien, from London, England, has such an incredible memory—he can memorize a full deck of cards in a few seconds—that he is banned from casinos all over the world. He has used his technique to memorize the order of 2,808 random playing cards from 54 decks after seeing each card only once.

PUMPKIN PADDLER ▶
On October 15, 2017, Rick Swenson, of Fergus Falls, Minnesota, paddled a 1,086-lb (493-kg) pumpkin for 26 mi (42 km) along the Red River. He had been growing his "boat"—a Howard Dill's Atlantic Giant—since the previous March, and the journey took him 13 hours at an average speed of 2 mph (3.2 kmph).

PERFECT GAME ▶ On April 5, 2017, bowler Ben Ketola, of Preble, New York, rolled a perfect 300 game in less than 90 seconds at 281 Bowl in Cortland. He hurried from one lane to the next at the 10-lane facility and registered the strikes using a different ball on each lane.

SIDE WHEELIE ▶ Using special heavy-duty reinforced tires, Finnish stunt driver Vesa Kivimäki drove a BMW 330 car on two wheels—a side wheelie—at a speed of 116 mph (187 kmph) at the country's Seinäjoki Airport.

GREAT ESCAPES

FAST PUNCHER ▶ Satyapira Pradhan, from Odisha, India, can deliver 393 punches with one hand in a minute—more than six punches every second.

BASKETBALL GIANT ▶ Romanian-born Robert Bobroczky stands 7.6 ft (2.3 m) tall—at age 16. When he made his debut in January 2017 for the SPIRE Institute basketball team from Geneva, Ohio, he became the second tallest player in the world, an inch behind Englishman Paul Sturgess. Height runs in the family, as Robert's father, 7.1-ft-tall (2.1-m) Zsiga, was also a professional basketball player who represented the Romanian national team.

GIANT ROBOT ▶ Yin Huajun, from Shaoxing, China, built a 13-ft-tall (4-m), working mechanical robot as a toy for his teenage son. The yellow robot, which weighs four tons and cost $70,000 to construct, travels on wheels and has heavyweight arms that move.

FLYING PUMPKIN ▶ A giant trebuchet at an Extreme Chunkin pumpkin-destruction event at Loudon, New Hampshire, has flung a 1,300-lb (590-kg) pumpkin, a piano, a boat, and even a VW Beetle car. The trebuchet, Yankee Siege II, stands 56 ft (17 m) tall and weighs 55,000 lb (25,000 kg).

Allied soldiers in World War II escaped from German prison camps with the help of decks of **PLAYING CARDS** that revealed maps when soaked in **WATER**.

In November 2013, a Swedish **INMATE** with a toothache escaped prison to visit a **DENTIST** before turning himself in a day later.

When caught in a _____ and trapped in an icy tomb, Danish explorer Peter Freuchen escaped using a knife-like tool made from his _____

World War II _____ Virginia Hall—who had one prosthetic leg—escaped Nazi-occupied France through the Pyrenees Mountains on _____

When _____ blazed through Western Australia in November 2011, Peter Fabrici survived the approaching fire by scuba-diving in a neighbor's _____

Twelve _____ escaped Jasper, Alabama's Walker County Jail in July 2017 by using _____

In 1542, French aristocrat Marguerite de la Roque survived for _____ alone on a remote island off the coast of _____

In April 2013, hotelier Thomas Fleetwood survived _____ in a broken elevator in his Austrian ski resort hotel with no food, water, or _____

Melvin Roberts, of Seneca, South Carolina, has _____ being struck by lightning

ANACONDA CONQUERED ▶ In 2016, competitive eater Pablo Martinez became the first person to finish the 3-ft-long (0.9-m), 5.5 lb (2.5 kg) Anaconda Burrito at Taqueria Yareli Mexican restaurant in Fresno, California. It took him just 13 minutes to devour the dish, which features beans, meat, cheese, rice, and sauce, all rolled into five tortillas.

REVERSE RACE ▶ On May 28, 2017, more than 1,000 people took part in a 150-meter race in Mumbai, India—all running backward.

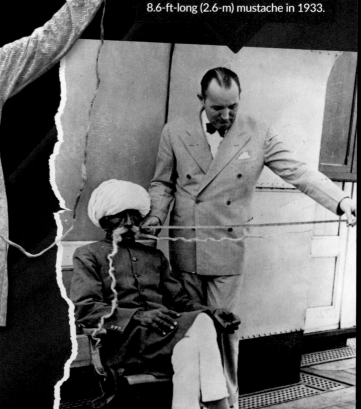

Robert Ripley measures Indian policeman Desar Arjan Dangar's 8.6-ft-long (2.6-m) mustache in 1933.

RIPPED from HISTORY

LONG MUSTACHE

For the past 25 years, 78-year-old Ramesh of Uttar Pradesh, India, has grown his mustache to an astonishing 9 ft (2.7 m)! He keeps his mustache safely coiled in a ball on his head and refuses to see his daughter or grandchildren, for fear that they'd break his fragile mustache. He says he keeps the hair healthy by washing it in milk and applying curd and cream every day.

FOUR-DAY CRAWL ▶ After breaking two bones in his lower right leg stumbling on logs in the Idaho wilderness, 50-year-old John Sain, of Riverside, California, crawled for nearly four days in a makeshift splint. With little food or water, no cell phone reception, and knowing that he was miles from the nearest trail, he used sticks and a ripped up cloth to make a splint for his injured leg and dragged himself along the ground until he was finally found by two motorcyclists who had taken a wrong turn.

SEVEN-TON PIZZA ▶ On June 10, 2017, seven pizza makers in Fontana, California, assisted by 100 volunteers, created a pizza that stretched for 1.2 mi (2 km) and weighed more than seven tons, making it heavier than an elephant. The giant pizza could be sliced into 63,000 6 × 4-in (15 × 10 cm) servings—enough to feed 10,000 people.

FAIRGROUND RACER ▶
Inventor Colin Furze, from Lincolnshire, England, designed a fairground bumper car that can travel at more than 100 mph (160 kmph)—20 times faster than its regular speed. Over a period of three weeks, he fitted a 600 cc, 100 bhp Honda motorcycle engine inside the chassis of a 1960s bumper car.

MASS HAKA ▶ On June 17, 2017, a huge crowd of 7,700 people gathered in a field in Rotorua, New Zealand, to perform a haka—a traditional Maori war dance that is performed by New Zealand rugby teams before international matches. The steps were so vigorous that the ground shook.

KEEPS PEDALING ▶ Bill Grun, of Doylestown, Pennsylvania, celebrated his 96th birthday by joining a local cycle club on a ride to mark the fact that he still rode up to 10 mi (16 km) a day.

MEDAL TABLE ▶ If U.S. swimmer Michael Phelps were a country, his haul of 23 Olympic gold medals, three silver, and two bronze would place him 39th in the all-time Summer Olympics nations' medal table, ahead of countries such as Argentina, Austria, and Mexico.

> ❯ **Off the coast of Scotland, four climbers scaled the tough North Gaulton Castle—a tower of sandstone 165 ft (50 m) high rising out of the ocean and completely surrounded by water.**
>
> The men lowered themselves onto a rocky ledge using a rope attached to two points on the mainland and then climbed their way up the sea stack. In the end, they stood atop the tower while choppy waves crashed at the base below. The photos of the precarious ascent were captured during the filming of a BBC series.

COCONUT SPLIT ▶ Shankar Budati, of Chirala Mandal, India, can use a machete to split a coconut balanced on his wife Bhramaramba's throat without harming her.

NEW HANDS ▶ Less than a year after being given the United Kingdom's first double hand transplant, Chris King, from South Yorkshire, England, was able to write to surgeons to thank them. He had lost all his digits in an accident at work, leaving him with only his thumbs.

BIRTHDAY RIDE ▶ In April 2017, Jack Reynolds, from Chesterfield, Derbyshire, England, celebrated his 105th birthday by riding a rollercoaster. On his 104th birthday, he had received his first tattoo.

STRONG SHOULDERS ▶ Austrian strongman Franz Muellner can support a 1,980-lb (900-kg) helicopter on his shoulders.

ESSENTIAL VIEWING ▶ Believe it or not, 99.8 percent of Icelandic TV viewers watched their country's 2-1 victory over England at the Euro 2016 soccer tournament. Only 298 people out of Iceland's total population of 339,000 watched another channel.

HIGHLINE WALK

> In September 2016, French daredevil Thibault Cheval walked across a slackline held up by two paragliders high in the sky above the French Alps.

After months of preparing for the stunt, he tiptoed across the wobbly line while paragliders Eliot Nochez and Julien Millot flew through the clouds about 66 ft (20 m) apart. The pair desperately tried to keep at the same altitude to make his crossing less hazardous. After taking several steps across the slackline, Cheval safely parachuted down.

BURGER BASE JUMP

» BASE jumper Quentin Luçon filmed himself jumping off a Swiss mountainside with a cheeseburger wedged in his mouth. The burger fell apart abruptly when Luçon deployed his parachute, with the top bun flying into his face as he tried to keep a hold of it in his mouth.

DIFFERENT SCENERY ▶
Between February 28 and December 27, 2016, Costin Boldisor ran 1,300 mi (2,092 km) through 4,880 different streets in London, England, simply because he was bored with his usual running route. His 10-month exercise regime was the equivalent of running 50 marathons.

LEFT-HANDER ▶
Only two former NFL quarterbacks inducted into the Pro Football Hall of Fame were left-handed.

BUNGEE DIP ▶ Simon Berry, from Sheffield, England, bungee jumped more than 240 ft (73 m) to dunk a chocolate cookie in a cup of tea.

HOCKEY VETERAN ▶ Anne Graves, from Stevenage, England, still played competitive field hockey for almost a full season at age 80. She took up the sport when she was 10 and joined the Hertfordshire club in 1951 when she was 16.

SUPER HOOPER ▶ Australian entertainer Marawa Wamp, who performs under the name "Marawa the Amazing," can spin 200 hula hoops simultaneously—while wearing high heels.

POOL MARATHON ▶ Graham Cuthbert, landlord of the Bell Inn at Kingsteignton, Devon, England, played pool with customer Darren Stocks for 106 hours straight—more than four days.

WORLD TRAVEL ▶ Since turning 65 in 2003, Ethel MacDonald, a great-grandmother from Missoula, Montana, has cycled more than 10,000 mi (16,000 km) across North America and Europe.

SOLE SURVIVOR ▶ Jose Antonio Garcia, from Puerto de Santa Maria, Spain, trekked 67,000 mi (107,826 km) in 11 years—after doctors had told him he might never be able to walk again. In 1999, he was the sole survivor of a crew of 17 after the fishing boat on which he was working capsized off the coast of Norway. He was stranded for hours in the freezing water, and his injuries were so bad that he spent the next two years in a wheelchair and two more after that walking with crutches. When he was finally able to move again unaided, he set off walking to holy sites around the world, through the Middle East, across Asia, and from Alaska down to South America.

NATIONAL PARKS ▶ Photographer Jonathan Irish and NASA employee Stefanie Payne visited all 59 U.S. national parks in one year. In the course of their journey, they traveled along 45,674 mi (73,505 km) of road, hiked 271 trails, and took 322,405 photos, an average of nearly 884 photos per day.

BMX HOPS ▶ Martin Tuson, from Bangor, Northern Ireland, can complete 46 front hops on a BMX bike in just 10 seconds. He can also perform nearly 100 BMX front hops in succession while standing on the frame of the bike.

UNDERWATER CYCLIST ▶ Riding a stationary bike, Italian underwater cyclist Homar Leuci cycled a distance of 2,800 ft (854 m) underwater in a single breath. After climbing into a water-filled tank, he took one long breath before submerging himself and pedaling furiously for about four minutes.

PERFECT BALANCE ▶ Abdul Halim, from Magura, Bangladesh, cycled for 8.6 mi (13.7 km) with a soccer ball balanced on his head. He rode around a roller-skating complex in Dhaka for 1 hour 19 minutes, completing 91 laps before finally losing his control over the ball.

JET FLIPPER ▶ At Bahe Lake, Xi'an, China, Liu He completed 29 full, 360-degree backflips in one minute using a water-propelled jet pack.

ENORMOUS BUBBLE ▶ Czech bubble artist Matej Kodes surrounded 275 people and a car inside a single soap bubble. The enormous bubble covered an area of 36 × 25 ft (11 × 7.5 m).

BLOOD DONOR ▶ Dale Faughn, of Fredonia, Kentucky, still gives blood at age 91. He first gave blood in the mid-1950s but has been a regular donor for more than 40 years, since 1975.

UNBEATEN TEAM ▶ Soccer club Glasgow Celtic did not lose a single match in the regular, 38-game, 2016–17 Scottish League season—the first team to achieve the feat since 1899.

◀ Cindy Dunlow, of Ocala, Florida, has a collection of nearly 800 flamingo items. ▶

SCARY STUNT ▶ Austrian stunt cyclist Fabio Wibmer rode along the narrow top of a safety railing, which was barely wider than his bicycle tire, above the 650-ft-high (198-m) Kolnbrein Dam near Klagenfurt.

EXTENDED SKIS ▶ A team of 130 employees of Finnish energy company St1 traveled on a single pair of skis that were 460 ft (140 m) long.

DEATH SPIN ▶ BMX rider Matti Hemmings from England can complete 46 "deathtruck spins" in one minute. The stunt involves balancing with just the rear wheel of the bike on the ground and spinning 360 degrees—with his hands off the handles!

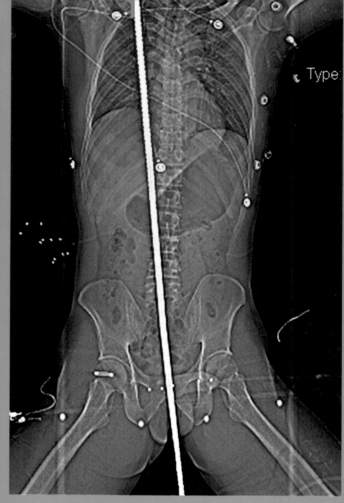

Type

STUCK IN THE MIDDLE

» A construction worker in Chengdu City, China, miraculously survived after suffering an electric shock and falling vertically onto a 4-ft-long (1.2-m) steel bar. The bar missed all of his vital organs when it entered his body through his buttocks and exited his right shoulder.

PUSH-UPS ▶ Chakkanath Pradeep, a 48-year-old former soccer player from Malappuram, India, can do 99 push-ups in one minute.

BIKER MARATHON ▶ Gaurav Siddharth, from Lucknow, India, rode a motorcycle solo around the country for more than 14 months, covering a distance of more than 62,100 mi (100,000 km).

BLOOD RAIN ▶ Elaine Hopley, a 45-year-old mother-of-two from Dunblane, Scotland, rowed more than 2,000 mi (3,200 km) solo across the Atlantic Ocean from the Canary Islands to Antigua in 59 days—and at one point had to row through blood rain, caused by winds picking up red sand from the Sahara Desert.

MICROSCOPIC FLAG ▶ Scientists at the University of Waterloo, Ontario, created a microscopic Canadian flag that measured just 1.178 micrometers long—about one-hundredth the width of a human hair. The flag is so tiny it cannot be seen with the naked eye.

ACCURATE KICKER ▶
Parker Hannon, a 15-year-old student at Roswell High School, Georgia, kicked 31 football field goals from a distance of 20 yards in one minute.

BIKE BURNOUT ▶
On May 20, 2017, Polish stunt rider Maciej Bielicki performed a continuous motorcycle burnout for a distance of almost 2.8 mi (4.5 km).

TOY BOAT ▶ A 3-ft-long (0.9-m) toy boat launched in 2013 by fifth-graders of Summit-Questa Montessori School in Davie, Florida, washed up four years later 500 mi (800 km) away on Edisto Beach in South Carolina.

BREATHLESS SHOUT ▶
At the Radio Romania studio in Bucharest on March 7, 2017, sports commentator Ilie Dobre shouted "goal" for 52 seconds without pausing for breath.

STATE CAPITOLS ▶
John and Ruth Pace, from Baton Rouge, Louisiana, visited all 50 state capitol buildings in the United States over a period of 20 years. Their final statehouse, on August 16, 2016, was Helena, Montana.

SENIOR CYCLIST ▶
On January 4, 2017, French cyclist Robert Marchand rode 14 mi (22.4 km) in one hour around the St Quentin-en-Yvelines national velodrome in Paris—a total of 92 laps—at age 105. After cycling in his youth, Marchand, who is only 5 ft (1.5 m) tall, returned to the sport in his late sixties, and when he was 80, he cycled all the way from Moscow, Russia, to Paris—a distance of 1,758 mi (2,812 km).

SPINNING CUSHION ▶ Thomas "Bounce" Senior, from Lancashire, England, can spin a cushion on his right index finger for 15 minutes. He says the secret is to place the finger off-center—otherwise the cushion will stop spinning.

HEIGHT DIFFERENCE ▶ In 1987-88, the shortest man ever to play in the NBA, 5-ft-3 in-tall (1.6-m) Tyrone "Muggsy" Bogues, played on the same Washington Bullets team as 7-ft-7-in-tall (2.3-m) Manute Bol, who was at the time the tallest player ever to have appeared in the NBA. The height difference between them was 28 in (71 cm).

Visible HEART

> Russian eight-year-old Virsaviya Borun-Goncharova's heart beats outside of her chest.

Virsaviya has a rare birth disorder known as Pentalogy of Cantrell, which resulted in a defective sternum that does not keep her heart within her ribcage. Doctors thought she would not live long past infancy, but she has defied expectations and now lives with her mother in Florida. Virsaviya enjoys hip-hop dancing and running but must always be careful not to fall onto her partially exposed heart.

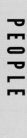

AIRPORT HOME ▶ A 50-year-old woman has spent more than eight years living in Changi Airport, Singapore, while renting out her own three-room apartment. Using only a small part of the $1,000 she collects each month in rent, she eats at the airport food court, shops at the supermarket, has access to showers, and uses the free Wi-Fi.

TURTLE SMUGGLER ▶ Kai Xu, a student from Windsor, Ontario, Canada, admitted to attempting to smuggle more than 1,000 turtles out of southeastern Michigan. He was finally caught at an Ontario border crossing with 51 live turtles taped to his legs.

COMMITTED STUDENT ▶ In a two-hour operation, doctors at a hospital in Yiwu, China, removed an 8-in-long (20-cm) metal spoon from the stomach of an 18-year-old student who had swallowed it accidentally. After swallowing the spoon, she had waited three days before seeking medical treatment because she wanted to finish her school exams.

BAD EYESIGHT ▶ While trying to apply her false eyelashes without wearing her eyeglasses, Judy Robbins, from England, accidentally picked up a dead fly instead and tried to glue the insect to her eyelid.

PARKOUR PLUNGE ▶ While making a parkour video with friends on the roof of an apartment building in Denver, Colorado, 26-year-old Dustin Hinkle accidentally fell 40 ft (12 m) down a chimney. He survived because a cable broke his fall, but he was stuck in the chimney for nearly two hours until firefighters broke through a brick wall to free him.

HORROR WEDDING ▶ Becca and Jack Cain's horror-themed wedding in Edinburgh, Scotland, took place in a haunted underground vault filled with cobwebs. It included a ghost tour, and in keeping with the theme, the bride's white wedding gown was decorated with fake blood-stained handprints.

WRONG COUPLE ▶ Hired to photograph a surprise sunrise marriage proposal at Hawksbill Crag, Arkansas, Jacob Peters woke at 2 a.m., hiked for an hour to the remote spot carrying 30 lb (13 kg) of equipment—and ended up taking pictures of the wrong couple. Unbeknownst to him, the couple who had hired him were running an hour late, but another couple had chosen the same location and the same time.

WRONG TURN ▶ Keen amateur cyclist Roger Armstrong took a wrong turn and accidentally found himself leading a pack of more than 120 professional cyclists on the fourth stage of the 2016 Tour of Britain race. The 56-year-old had set off for his regular morning ride in North Wales but inadvertently strayed to the head of the group as it passed near his home village of Mynydd Isa. He wondered why hundreds of people cheered as he rode past, until after 1 mi (1.6 km) when he realized what had happened and pulled over red-faced.

WASHER RESCUE ▶ While playing a game of hide-and-seek with his sister at their home in Kharkiv, Ukraine, a seven-year-old boy became stuck inside a washing machine. Emergency services eventually managed to pull him out of the drum by covering his body in sunflower oil.

HIDDEN LIZARD ▶ A suspected drunk driver who hit six mailboxes and several cars before crashing into the garden of a house in Taunton, Massachusetts, was found to have a bearded dragon lizard in her bra when she was arrested.

RISKY BUSINESS ▶

MUG SHOT ▶ Wanted on suspicion of assault, Wayne Esmonde turned himself in to police in South Wales on the condition that they remove an unflattering photo of him that had been posted on the department's Facebook page.

WRONG SYDNEY ▶ Dutch teen Milan Schipper bought a cheap flight from Amsterdam to Sydney, but realized too late that instead of taking him to Sydney, Australia, it was flying him to Sydney, Nova Scotia, Canada, some 10,500 mi (16,800 km) from his intended destination. It was only after boarding a second plane at Toronto that he realized there was another Sydney.

CHEATED DEATH ▶ Kumar Marewad, a 17-year-old boy from Managundi, India, woke up on the way to his own funeral. After being bitten by a stray dog, he developed an infection and was thought to have died. He did not move or breathe for days, but then he suddenly jerked awake on the stretcher, minutes before he was due to be cremated.

PARTING SHOT ▶ The 2017 obituary of long-suffering Philadelphia Eagles fan Jeffrey Riegel, from Port Republic, New Jersey, requested "eight Philadelphia Eagles as pall bearers so the Eagles can let him down one last time."

Getting on and off the contraption also carries the potential for injury.

❯ A symbol of the Victorian era, the penny-farthing bicycle paved the way for cycling to become a sport, and believe it or not, brave enthusiasts still race penny-farthings today!

A dangerous vehicle that sees riders sit high atop a massive front wheel, the biggest threat is being thrown headfirst overboard, so to speak. Developed in the 1870s, racing high wheelers was—and still is—risky, although competitors don't seem to mind. Today a handful of races draws cyclists from all over the world, with the most iconic competition, the Knutsford Great Race, only taking place once a decade.

HAIR-RAISING WEDDING

» A one-of-a-kind wedding ceremony in 1970s Germany found couple Tsen Hai Sun and Hay Gy Sun exchanging rings 180 ft (55 m) above the ground—while dangling below a helicopter by their hair!

HANGING FROM THEIR HAIR!

STIFF PERSON ▶ Rhonda Hodges, from Toowoomba, Queensland, Australia, suffers from stiff person syndrome, a rare neurological condition that left her unable to walk for 12 years. The one-in-a-million disorder causes the body to tense up and become rigid, resulting in impaired mobility. In November 2016, doctors at the Mater Hospital inserted a pump that injects a drug into her spinal cord, giving her mobility again.

LAW STUDIES ▶ Farmer Wang Enlin spent 16 years studying law so that he could sue the chemical company that he claims polluted his village of Yushutun, in China's Heilongjiang Province, in 2001. Since the villagers could not afford professional legal advice, Wang, who had only attended school for three years, spent every day reading law books at a local book store, copying important information from them by hand. In return for letting him read the books, he gave bags of free corn to the shopkeeper.

HUSBAND ALLERGY ▶ Johanna Watkins, of Minneapolis, Minnesota, suffers from a rare genetic disorder that has left her allergic to virtually everything, including her husband Scott. She was diagnosed with mast cell activation syndrome, which causes her body to develop life-threatening anaphylactic reactions. She has hundreds of allergies, including foods, scents, pollen, and even natural chemicals and body odors that people—including her husband—release. At present, her body only tolerates 15 foods. To avoid these triggers, she lives 24/7 in an air-locked bedroom, and anyone who comes into contact with her must use a special scent-free soap and not wear any scented products or eat onions, garlic, or pepper in their diet.

CITY SCENTS ▶ In 2017, to mark the Canadian city's 375th anniversary, perfume-maker Claude André Hébert created five scents to reflect different districts of Montreal, Quebec. They include a Mount Royal–inspired scent featuring pine and incense, and a downtown scent incorporating tobacco and hops.

NUMBER FEAR ▶ People with octophobia have a morbid fear of the number eight, and will not only refuse to live in a house containing the number but may also refuse to climb stairs if there are eight in total.

DIAMOND RING ▶ A ring that was bought for $13 from a London junk market in the 1980s in the belief that it was cheap costume jewelry turned out to feature a genuine 26-carat white diamond and sold at auction in 2017 for nearly $850,000.

ROTATING BED ▶ Zhu Qinghua, a rice farmer from Jiangxi Province, China, invented a rotating, vibrating bed specially designed to help his wife pass kidney stones. When doctors advised his wife to stand upside down for a few minutes every day to help dislodge the stones, Zhu had the idea for his bed. He spent a month drawing up plans and then built it from scrap materials. The bed rotates 360 degrees while keeping the user upside down at a sharp angle and also vibrates with the aid of a tractor driving wheel. Zhu says that after spending just 10 minutes in the bed for five days, his wife passed all her stones.

ONE WING ▶ Shuttlecocks used in the Summer Olympic sport of badminton are always made of feathers from one wing (left or right) of a goose or duck.

SIGN THIEF ▶ John Hoelzl, of Avon Lake, Ohio, stole more than 500 advertising signs from public land over a period of 10 years because he claimed they were an eyesore and a distraction to drivers.

SOFA TESTER ▶ Anna Cherdantseva, from Ufa, Russia, spends up to 10 hours a day sitting on sofas in her job as a full-time sofa tester.

YOUR UPLOADS

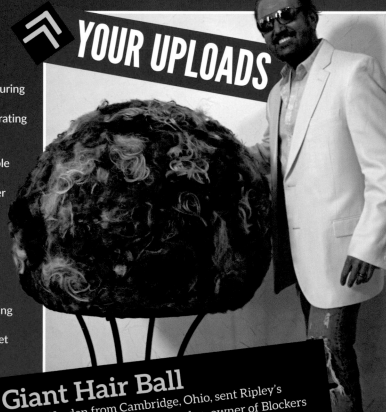

Giant Hair Ball

Steven Warden from Cambridge, Ohio, sent Ripley's photos of this giant hair ball! Warden, owner of Blockers Salon, has been collecting hair from his studio clients for two years, keeping the mass together with Gorilla Glue and hair spray. It currently weighs 96 lb (43.5 kg) and measures 4 × 4 ft (1.2 × 1.2 m)...and counting!

BULLHEADED

In 2011, a two-headed bull shark fetus was discovered off the Florida Keys—the first known case of dicephalus (conjoined twins that share a torso) in bull sharks.

Two-headed sharks are exceedingly rare, since they likely don't live long enough for people to find them. Interestingly, the conjoined bull shark sold for $10,600 (£6,930) in an eBay auction, and the profits were used to fund further shark conservation research.

Although shark skeletons are made of cartilage (not bone), the cartilage is dense enough to be captured by X-ray.

PLAY WITH WIRE

> In 2017, Italian artist Edoardo Tresoldi created a massive 75,347-sq-ft (7,000-sq-m) pavilion made entirely out of wire mesh.

Tresoldi created the elegant masterpiece for a royal event in Abu Dhabi, and it took three months to design and construct.

The suspended architecture was lit from both above and below.

ROASTED GUINEA PIG

» Best known as a favorite furry pet, guinea pigs are actually one of Peru's most famous delicacies. Called *cuy* (pronounced KWEE), the rodents are skinned and skewered over a fire, roasted with the head, arms, teeth, ears, and other parts left intact. Tasting like a cross between rabbit and chicken, Peruvians feast on about 65 million guinea pigs a year. It's no wonder that Peru declared October 11 National Guinea Pig Day.

DOG MILK ▶

For more than six years, Mohit Kumar, a boy from Manaitand, India, has been sucking the milk of stray female dogs in the town. He developed his craving for dog milk at age four, and although most of the local canines know him and allow it, he had to go to the hospital for a rabies vaccine after a dog from another pack bit him. Mohit was born mute, so his worried parents struggle to understand why he loves dog milk so much. They try not to allow him out of the home unsupervised, but he sometimes slips out behind their backs.

HIDDEN CASH ▶ A worker at a recycling plant in Barrie, Ontario, Canada, discovered more than Can$100,000 (about US$75,000) in cash stashed inside a 30-year-old TV set. The money was returned to its rightful owner, who said he had inherited it from his parents, stored it in the TV for safekeeping, but then had forgotten about it and given the TV to a friend.

JUNK MAIL ▶

After 18-year-old student Connor Cox forgot to empty the trash on a visit home, his mother Connie mailed the bag of garbage to him at Westminster College, New Wilmington, Pennsylvania.

TINSEL TOWN ▶

For Christmas 2016, Thomas Jeromin filled the interior of his house in Rinteln, Germany, with more than 110 artificial Christmas trees, decorated with a total of 16,000 ornaments and hundreds of LED lights. It took him eight weeks to prepare, and he put trees in every room except, at his wife Susanne's request, the master bedroom.

VIKING *Festival*

❯ **Every year on the last Tuesday in January, the city of Lerwick in the Shetland Islands, Scotland, hosts Up Helly Aa—a Viking festival celebrating its Scandinavian history.**

The day consists of a series of marches and visitations, ending in the triumphant burning of a galley, or Viking longboat, with up to 1,000 torches! The entire procession is led by the elected Guizer Jarl and his Jarl Squad, along with another 45 squads, who are all costumed Vikings for the day. Each year, the suit of armor—the helmet, breastplate, shield, axe, dagger, and belt—is passed down to the next Guizer Jarl. The Guizer Jarl then designs his kirtle (tunic) and cloak to distinguish him from the group, while the rest of his squad design and make their own unique costumes every year.

SALAD DRESSING

> U.K. bakery chain Greggs commissioned two fresh, couture-inspired dresses—made entirely of vegetables!

Using 5,000 lettuce leaves, 200 cabbages, 150 chilies, 100 limes, 80 peppers, and 50 bulbs of garlic, it took four designers (including Kate Tabor, who has designed costumes for Katy Perry) 200 hours to assemble the dresses. The designers put each dress together "peas by peas" before their grand reveal on the streets of London.

FAST VOWS ▶
In July 2016, James Music and Cortni Bryant got married on the 95 mph (152 kmph) Fury 325 roller coaster at Carowinds amusement park in Charlotte, North Carolina. Their first date had also been on the 325-ft-tall (100-m) ride.

BORROWED TIME ▶ To deter people from borrowing books and then returning them late, the Athens-Limestone public library in Athens, Alabama, has introduced a range of tough punishments for overdue returns, including a $100 fine or 30 days in jail.

HEADSTONE ERROR ▶ An American Civil War soldier buried under the wrong name at an Ohio cemetery finally received a new headstone 154 years later. Confederate soldier Augustus Beckmann was fatally wounded in the Battle of Shiloh on April 7, 1862, but was buried at the Camp Chase Confederate Cemetery in Columbus as A. Bergman. The National Cemetery Administration agreed to fix the headstone after Beckmann's brother's great-great grandson Greg pointed out the error.

SIBLING WORKERS ▶ In 2016, 18-year-old non-identical quintuplets—three brothers and two sisters—all worked together at the same McDonald's restaurant in Potterville, Michigan. Leith, Logan, and Lucas Curtis all worked in the kitchen while Lauren served at the front counter and drive-thru and Lindsey handled the lobby.

PIZZA ATM ▶ An ATM installed at Xavier University, in Cincinnati, Ohio, dispenses pizza instead of cash. The machine holds 70 pizzas, and customers use a touchscreen to select their choice, which is then heated for several minutes, placed in a cardboard box, and ejected through a slot.

NASAL BLOCKAGE ▶ After suffering from a mysterious runny nose for six months, five-year-old Khloe Russell, of Hemet, California, finally managed to blow out the cause—a 1.5-in-long (3.7-cm) safety pin.

CHASED ROBBER ▶ Store worker Raffique Chaudhery fought off an armed robber in Derby, England, by chasing him with a Hoover vacuum cleaner.

FLUTE OF SHAME ▶ In medieval Germany, untalented musicians were punished with the *schand flöte*—the flute of shame. Bad musicians would face the public wearing the heavy iron "flute," their neck and fingers locked in the contraption. Did we mention the tough crowd hurling rotten fruit at the culprit?

FREE SPIRIT ▶ Jerry Kimball was fined $190 for letting his pet ball python slither around a park in Sioux Falls, South Dakota, without a leash. A city ordinance requires all pets to be leashed or restrained in public.

FAT HOUSE

» Austrian sculptor Erwin Wurm created an obese house sculpture called *Fat House*. Originally finished in 2003, the bulky building plays a video inside in which the house speaks emotional sentences, asking itself "Am I a house?" and saying "I think I'm a piece of art."

YOUR UPLOADS

Kilimanjaro Kid

In June 2017, 10-year-old Wakeland Branz of DeLand, Florida, climbed the highest mountain in Africa! Mount Kilimanjaro is 19,341 ft (5,895 m) above sea level. Wakeland and a group including his family and friends also stayed overnight in one of its (dormant) volcanic craters!

BROKENBACK MOUNTAIN ▶ After slipping on ice and falling 80 ft (25 m) while hiking a mountain in the Scottish Highlands, Ashley Simpson, a 27-year-old doctor from Edinburgh, walked for two hours back to a car and then traveled 70 mi (122 km) home to feed her dog before going to the hospital, where she discovered she had fractured several ribs and had broken her back in 12 places. She had been so unaware of the extent of her injuries that she had smiled for a picture taken by her boyfriend as she lay in the snow after the fall.

MINI GOLF ▶ Over a period of just 78 days, Dan Caprera, of Denver, Colorado, played mini golf in all 50 U.S. states. After driving 20,681 mi (33,089 km) to visit every mainland state, including Alaska, he headed to his final destination, Hawaii. He played mini golf on an 80-ft-long (24-m) schooner in Maine, on a coal mining–themed course in West Virginia, in a five-story temple in South Carolina, and on a biblical-themed course in Kentucky.

TINY CUBE ▶ Tony Fisher, of Ipswich, Suffolk, England, built a Rubik's Cube puzzle measuring just 0.22 in (0.55 cm) on each side. He solves it using tweezers and a magnifying glass. He has also built a 220-lb (100-kg) Rubik's Cube that measured just over 5 ft (1.5 m) from edge to edge.

UNINTERRUPTED PRAYER ▶ Nuns from the Franciscan Sisters of Perpetual Adoration, based in La Crosse, Wisconsin, have taken turns praying nonstop for more than 135 years. Members of the order have been praying continuously night and day for the sick and the suffering of the world since 11 a.m. on August 1, 1878.

GIANT PUPPET ▶ Engineers in England built a mechanical puppet that is 33 ft (10 m) tall—about twice the height of an adult giraffe—and weighs 44 tons. In 2016, the metal "Man Engine" puppet marched 130 mi (208 km) on a two-week tour of mining heritage sites in Devon and Cornwall.

STRANGE ACCENT ▶ Michaela Armer, from Lancashire, England, suffers from foreign accent syndrome, and wakes up with a different foreign accent every day, including Italian, French, Chinese, Filipino, South African, or Polish. The rare speech disorder is thought to be caused by damage to the area of the brain that controls language.

SCI-FI RELIGION ▶ In the official 2001 census for England and Wales, 390,127 people (nearly 0.8 percent of the population) listed their religion as Jedi, making it the fourth largest religion in those countries.

MYSTERY MEAT ▶ Woken by a loud thud at their house in Deerfield Beach, Florida, Travis Adair and his family discovered 15 lb (6.8 kg) of frozen sausage in the side yard and on the roof. It is thought that the five packages of Italian sausage had landed on their home after falling from a plane.

FLYING HIGH ▶ Russian adventurer Fyodor Konyukhov, 65, circumnavigated the Earth solo in a 200-ft-high (60-m) hot-air balloon, called the *Morton*, in just over 11 days. Starting and landing in Western Australia, he traveled 21,200 mi (34,000 km) around the world, battling freezing winds and temperatures as low as –69°F (–56°C) while flying at altitudes of up to 33,000 ft (10,000 m). Hooked up to oxygen tanks for most of the journey, he hardly slept, even though a small bed was fitted into the balloon's 6.6-ft-wide (2-m) carbon fiber gondola.

SKATER BOY ▶ Eight-year-old limbo skater Devi Sri Prasad, from Tirupati, India, skated backward under a line of 53 cars with a clearance of just 7 in (17.5 cm) above the ground. Contorting his super-flexible body into a seemingly impossible position, he covered the 330-ft (100-m) distance in 22.59 seconds.

RIVER PADDLE ▶ Tom Dunn, of Horsham, Victoria, steered a stand-up paddleboard down the Darling and Murray river system to Goolwa, South Australia, to complete a journey of 2,300 mi (3,700 km) in 113 days. He set off from Warwick, Queensland, in January 2017 with the intention of paddling all the way, but at that time of the year the rivers were dry in many places, and so he was forced to run most of the first 560 mi (900 km).

FACIAL ILLUSIONS ▶ Former teacher Mimi Choi, from Vancouver, British Columbia, Canada, uses nothing more than regular makeup to create incredible facial optical illusions that appear to quadruple her eyes or slice her entire head in half. Treating her face as a blank canvas, she spends up to five hours on each spectacular effect and has also perfected the illusion of melting her face, cracking it like a sheet of glass, lacing up her eye sockets with tiny bows, and covering her face with a fake hand.

BACKWARD SKIER ▶ At the Arosa ski resort in Switzerland in 2017, Swiss freestyle skier Elias Ambuhl reached 81.5 mph (131 kmph) while skiing backward down a mountain! His speed was only 19 mph (30 kmph) slower than the fastest skiers achieve in competition. . . going forward.

PENNY PROTEST ▶ Following a prolonged dispute, Nick Stafford, of Cedar Bluff, Virginia, paid the $3,000 sales tax on two new cars by delivering 300,000 pennies to the Department of Motor Vehicles. He transported the coins, which weighed a total of 1,600 lb (726 kg), in five wheelbarrows. He spent almost $1,000 on buying the wheelbarrows and on hiring 11 people to open the countless rolls of pennies, a process that took four hours.

Mutant of DANCE

> Los Angeles, California, dancer Solto Esengulov moves and morphs his body in ways that seem to go against ordinary human anatomy.

Some of Solto's moves include flipping onto the top of his head, bulging his shoulder blades out of his back, and displacing his abdomen while seemingly moving his ribcage up and down. Perhaps the most alarming to watch is his signature move of grabbing his windpipe and shifting it from one side of his throat to the other.

BACK-BREAKING MOVES!

BALANCING ON HIS HEAD!

DISPLACED ABDOMEN

CRAZY CHOREOGRAPHY

> In July 2017, a shrinking Swiss glacier revealed the perfectly preserved bodies of a couple who had gone missing 75 years earlier.

After going to milk cows in a high-altitude pasture, Marcelin and Francine Dumoulin vanished in 1942. Search parties persisted for more than two months before giving up, leaving the bodies entombed at more than 8,500 ft (2,600 m) elevation.

Icy TOMB

CAR SEARCH ▶ Gavin Strickland drove from his home in Syracuse, New York, to Toronto, Ontario, Canada, for a Metallica concert, but then completely forgot where he parked his car. Joined by police officers, he spent 24 hours searching the city's underground garages in vain and was only reunited with his vehicle three days later after posting an ad on Craigslist appealing for help and offering a $100 reward.

ROBOT BRIDE ▶ Disillusioned with dating, 31-year-old Zheng Jiajia, of Hangzhou, China, ended up marrying a robot that he had built himself. The robot designer and artificial intelligence planner had tried in vain to find his perfect match for six years, so he decided instead to build his own dream wife—a lifelike humanoid machine named Yingying. She can say a few words, but because she was not yet able to walk, he had to carry her to and from their wedding. He hopes to upgrade her eventually so that she can help with chores around the house.

DANCING PALLBEARERS ▶ Benjamin Aidoo employs around 100 men and women to perform at funerals in Ghana as dancing pallbearers. While carrying the casket on their backs and shoulders, they lighten the solemn mood by executing a precise choreographed routine that involves spinning around, sinking to their knees, and even pretending to drop the corpse.

SPELLING MISTAKE ▶ A misspelled sign at North Branford High School, Connecticut, went unnoticed for several months. The sign that wrongly spelled "entrance" as "enterance" was put up in August 2016, but the error was not spotted until spring 2017.

PREMATURE CELEBRATION ▶
At the 2016 National Cycling Championships in Erfurt, Germany, Martin Gluth punched the air with delight, thinking that he had won the 133-mi (214-km) race, but then realized there was still one lap to go. He eventually finished 73rd.

GRAMMAR VIGILANTE ▶ For more than 13 years, an anonymous "grammar vigilante" has been going out undercover in the dead of night in Bristol, England, correcting street signs and storefronts where the apostrophes are in the wrong place.

ELABORATE PRANK ▶ Customs officer Yuri Petruk shocked his girlfriend by disguising his marriage proposal as an authentic drugs bust. Oksana Tichkovskaya was returning to her native Ukraine with her mother when customs officers stopped their car at the Polish border. Sniffer dogs searched the vehicle, and when suspicious packages were suddenly produced, the innocent Tichkovskaya was told that she could be facing years in prison for trafficking heroin. It was only then that Petruk appeared carrying a bouquet of 101 red roses, got down on one knee, and admitted that the drugs bust was a prank. Luckily for him, she accepted his proposal.

POPSICLE NIGHTMARE
» Students from the National Taiwan University of the Arts created popsicles using polluted water that contain dirt, cigarette butts, bottle caps, bugs, and even dead fish! Designed to bring awareness to pollution problems in Taiwan, these frozen treats are strictly artistic and should not be eaten, no matter how tasty they might look.

MATH HOMEWORK ▶ When 10-year-old Lena Draper, of Marion, Ohio, messaged police on Facebook for help with her math homework, Lt. B. J. Gruber replied and walked her through her tricky equations.

HUMAN SKULL ▶ A homeless woman led police in Sacramento, California, to a decomposed body after she was seen walking down the street with a human skull on a stick.

DIVIDED HOUSE ▶ After Margarita Tsvitnenko and her husband Sergei divorced, they were ordered to split their $3.2 million, three-story house in Moscow, Russia, in two—but then Sergei decided to divide it with a brick wall, which left his ex-wife unable to access the upper floors in her half because the stairway is on his side.

TRASH!

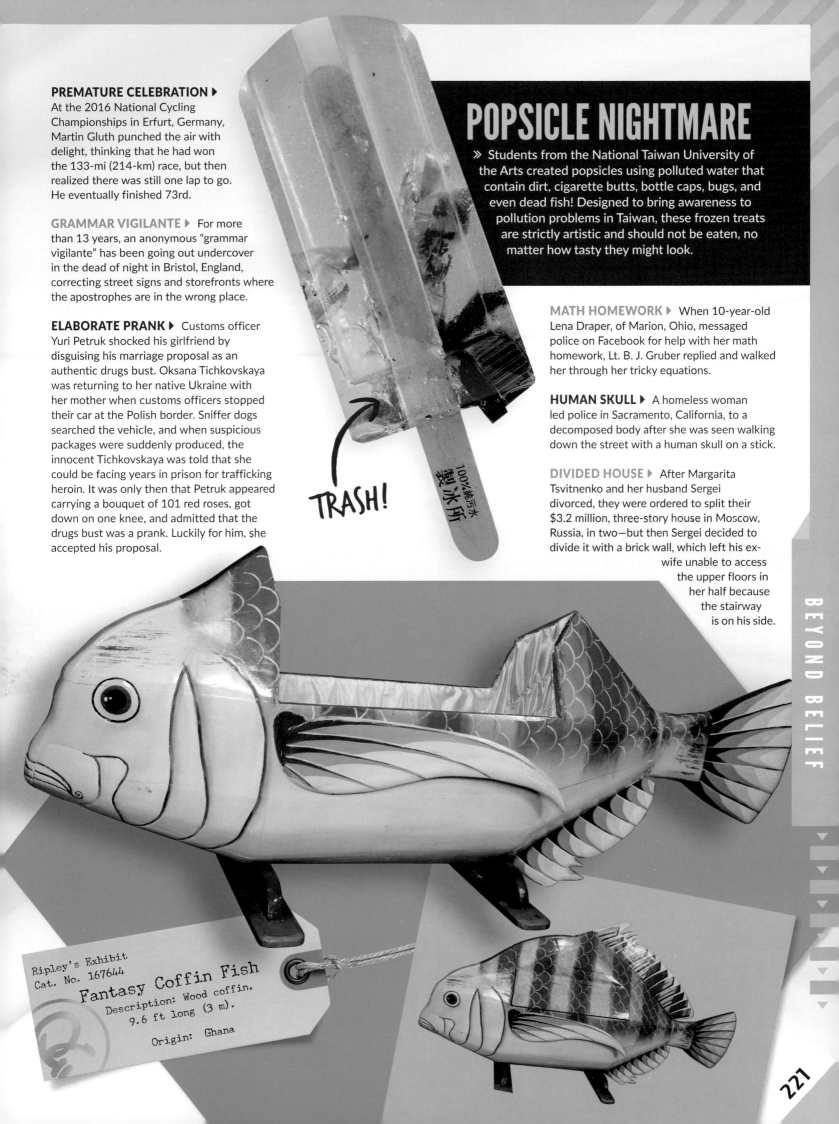

100%純污水
製冰所

Ripley's Exhibit
Cat. No. 167644
Fantasy Coffin Fish
Description: Wood coffin,
9.6 ft long (3 m).
Origin: Ghana

BABY ON BOARD ▶ Car seats are a protective fixture for today's families, yet in the 1930s and '40s, they were not made for safety but for convenience. Driving with a baby crawling around the vehicle was troublesome, so the first car seats were meant to keep kids contained—a simple baby sack hooked onto the back of a seat did the trick. It wasn't until 1985 that all states had child passenger safety laws in the United States.

Baby CAGES

❯ The 1884 book *The Care and Feeding of Children* put forth the idea that babies need to be "aired" out to "renew and purify the blood," which evolved into mothers dangling "baby cages" out of their apartment windows.

Invented in 1922, the infant-sized cages became all the rage in early 1930s London, where city living meant outdoor space was limited. The preposterous chicken coop-like baby bins have thankfully gone the way of the dinosaur.

SAFETY

CHILD'S PLAY ▶ The idea of playgrounds being a wholesome and safe way for kids to have fun is apparently rather new—in the early 1900s, they were a little more scary and dangerous. This surreal photo of a Dallas, Texas, playground in then Trinity Play Park features a massive structure made of iron that towers above the ground.

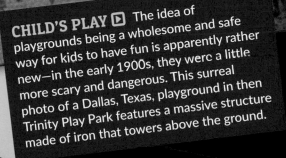

SKY-COT

» In the early days of flying, parents traveling with babies merely placed the infants in cradles that hung on the overhead luggage bin, supposedly ensuring the little ones did not tumble out. This image from the 1950s shows a stewardess tucking in a small passenger in the "Sky-Cot," which was introduced by the British Overseas Airways Corporation. Cozy? Sure. Turbulence-proof? Perhaps not.

FIRST

❯ The 19th century saw many technological achievements and improvements in the quality of life, but things sometimes needed to get worse before they got better—which was especially the case for children. A little trial and error never hurt anybody. . . that we know of.

HERE LIES OLD JACK CROW IT WAS TOO BAD HE HAD TO GO
WHILE ON THIS EARTH HE WAS HELL BENT
AND WE KNEW SOME DAY HE WOULD UP AND WENT

CLOTHESPIN GRAVE ▶ The Middlesex Center Cemetery in Vermont features a giant granite clothespin grave, marking the final resting place of W. Jack Crowell, a clothespin manufacturer. His factory in Montpelier, Vermont, was the last wooden clothespin manufacturer in the United States, and the building is now listed on the National Register of Historic Places.

SEVERED FINGER ▶ Normand Lariviere, of Olympia, Washington, was charged with mailing his own severed finger to the IRS as a way of protesting his taxes.

TIGHT SQUEEZE ▶ Police in Chongqing, China, pulled over a small six-seater van and found 40 construction workers squashed inside.

TOUGH TOY ▶ Eleven-year-old Sam Rhodes, of Tempe, Arizona, had a fidget spinner stuck on his finger for 16 hours. Soap, oil, and even a ring cutter failed to remove the tough, alloy metal toy until a hospital maintenance worker finally managed to slice through it—but only after it had broken four fiberglass saw blades.

INCRIMINATING POOP ▶ A man was identified and arrested on suspicion of burglary because he forgot to flush away his poop. After breaking into a house in Thousand Oaks, California, he used the bathroom, but his failure to flush allowed investigators to carry out DNA analysis on the fecal matter.

SURREAL CHASE ▶ A suspected thief seen running from a store in London, England, was chased and caught by an off-duty police officer dressed as a giraffe. Police Constable Ben Perkins was wearing the wild animal costume for a bar crawl.

CHICKEN WALKER ▶ Milt Strong, of Dallas, Texas, takes his pet chickens out for daily walks in a baby stroller.

BACH CONCERT? ▶ A Labrador dog calmly wandered onto the stage during a classical music concert by the Vienna Chamber Orchestra in Ephesus, Turkey. The dog eventually sat down next to the string section, who, along with the rest of the orchestra, tried to ignore the gate-crasher and continued playing. The audience was more impressed with the canine and gave the dog a round of applause.

ZERO TURNOUT ▶ A 2017 election in McIntire, Iowa, failed to attract a single vote after not one of the town's 70 registered voters showed up to cast their ballot.

FROZEN FOX

» In January 2017, Jäger Franz Stehle and his son used a chainsaw to carve a frozen fox out of the Danube River near their family's hotel in Fridingen, Germany. Stehle believes the fox fell through thin ice and drowned. The block of ice containing the unfortunate fox was put on display outside their hotel to warn others of the dangers of the icy river.

Jet-Powered TRUCK

> Car enthusiast Perry Watkins from Buckinghamshire, England, transformed a rusty pick-up into a jet-powered truck that can reach speeds of more than 300 mph (482.8 kmph)!

He first imported the 1958 Volkswagen vehicle from Oklahoma and then spent the next five years perfecting his creation, which he dubbed Oklahoma Willy, by attaching a 5,000-brake horsepower fighter jet engine to it. With a standard engine hidden in the trunk, the final truck is a road-legal $64,555 (£50,000) monstrosity.

1978 ROLLS ROYCE VIPER 535 JET ENGINE!

CRAB
Fashion Show

> The Hongze Lake Harvest Festival in Jiangsu Province, China, stages a fashion show for crabs.

The show celebrates the harvest of mitten crabs, nearly 6,000 tons of which are caught locally each year. Some of the 150 entrants decorate their crabs in ornate, miniature wedding dresses or colorful costumes, while others just paint the shells. Last year, a drone flew the fashionistas down the runway! The good news for the crabs is that by taking part, they will live for at least another 12 months, as it is considered bad luck to eat one of that year's models.

PUDDING PUPS

» Wilaiwan Mee-Nguen, owner of a dessert shop Wilaiwan, in Pathum Thani, Thailand, uses special molds to make coconut cream puddings that look just like puppies.

BUBBLE TUMORS ▶ A 60-year-old man named Shiti Charoenrattanaprapa has lived as a recluse in Thailand for more than 45 years because he suffers from neurofibromatosis, a condition that has caused hundreds of large bubble-like tumors to form all over his face and body. Nurses from a nearby hospital regularly visit Shiti to bring him food and check on his health.

BEER DIET ▶ Hugues Derzelle, a cattle breeder from Chimay, Belgium, gives his cows 1 gal (4 l) of dark beer every day to improve the marbling of their meat. The cows do not get drunk from their daily beer diet because the bacteria in their digestive system immediately metabolize most of the alcohol, so that only a small amount reaches their bloodstream.

LIVE COCKROACH ▶ In 2017, doctors in Injambakkam, India, removed a live cockroach from the skull of a 42-year-old woman named Selvi. She had woken in the night with a crawling sensation in her right nostril, followed by a burning feeling in her head. The insect was discovered sitting in the skull base, between her eyes and close to her brain. If she had not reported it and the cockroach had died inside her, it could have caused an infection that would have spread to her brain.

FAKE EMBASSY ▶ A fake U.S. embassy operated in Accra, Ghana, for 10 years, convincing people to pay thousands of dollars for visas and identification documents. Located well away from the real U.S. embassy in Accra, it was housed in a rundown, two-story building with an American flag flying outside. No Americans worked there, just members of organized crime syndicates from Ghana and Turkey.

RARE PENNY ▶ A 1943 Lincoln Penny—one of no more than 20 still in existence—sold at auction in Denver, Colorado, in 2017 for $282,000. Due to copper shortages in World War II, the coin should have been made of zinc-coated steel but was mistakenly struck in bronze instead.

MEDIEVAL HOME ▶ Jousting champion Martin Townley and his wife Jayne, a magician, have turned their three-bedroom, semi-detached house in Weston-super-Mare, Somerset, England, into a replica of a medieval castle. They had the exterior painted to resemble gray stone and added battlements and archways over their windows. The interior is decorated with swords and suits of armor, while the couple and their two children eat on a long, wooden banquet table in a baronial-style dining room and drink from goblets to the sound of lute music.

HEADS WOOL ROLL

» A traditional dish of western Norway, *smalahove*, is an entire sheep's head cooked and served as a main course. Eaten right before Christmas, the slaughtered sheep head is first split in two and the brain removed while the two pieces are soaked in water for a couple days. Afterward, the head is salted to preserve it and then smoked to remove the fleece, or fur. In the end, a boiled or steamed sheep head—still with tongue and eyes—is served with a side of potatoes and mashed swede (rutabaga).

STICKY SWIM ▶
Scientists at the University of Minnesota discovered that people can swim just as fast in syrup as they can in water.

DEDICATED MOTHER ▶
Sixty-nine-year-old Julieta Lorenzo, from Roxas in the Philippines, carries her 30-year-old disabled daughter, Mary Jane, on her back whenever they go out. Mary Jane was paralyzed at age three, so her mother has been carrying her everywhere for three decades.

DENTAL BRACES ▶ After a woman in Perth, Western Australia, complained of severe stomach pains, surgeons removed a 2.8-in-long (7-cm) piece of orthodontic wire from her abdomen. The woman had once worn braces on her teeth and had somehow swallowed part of the wire, which was then lodged in her body for at least 10 years.

HIDDEN BILL ▶
A 700-year-old Ming Dynasty banknote was found hidden inside the head of an ancient wooden Chinese Buddhist sculpture when it went up for auction in Armadale, Western Australia, in 2016.

SMART STRAP ▶ A South Korean company has developed a smart watch strap that turns the wearer's hand into a cell phone. The gadget, which connects to a person's phone via Bluetooth, contains a unit that transmits sound through their body, allowing them to hear the caller just by touching their ear with their fingertip and then to conduct a conversation via a microphone embedded into the watch strap.

THIRD WIN ▶
In 2017, Barbara and Douglas Fink, from Edmonton, Alberta, Canada, won the lottery for the third time. They picked up more than $8 million in the Western Canada Lottery Corporation draw after collecting smaller wins in 1989 and 2010.

BURRYMAN ▶ Every year on the second Friday in August, the town of South Queensferry, Scotland, celebrates a mysterious tradition that sees a single resident parade through the streets covered in burrs. Andrew Taylor has been the burryman for five years and counting, suiting up in the sticky, prickly burrs, all while braving the summer heat. The meaning of this bizarre tradition has been lost to time, but the townspeople believe giving the burryman money (or more importantly, whiskey through a straw) will bring good luck and ward off evil.

Suite SAFARI

> Nestled between natural rock formations, the open-air Stars Suite at the Kagga Kamma Nature Reserve in South Africa promises luxurious nights underneath the Milky Way.

With no walls, no cell phone reception, and no Wi-Fi, isolated visitors can tough it out in the wilderness—while sleeping on a queen-size bed and bathing in a natural rock pool. Thankfully, mosquitoes don't thrive in the dry environment.

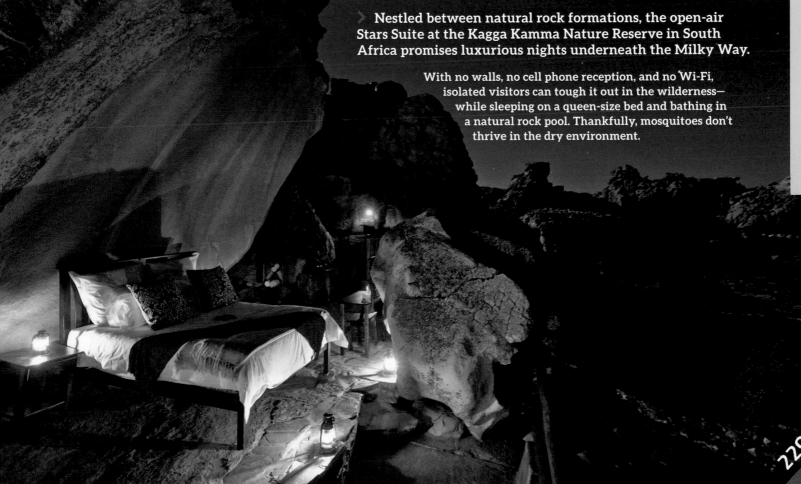

Some of the 300 Krampusses that showed up for the 2017 Krampus Run at Germany's Munich Christmas Market.

❯ The Grinch and Ebenezer Scrooge have nothing on Krampus, an Alpine legend who travels with St. Nicholas during the Christmas season, beating naughty children with a bundle of twigs or even stealing them away to his lair.

The origins of Krampus aren't clear, but the mythological demon is most well-known in the countries of Austria, Germany, Hungary, Slovenia, and the Czech Republic. His popularity has soared in recent history thanks in part to media coverage of *Krampuslauf*, or "Krampus Run," a festival during which people take to the streets dressed in elaborate, fur-covered costumes complete with giant horns and fanged masks. Krampus has been the subject of several horror movies, has appeared in a 2012 episode of *Scooby-Doo! Mystery Incorporated*, and even has his own graphic novel.

A Krampus postcard from 1900s Germany, stating "Greetings from Krampus!" in German.

Gruss vom Krampus!

Ripley's Exhibit
Cat. No. 172327
**Mesh Wire
Ryan Gosling**
Made by Fekadu Mekasha
Origin: Addis Ababa, Ethiopia

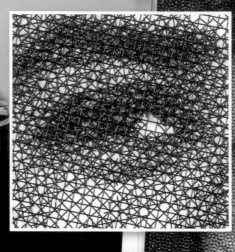

WORM COCKTAIL ▶ A company in Shaanxi Province, China, punished employees who failed to meet their sales targets by feeding them a cocktail of rice wine containing live mealworms.

TRUE GRIT ▶ Hans Raj, from Uttar Pradesh, India, has eaten a plate of gravel and sand every day for more than 25 years—and has never been sick. To vary his diet, he sometimes snacks on rocks and pieces of brick.

FAULTY GPS ▶ A 21-year-old Canadian driver was fined $425 after, as his GPS instructed, he drove his car 2,624 ft (800 m) into a streetcar tunnel. The vehicle had to be lifted by crane from inside Union Station, Toronto, Ontario.

MULTIPLE WIVES ▶ Fifty-eight-year-old Tambon Prasert, from Nakorn Nayok, Thailand, has 120 wives and 28 children—and all of his brides know each other.

MEAT BOUQUET ▶ Mu Siyao proposed to girlfriend Wang Qiqi at a restaurant in Changchun, China, by presenting her with a bouquet of chopped beef on a bed of lettuce. She said yes.

WRONG TURN ▶ A driver escaped unhurt after his car's GPS device directed him to drive along a bicycle path through a park and into the Lehigh River in Easton, Pennsylvania.

DEAD MAN ELECTED ▶ Polling 17,659 votes, Gary Ernst was reelected as treasurer in Oceanside, California, in November 2016, even though he had died two months earlier.

HAUNTING THREAT ▶ The newspaper obituary for Canadian hockey fan Loretta Workun, who died on May 30, 2017, at age 85, warned her beloved Edmonton Oilers that she would haunt the team's arena if they failed to win the NHL championship again soon.

EMPIRE STATE OF BALANCE

≫ On August 21, 1934, acrobats Jarley Smith, Jewell Waddell, and Jimmy Kirigin performed a balancing act while standing on the edge of the Empire State Building—1,245 ft (379 m) above ground! The three brave daredevils completed several different movements before finishing their high-altitude stunt.

FLYING RATS ▶ Fans of Danish soccer team Brondby threw dead rats at a player from rival FC Copenhagen as he prepared to take a corner kick near the end of their match in April 2017. Brondby lost 1-0.

BOARDER NUN ▶ Sister Fabienne, a 78-year-old nun in Baugé, France, glided into a voting booth for the 2017 French legislature elections on a hoverboard. She said she had been taught how to use it by a priest.

SHORTS RITUAL ▶ In the hope of bringing good luck, the Milwaukee Bucks basketball team's shooting guard Jason Terry goes to bed the night before every game wearing the uniform shorts of the next day's opposing team.

DOG RADIO ▶ German radio host Stephan Stock broadcasts a regular program for lonely dogs. Hallo Hasso, on Radio Ton in the Baden-Württemberg region, plays soothing music to help dogs relax while their owners are out.

SAVE SKIN

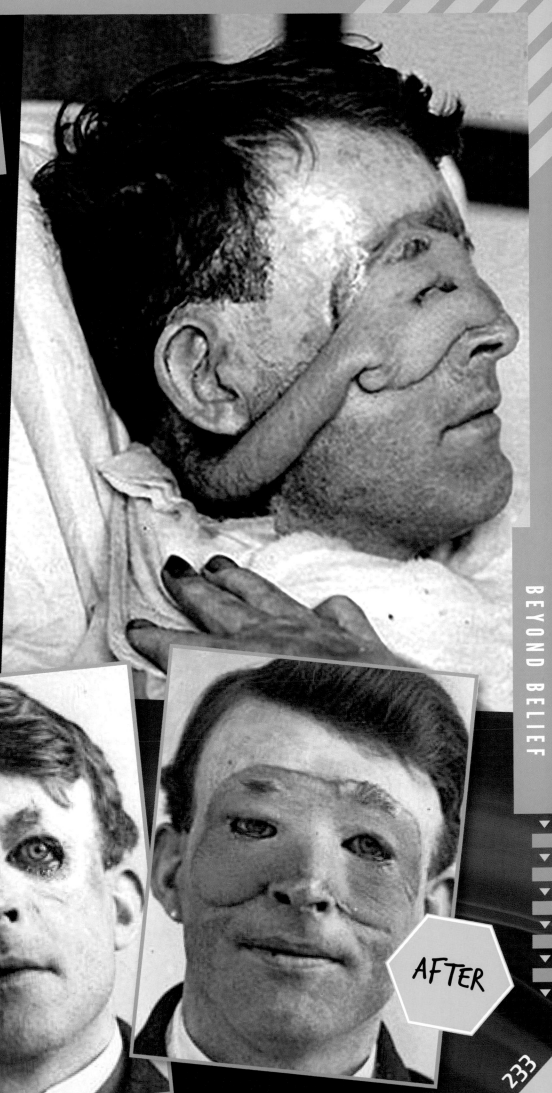

> Walter Yeo of Plymouth, England, was one of the first patients to receive innovative skin graft surgery in 1917.

The 27-year-old World War I sailor sustained facial burn injuries, including losing his upper and lower eyelids, in battle while manning the guns aboard the HMS Warspite in 1916. A year later, Sir Harold Gillies performed the medical procedure, grafting a flap of skin across Walter's face and eyes like a mask, thereby giving him new eyelids.

Walter's new kind of skin graft, called the "tubed pedicle graft," involved lifting a flap of skin and moving it to a new area, while keeping one end attached to the body and stitching part of it into a tube, so that the original blood flow was kept intact. This reduced the infection rate, as antibiotics had not been invented yet. In Walter's case, skin was moved from his chest to his face.

Documents show that Walter's condition improved, although he still had severe disfigurement. After further treatment at the Royal Naval Hospital in Plymouth in 1938, nothing else is known about him.

BEFORE

AFTER

NOT FAR FROM THE TREES ▶

During Hurricane Ophelia, tens of thousands of apples were blown from the trees in an orchard in Clonmel, Ireland— but the fruits landed unbruised and ready for cider processing. The nearby River Suir flooded at the same time the apples were stripped from the trees, and when the waters receded, the apples were laid to rest gently, blanketing the orchard floor. It turns out nature might be the best apple picker.

SNIFFER DOG ▶ A Japanese company has created Hana-chan, a robot dog that faints if your feet smell bad. The robot, which has a powerful sensor embedded in its nose, wags its tail if your feet smell fresh.

BAD DAY ▶ Georgiy Karpekin's two vehicles were both crushed by trees on the same day—January 18, 2017. After high winds had caused a tree to fall onto his truck in a parking lot in Sacramento, California, he returned to his home in West Sacramento to find that another tree had crashed down onto his car while it was parked outside his house.

KITTEN PERFUME ▶ New York fragrance company Demeter released a new perfume that recreates the scent of kitten fur.

SOUL MATES ▶ Jessica Gomes and Aaron Bairos were born at the same hospital (Morton Hospital in Taunton, Massachusetts) on the same day (April 28, 1990)—and 27 years later, on September 9, 2017, they got married.

SKYDIVING SUITOR ▶ To ask girlfriend Katie Potter to their high school prom, 19-year-old senior Ty Myers, from Bristol, Tennessee, leapt from an airplane while dressed in a tuxedo and parachuted down to the ground holding a sign that read: "I'm Falling 4 U, Prom?" She said yes.

LEAF Canvas

❯ Indian artist Sandesh S. Rangnekar paints beautiful works of art on to the large but fragile leaves of the peepal tree.

Preparing each 7.8-in (20-cm) leaf for use takes about 40 days. The leaf is kept in water for a month until its green skin can be brushed away to leave only a flimsy, translucent net. Once his leafy canvas is ready, he gently applies the paint with a fine-tip brush. As the leaves are so fragile, the finished artworks must be framed for preservation.

9,600 U.S. PENNIES!

Ripley's Exhibit
Cat. No. 5864
Lincoln Log Cabin
Scale model of President Lincoln's
Kentucky birthplace made from
Lincoln pennies, by Ernie Hood.

CAMERA STICK ▶ Becky Apperley-Gawn, a zookeeper at Chessington World of Adventures, Surrey, England, has developed a 20-ft-tall (6-m) camera stick so that visitors can take full-body selfies with the giraffes.

LUCKY PUB ▶ When Ian Brooke, landlord of The Mallard pub in Scunthorpe, England, won £1 million ($1.3 million) on the lottery in 2017, he became the third person at the bar to win the jackpot in four years, beating odds of 283 billion to one.

HEART FAILURES ▶ Ray Woodhall, 54, of the West Midlands, England, suffered 27 heart attacks in 24 hours—and survived. He collapsed while playing "walking soccer" and then "died" in a hospital 26 times, even though he had no previous history of cardiac problems.

HUGE DIAMOND ▶ In 2017, Pastor Emmanuel Momoh found a 706-carat diamond in Yakadu village, Sierra Leone—the largest uncut diamond found in the country since 1972. The huge diamond is worth an estimated $60 million.

WEEPING STATUE ▶ Over several days in April 2017, hundreds of worshippers rushed to the Frias Mendoza family home in San José de Metán, Argentina, after a statue of the Virgin Mary appeared to start weeping blood.

PRESIDENTIAL AUCTION BLOCK

George H. W. Bush's **GOLF BAG**, shoes, and putter garnered **$30,000** at an auction in 2016.

George Washington's **PERSONAL COPY** of the United States **CONSTITUTION** and Bill of Rights sold for a cool $9,826,500 in 2012.

An ornate **GOLD HUNTING KNIFE** given to Theodore Roosevelt for his years of service was purchased for $414,000—a **RECORD HIGH** for American knives at auction.

For $6,875, an anonymous buyer became the owner of **14 STRANDS** of Thomas Jefferson's hair that were taken at the time of his **DEATH**.

A page of White House stationery covered in **DOODLES** and signed by **RONALD REAGAN**, estimated to sell at $3,500, went for $100,000!

MARY TODD LINCOLN'S black mourning dress had a starting auction price of $5,000 and ended at $100,000 after a **BIDDING WAR**.

The gold **WEDDING BAND** of John F. Kennedy's **ASSASSIN**, Lee Harvey Oswald, sold for $108,000 in 2013.

S. RANGNEKAR

FLYING
Colors

❯ As Día de los Muertos (or Day of the Dead) celebrations take place across Latin America, Guatemalans not only pay visits to cemeteries and prepare special dishes but also fly "barilletes gigantes"—giant kites 100 ft (30 m) in diameter!

On November 1, the Kite Festivals of neighboring towns Santiago and Sumpango honor the dead with local competitions for the most beautiful kite and the longest-flying kite. Groups of participants spend weeks preparing for the festival, as each kite is made of cloth and paper tied to a bamboo frame. The colorful designs, both religious- and folklore-themed, are awarded prizes. Interestingly, the giant kites are too big to fly normally, but instead they stand upright as behemoth banners.

SOME KITES CAN BE AS BIG AS 118 FT (36 M)!

Believe it or not, the festival takes place in a nearby cemetery, where the locals also clean up the graves and decorate them with flowers.

KNOCK ON WOOD

Canadian artist Maskull Lasserre hand-carved his latest work "Schrödinger's Wood" from the giant trunk of an ash tree, carefully chiseling the wood down to what looks like a frayed rope and then suspending the entire 13-ft-tall (4-m) piece.

Robert Ripley stands outside in his garden with the world's largest wood-carved chain draped all around his neck and arms (c. 1935).

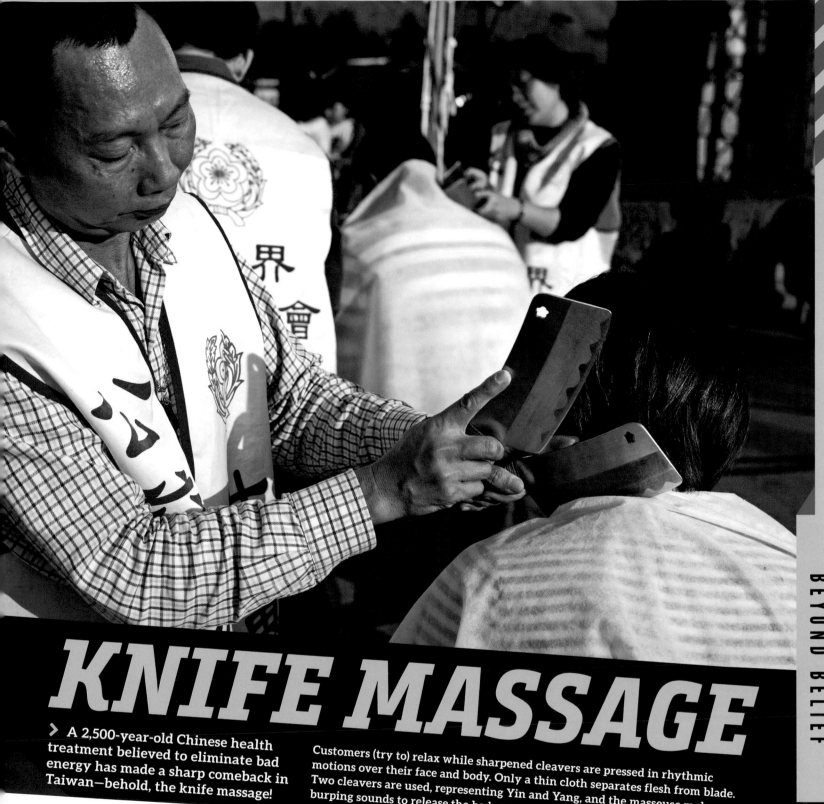

KNIFE MASSAGE

> A 2,500-year-old Chinese health treatment believed to eliminate bad energy has made a sharp comeback in Taiwan—behold, the knife massage!

Customers (try to) relax while sharpened cleavers are pressed in rhythmic motions over their face and body. Only a thin cloth separates flesh from blade. Two cleavers are used, representing Yin and Yang, and the masseuse makes burping sounds to release the bad energy drawn out from the customer.

ANTIQUE COOKIE ▶ Penny Rickhoff, of Scottsdale, Arizona, keeps an 85-year-old cookie inside a jewelry box as a family heirloom. The heart-shaped cookie was given to her mother in the early 1930s as a Valentine's Day gift.

FAKE FERRARIS ▶ Police in Sils, Spain, uncovered a gang that had been converting old Toyotas into fake Ferraris and Lamborghinis. Officers found badges, stickers, and body kits designed to transform the cars into replica luxury vehicles, which were then being sold to unsuspecting customers on the internet.

CANNED POLLUTION ▶ British-born Dominic Johnson-Hill, owner of a souvenir shop in Beijing, China, sells cans of polluted Beijing city air to tourists for $4 each.

FLUSHES ASHES ▶ For more than eight years, New Yorker Tom McDonald has been flushing the cremated remains of his lifelong friend down ballpark toilets across the United States. Roy Riegel, a fellow baseball fan, died in 2008, and, with the family's permission, McDonald has tipped a small portion of ashes into stadium toilets from a little plastic bottle—always while the game is in progress.

PARALLEL LIVES ▶ Identical twins Steven and David Bisset, from Black Isle in the Scottish Highlands, became fathers on the same day—August 15, 2016—beating odds of 150,000 to one.

ROYAL UNDERWEAR ▶ A pair of Queen Victoria's 120-year-old undergarments, embroidered with VR (Victoria Regina), sold for more than $20,000 at an auction in London, England, in 2016, five times the estimated price.

FirePAAN

> A new trend has been heating up India. . . literally. Street vendors have been setting their food on fire before stuffing it in their patrons' mouths.

Paan stalls sell spices, dried fruits, sugar, areca nuts, or sometimes tobacco wrapped in betel leaves, with locals chewing the snack as a stimulant and then spitting it out or swallowing it. Fire paan takes things up a notch as the morsel is set aflame and shoved into open mouths that are happy to experience the peculiar novelty.

FOOD ON FIRE!

THAKUR'S
DEON

KETCHUP LEATHER

» Plan Check, a series of restaurants in Los Angeles, California, serves their burgers with a dehydrated slice of ketchup! The innovative condiment, known as Ketchup Leather™, is said to prevent soggy buns and tastes just like the tomato topping you know and love.

BLOCKED DRAINS ▶ Since 2012, Bryan Gibson has taken more than 15,000 pictures of blocked drains in Cornwall, England, trying to draw attention to "the scandal of drainage maintenance in Cornwall."

WRONG RESTAURANT ▶ Gourmet customers and TV crews suddenly flocked to Le Bouche à Oreille, a small roadside café in Bourges, France, in 2017 after it was mistakenly awarded a coveted Michelin star, the prize given to the world's top restaurants. The Michelin Guide website had confused the humble café with an upscale restaurant of the same name 120 mi (192 km) away in Boutervilliers.

INFLATABLE POOP ▶ A 6-ft-high (1.8-m) inflatable poop was installed in Torrelodones, Spain, in June 2016 to deter dog owners from leaving their pets' excrement on the town's streets. A week later, it was stolen. Torrelodones has about 6,000 dogs who produce an estimated 1,100 lb (500 kg) of excrement every day.

FEATHER COAT ▶ The Museum of the Arkansas Grand Prairie in Stuttgart displays the Coat of Many Feathers, made in the 1960s by restaurant owner and champion duck caller Ruby Abel, who spent 600 hours sewing the green head feathers of 450 male mallard ducks into a coat. She subsequently wore the coat on two trips to New York City, where she appeared as a contestant on TV panel game shows.

TRUNK DRUNK ▶ Carl Webb drove 14 mi (22 km) toward home from a barbecue in Memphis, Tennessee, unaware that a drunk man was curled up asleep on top of the 14-in-wide (35-cm) trunk of his car. Unbelievably, the lip of the trunk kept him from falling off at speeds of up to 65 mph (104 kmph), and Webb only learned that he had an extra passenger when a police officer stopped him on the exit road from Interstate 55. The man had passed out on the vehicle while it was parked at the barbecue.

VOMIT BEER ▶ Australia's Robe Town Brewery launched a new beer made from whale vomit. Its limited run Moby Dick Ambergris Ale features hints of ambergris, or whale vomit, a substance that is excreted by sperm whales and is commonly used in perfumes. The beer is described by its makers as having a "pungent, animalistic aroma" and a "challenging" taste.

MIXED FEELINGS ▶ Brandon Thomas, a minor league baseball player with the Gateway Grizzlies of Sauget, Illinois, hit a grand slam homerun against the Joliet Slammers, only to find that the ball had smashed through the windshield of his own truck. He sent the ball sailing into the parking lot, where his 2008 Toyota Tundra was standing some 60 ft (18 m) behind the left field wall.

NEWS BLACKOUT ▶ Joseph Talbot, of Newark, New York, bought nearly 1,000 newsstand copies of the 12,000-circulation *Times of Wayne County* at $1.25 each because he did not want people to read about his arrest for drunk driving.

GHOST REPELLENT ▶ The Trisaksri Ghost Repellent device, made by Thai company Boondee Workshop, claims to ward off ghosts for just $1,500 plus $140 for U.S. shipping. The machine uses an infrared camera and electromagnetic field meters to detect the presence of ghosts, and then it emits a blast of radio energy to scare them away.

SPACE CAKE ◉ In October 2017, researchers from the Glasgow Science Centre sent a chocolate teacake into space just to see what would happen to it. The fun experiment saw "Terry the Teacake" launched on a hydrogen weather balloon, with the attached camera broadcasting to Facebook Live and thousands of expectant viewers. The teacake went 23 mi (37 km) up before it made its descent back to Earth and landed in good condition.

23 MI (37 KM) UP IN SPACE!

HAIRCULESE

> **Strongman Chris "Hairculese" Rider of Thomasville, Pennsylvania, can pull a car with his hair!**

To pull off this amazing stunt, Hairculese parts his long locks into two braids, and then weaves those below his chin and around a tow cable that's attached to the car. Facing the car, he walks backward, pulling the cable taut and hauling the car—sometimes up to 0.25 mi (0.4 km)! Hairculese is also able to perform other strongman feats like bending steel bars, ripping phone books in half, and folding coins with his bare hands!

From the top of his head to the ends of his hair, Hairculese's mane is 42 in (106.6 cm) long!

SPEEDY STRENGTH ▶ Nearing 70 years old, Reverend Les Davis of Dothan, Alabama, impressed hundreds of onlookers in 2017 as he bent 20 steel bars around the back of his head in under a minute. Directly after that, he broke through three handcuffs in just 52 seconds, using only his body strength!

PAPER SNACK ▶ At age 10, Caden Benjamin, from Mpumalanga, South Africa, already weighs 198 lb (90 kg)—more than twice the weight of an average 10 year old. He suffers from a rare genetic disorder, Prader-Willi syndrome, which leaves him feeling permanently hungry—so much so that if he cannot find any food he sometimes eats rolls of toilet paper.

FIERY FERRARI ▶ A man totaled his $300,000 Ferrari 430 Scuderia supercar in a crash in South Yorkshire, England, just one hour after buying it. The brand-new luxury car skidded off the road into a field where it caught fire, reducing it to a mass of burned-out, crumpled metal.

WRONG PLANE ▶ Hoping to make the short flight from Cologne, Germany, to London, England, British businessman Samuel Jankowsky accidentally boarded the wrong plane and ended up 5,325 mi (8,424 km) from his intended destination in Las Vegas, Nevada. He only knew something was wrong when he woke from an hour-long nap and saw that the in-flight tracker showed the plane had flown over the United Kingdom and was now above the Atlantic Ocean.

WRAPPER'S REVENGE ▶ Annoyed by a stranger's car that had been left parked outside his house in Liverpool, England, for two days, homeowner Neil Junglas took his revenge by encasing the entire vehicle in Saran Wrap.

GRAVESIDE DRINK ▶ Visitors to the burial place of Irish-born Antarctic explorer Sir Ernest Shackleton (1874–1922) on the remote southern Atlantic island of South Georgia are encouraged to drink a shot of whiskey to quench his thirst.

FREE BEERS ▶ A group of seven trainee Roman Catholic priests who came to a pub in Cardiff, Wales, for a drink were initially turned away because the doorman mistook them for bachelor-party revelers in costume. The manager eventually allowed them in after realizing they were genuine and gave them free beers by way of apology.

BRAIDED TO A TOW CABLE!!

GOLDEN EGG

» Artists Bigert and Bergstrom designed a giant golden egg that is actually a portable sauna with room for eight people. Located in Sweden, the Solar Egg, as it's called, can heat up to a steaming 185°F (85°C), stands an impressive 16 ft (5 m) tall, and has a shell of gold-plated stainless steel to reflect its gorgeous surroundings. When not in use, the art installation can be dismantled into 69 separate pieces.

INSIDE VIEW!

ENTHUSIASTIC POLYGAMIST ▶ By the time he died in 2017 at age 93, Nigeria's Mohammed Bello Abubakar had married 130 wives, divorced 10, and fathered 203 children.

BODY PARTS ▶ Austrian customs officials found human intestines in the luggage of a Moroccan woman who had arrived at Graz Airport. The woman said the organ parts, which were packed in plastic containers and formaldehyde, were those of her dead husband and that she had brought them to Austria for examination because she thought he had been poisoned.

HIDING PLACE ▶ Police in Głogów, Poland, eventually tracked down a 30-year-old male suspect they were searching for—hiding inside a dishwasher.

FIRE THERAPY ▶ Weighing 322 lb (146 kg) at age 11, Li Hang was set on fire to lose weight. Doctors at a hospital in Changchun, China, set alight an alcohol-covered towel on his bare stomach in the hope of curing the condition that has affected him since he was three. He has been diagnosed with Prader-Willi Syndrome, a rare genetic disorder that leads to obsessive eating and abnormal growth. Fire therapy and fire cupping are part of traditional Chinese medicinal practices for treating obesity.

DINE AND DANCERS ▶ More than 100 people claiming to celebrate a baptism at the Hotel Carmen Restaurant in Bembibre, Spain, danced out on an unpaid bill of about $2,200 via a conga line. They made their getaway just as dessert was being served.

Ripley's Exhibit
Cat. No. 172636
Voodoo Chest
A wooden box containing a doll, Bible, keys, candles, and several other objects.
Origin: France

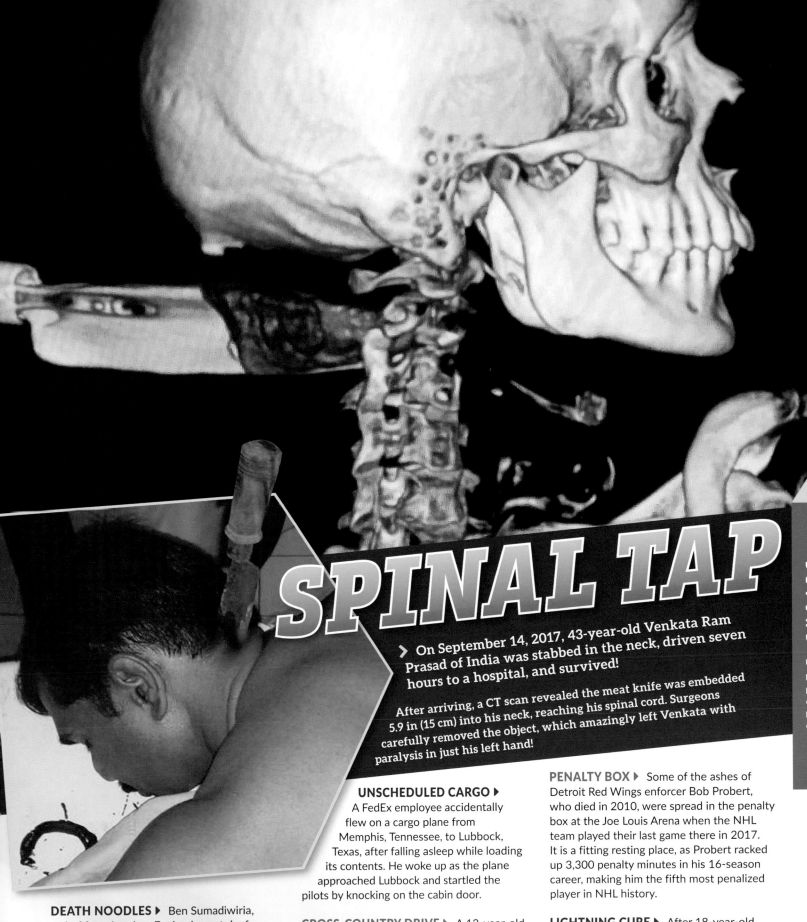

SPINAL TAP

> On September 14, 2017, 43-year-old Venkata Ram Prasad of India was stabbed in the neck, driven seven hours to a hospital, and survived!

After arriving, a CT scan revealed the meat knife was embedded 5.9 in (15 cm) into his neck, reaching his spinal cord. Surgeons carefully removed the object, which amazingly left Venkata with paralysis in just his left hand!

UNSCHEDULED CARGO ▶ A FedEx employee accidentally flew on a cargo plane from Memphis, Tennessee, to Lubbock, Texas, after falling asleep while loading its contents. He woke up as the plane approached Lubbock and startled the pilots by knocking on the cabin door.

DEATH NOODLES ▶ Ben Sumadiwiria, a chef from London, England, went deaf for two minutes after eating the world's hottest noodles at a restaurant in Jakarta, Indonesia. Known as "Death Noodles," the dish contained 100 bird's eye chilies crushed together, giving it a Scoville heat rating of 20 million, 4,000 times stronger than Tabasco sauce.

CROSS-COUNTRY DRIVE ▶ A 12-year-old boy drove 800 mi (1,280 km) alone across Australia for an entire day before being stopped by police officers. He had been planning to drive the family car all the way across the country, from Kendall, New South Wales, to Perth, Western Australia—a distance of 2,500 mi (4,023 km).

PENALTY BOX ▶ Some of the ashes of Detroit Red Wings enforcer Bob Probert, who died in 2010, were spread in the penalty box at the Joe Louis Arena when the NHL team played their last game there in 2017. It is a fitting resting place, as Probert racked up 3,300 penalty minutes in his 16-season career, making him the fifth most penalized player in NHL history.

LIGHTNING CURE ▶ After 18-year-old Ana Ballesteros, from Cereté, Colombia, was struck by lightning, she agreed to let relatives bury her alive in her garden in an attempt to cure her back pains. She was covered up to her neck in soil for four hours at a time over three days in the hope that it would take the heat out of the lightning energy.

INDEX

Page numbers in *italic*
refer to images.

www.ripleys.com/books

Ripley's Believe It or Not!

www.ripleys.com/books

ACKNOWLEDGMENTS

4 (tr) Courtesy of Laetitia Ky, (bl) © SATHIANPONG PHOOKIT/Shutterstock.com, (br) Caters News; **5** (tl) JOSH SAUNDERS/CATERS NEWS, (tr) Email: s.rangnekar01@gmail.com/peepalandme@gmail.com, Facebook: peepal&me, Instagram: peepalandme, (b) CATERS NEWS; **6** (tr) Courtesy of Jessica Firpi; **8** (bl) ABC Photo Archives/ABC via Getty Images; **9** (tl) Courtesy of Jessica Firpi; **12–13** (dps) Jane Barlow/PA Images via Getty Images; **14–15** (dps) Alasdair Turner via Getty Images; **16** (tr) Prisma by Dukas Presseagentur GmbH/Alamy Stock Photo, (t) robertharding/Alamy Stock Photo, (bl) Teshima Yasuhito/Cover Images; **17** Caters News; **18** (tl) Chandra Sena/Barcroft Media, (br) Imaginechina; **19** Jeremy Hunter/Exclusivepix Media; **20–21** Courtesy of Laetitia Ky; **22** (t) Barcroft Images/Barcroft Media via Getty Images, (bl) Imaginechina; **23** (tl, tr) Barcroft Images/Barcroft Media via Getty Images, (bl) Courtesy of Carmen Heroux/Rene Martin; **24–25** Alex Voyer/Caters News; **26** (tl) ASSOCIATED PRESS, (b) Imaginechina; **27** Courtesy of Autobahn Motors; **28** (t) Emy Gargiulo, (bl) Annette Reuther/picture-alliance/Cover Images, (b) Lorenzo Quinn Support 2017/Cover Images; **29** © SWNS.com; **30** (b) "Public Domain {{PD-US}} Library of Congress Prints and Photographs Division Washington, D.C. 20540 USA; http://www.loc.gov/pictures/item/00652085/"; **31** (t) Bettmann/Contributor/Getty Images, (b) Keystone-France/Gamma-Keystone via Getty Images; **32** (tl) U.S. Navy photo by Mass Communication Specialist 3rd Class Travis K. Mendoza/Released. The appearance of U.S. Department of Defense (DoD) visual information does not imply or constitute DoD endorsement, (t) Courtesy photo via U.S. Air Force, (b) U.S. Air Force photo; **33** (tl, t) Public Domain {{PD-US}} NASA, (bl) Photo by Pool/Solar Impulse/Bertrand Piccard/Anadolu Agency/Getty Images, (b) Photo by Jean Revillard/Solar Impulse2 via Getty Images; **34** Photo by Rafaela Ferraz (rafaelaferraz.com); **35** Arun Sankar/Getty Images; **36–37** ASSOCIATED PRESS; **37** (b) John Nordell/The Christian Science Monitor via Getty Images; **38** (b) Sean Pavone/Alamy Stock Photo; **38–39** (t) Courtesy of Shanell Papp; **39** (b) Romulus Whitiker; **40** (sp) Jim Dyson/Getty Images, (tl) Matthias Schickhofer/ASAblanca via Getty Images, (br) Deco/Alamy Stock Photo; **41** (t) Kyodo News via Getty Images; **42** (t) Sipa Asia/REX/Shutterstock, (br) Imaginechina; **43** Hi-Story/Alamy Stock Photo; **44–45** P. Sam Neill; **46** (tc) Photo contributed by Mandy Atkinson, (bl) EDWARD BOCHES/CATERS NEWS; **47** Public Domain {{PD-US}} https://www.flickr.com/photos/boston_public_library/4901555337/Panorama of the Molasses Disaster site, Globe Newspaper Co. (creator); **50** @spikethebeetle/Caters News; **51** (l) Feature China/Barcroft Images, (r, br) Cocona Inc./37.5® Technology/Cover Images; **52** (b) Jane Barlow/PA Images via Getty Images; **52–53** Jane Barlow/PA Images via Getty Images; **54–55** (dps) AFP/Getty Images; **56–57** (dps) Media Drum World/Alamy Stock Photo; **58** (tr) VCG via Getty Images; **58–59** (b) Jennifer Bolande/Cover Images; **59** (t) By Grand Velas Los Cabos; **60** Robert Luczun; **61** (l) Dinodia Photos/Alamy Stock Photo, (tr) Rajanish Kakade/Hindustan Times via Getty Images; **62** (c) TONY KARUMBA/AFP/Getty Images; **62–63** CARL DE SOUZA/AFP/Getty Images; **64–65** dbimages/Alamy Stock Photo; **66** © SATHIANPONG PHOOKIT/Shutterstock.com; **67** (t) Exotica/Alamy Stock Photo, (b) Theo Moye/Alamy Stock Photo; **68** (t) David R. Frazier Photolibrary, Inc./Alamy Stock Photo, (b) Evgeniya Vlasova/Alamy Stock Photo; **69** Prasit Rodphan/Alamy Stock Photo; **70** (t) AFP/Getty Images, (b) Wedding Glass/Orlando Durn/Caters News; **71** URS FLUEELER/EPA-EFE/REX/Shutterstock; **72** (b) Pablo Blazquez Dominguez/Getty Images, (sp) JAIME REINA/AFP/Getty Images; **73** (t) DeAgostini/Getty Images, (cr) Unknown/Alamy Stock Photo; **74** VCG/VCG via Getty Images; **75** (t) Tommy Lindholm/Pacific Press/LightRocket via Getty Images, (b) VCG/VCG via Getty Images; **76–77** VCG/VCG via Getty Images; **78** (tl) Vincent Belanger; **78–79** Liu Tao/VCG via Getty Images; **80** (t) In Pictures Ltd./Corbis via Getty Images, (b) KMWStock/Alamy Stock Photo; **81** AIZAR RALDES/AFP/Getty Images; **82–83** Eric Lafforgue/Exclusivepix Media; **84** (tl) Paul Nicholls Photography, (br) Celia Mannings/Alamy Stock Photo; **85** (t) Sipa Asia/REX/Shutterstock, (br) Allison Knight; **86–87** (dps) MICHAEL BUHOLZER/AFP/Getty Images; **87** (br) SEBASTIAN DERUNGS/AFP/Getty Images, (bl) MICHAEL BUHOLZER/AFP/Getty Images; **88** (t) STR/AFP/Getty Images, (b) Caters News; **89** Imaginechina; **90–91** (dps) Marc Dozier via Getty Images; **92–93** Courtesy of Piotr Naskrecki; **94** (t) Memphis Zoo, (br) Arif Avize/Solent News/REX/Shutterstock; **95** (t) REX/Shutterstock, (bl) Bazzano Photography/Alamy Stock Photo; **96** (sp) Laszlo Podor/Alamy Stock Photo; **97** (t) © Christine Blais-Soucy, (b) Rima Sharma/Barcroft Images; **98** (t) QUEENSLAND FIRE AND EMERGENCY HA/EPA/REX/Shutterstock, (bl) Jeff Rotman/Alamy Stock Photo; **99** Ruaridh Connellan/Barcroft Media; **100** (sp) MONROE MACKINNEY/CATERS; **101** (t) Frank Hecker/Alamy Stock Photo, (c) Caters News, (b) Marco Ledesma + his kitties Sunny and Milo; **102** (bl) Caters News Agency; **102–103** PC - Jeff Erickson; **104** NORBERT ROSING/National Geographic Creative; **105** (t) WEI FU/CATERS, (b) @TOKAITRICK_bot/Cover Images; **107** YouTube: tomaspasie Instagram: @tomaspasie; **108** (tl) Tim Spuckler; **108–109** Media Drum World/Alamy Stock Photo; **110** (t) SCOTTISH SPCA/MERCURY PRESS, (b) Chris Brunskill Ltd/Getty Images; **111** AP Photo/Sakchai Lalit; **112** (sp) Taylor Weidman/LightRocket via Getty Images; **113** (tr) E/V Nautilus (Supplied by WENN.com), (c) Taylor Weidman/Getty Images, (bl, br) Taylor Weidman/LightRocket via Getty Images; **114** blickwinkel/Alamy Stock Photo; **115** (t) Keystone-France/Gamma-Keystone via Getty Images, (b) Photo by Patrick Aventurier/Getty Images; **116** Solvin Zankl/Alamy Stock Photo; **117** (tr) © Franco Banfi/Solent News & Photo Agency, (br) Marcelo R. Nogueira, from Laboratório de Ciências Ambientais, Universidade Estadual do Norte Fluminense, (br) Laboratório de Radiografias, Museu Nacional, Universidade Federal do Rio de Janeiro; **118** (t) Zoo Creatures/Caters News, (b) Caters News; **119** (t) @omarvillafranca/CMS News; **120–121** (t) Cover Images; **121** (br) imageBROKER/Alamy Stock Photo; **122** (tl) Courtesy of Oregon Humane Society, (tr) Helena Bottemiller Evich, (b) WILDLIFE GmbH/Alamy Stock Photo; **123** (sp) Parramatta Veterinary Hospital/Caters News, (bl) Animal Referral Hospital Sydney/Caters News; **124** (b) Kindly donated by Graham Fox, Kingsclere, UK; **125** Courtesy of Piotr Naskrecki; **126** (tr) Darren5907/Alamy Stock Photo, (bl) GEORGES GOBET/AFP/Getty Images, (br) EMMANUEL DUNAND/AFP/Getty Images; **127** Cover Images; **128** Frank Glaw/Zoological State Collection Munich/dpa/picture-alliance/Cover Images; **129** (tl) Joel Sartore, (br) FLPA/Alamy Stock Photo; **130–131** Bluebowerbird/Bournemouth News/REX/Shutterstock; **132** (t) Hellen Die; **133** JOSH SAUNDERS/CATERS NEWS; **134** David Kawai/@teenytinyorigami; **136** (sp) Sunset Boulevard/Corbis via Getty Images; **137** (tr, bl) Public Domain {{PD-US}}, (br) Public Domain {{PD-US}} Henry Peabody, National Archives and Records Administration, NAID 520082; **138–139** Courtesy of @leekangbin91; **140–143** JP Lambiase and Julia Goolia; **144** (t) Dan Zemke/Cover Images, **144** (b) Steve Coupe - Steves Wooden Toys; **145** Fraser Coast Regional Council; **146** (tr) Firebox.com, (b) Bony/SIPA/REX/Shutterstock; **147** (t) Artiste:https://www.facebook.com/bleseagraffiti/, (bc) Pictorial Press Ltd/Alamy Stock Photo, (br) Drew Taylor Hill Country Visitor; **148** (t) Nestle Japan/Solent News/REX/Shutterstock, (b) MERCURY PRESS; **149** The Asahi Shimbun via Getty Images; **150** Caters News Agency; **151** (bl) REUTERS/Toru Hanai; **152** (t) David Lloyd; 154 (b) Cover Images; **155** (t) REUTERS/Vincent West, (b) Danielle York; **156** (cl) Moviestore collection Ltd/Alamy Stock Photo, (cr) PA Images/Alamy Stock Photo, (bl) Ronald Grant Archive/Alamy Stock Photo; **157** (tl) Moviestore collection Ltd/Alamy Stock Photo, (tr) Walker Art Library/Alamy Stock Photo, (bl) MARKA/Alamy Stock Photo, (br) Geoffrey Taunton/Alamy Stock Photo; **158** (tl) AF archive/Alamy Stock Photo, (tr) Archive Pics/Alamy Stock Photo, (bl) Pictorial Press Ltd/Alamy Stock Photo, (br) Heritage Image Partnership Ltd/Alamy Stock Photo; **159** (tl) AF archive/Alamy Stock Photo, (tr) Hercules Milas/Alamy Stock Photo, (bl) Moviestore collection Ltd/Alamy Stock Photo, (br) Public Domain {{PD-US}}; **160** Diane and Nick Nguyen/Cover Images; **161** (tr) Odeith; **162** (dps) KERI KILGO/MEDIA WORLD DRUM/CATERS NEWS, (bl) KERI KILGO/MEDIA WORLD DRUM/CATERS NEWS; **163** (br) FREDERIC J. BROWN/AFP/Getty Images; **164** EPA/MARKUS SCHOLZ; **165** Thomas Lohnes/Getty Images; **166** (b) © Kevin Burkett at http://flickr.com/photos/24514780@N02/2325309629, Wikimedia Commons//CC-BY-SA-2.0; **167** ASSOCIATED PRESS; **168** (tr) Geoff Robinson Photography/REX/Shutterstock, (bl) Jergens D. Correa (Founder/CEO) Brick Burger Restaurant (Pasig City, Philippines); **169** Bluebowerbird/Bournemouth News/REX/Shutterstock; **170–171** (dps) Caters News; **172–173** Tait Trautman/Caters News; **174** (tr) Newslions/Exclusivepix Media; **175** Courtesy of Ashley Glawe; **178–179** Lea Schaepe. Instagram: @lenia_lalea; **180** Exclusivepix Media; **181** Cover Asia Press; **182** (l) Public Domain {{PD-US}} George Eastman House museum (www.flickr.com/photos/george_eastman_house/2719965307/); **182–183** (b) Public Domain {{PD-US}} http://www.angelfire.com/art/rapunzellonghair/rapunzellonghairarchive/portrait4.htm; **183** (tl) Image via Sideshow World; **184** Kevin Smith/Caters News; **185** Michael Papadakis @Sunscribes; **186** (t) Caters News, (b) Abdulla Omar AlaAli/Barcroft; **187** Courtesy of Lehigh Valley Health Network; **188** (t) Sipa Asia/REX/Shutterstock, (b) MERCURY PRESS; **189** Armin Durgut/Caters News; **190** Lucy Gafford, AKA Shower Hair Master, Instagram: shower_hair_master; **191** PAU BARRENA/AFP/Getty Images; **192** (t) © SWNS.com, (b) Imaginechina; **193** (cr, bl, br) Robson Coelho/Barcroft Images; **194** (b) Bettmann/Contributor, (br) Francis Miller/Contributor; **195** (t) ATTA KENARE/Staff, (b) Christiaan Hart/Caters News; **196–197** Toofan Hashemi, Philippe Penel; **198** (t) Caters News, (b) Sipa Asia/REX/Shutterstock; **199** CATERS NEWS; **200** (bl) Cover Asia Press/Faisal Magray; **201** Dave Cuthbertson/Caters News; **202** (t) Barcroft India; **202–203** (b) GOUPIL STUDIO/CATERS NEWS; **203** (t) Caters News; **204** Imaginechina; **205** @dariborun - Instagram; **206–207** Neil Setchfield/Alamy Stock Photo; **208** Bryn Lennon/Getty Images for Jupiter London Nocturne; **209** (b) PA Images via Getty Images, (br) © Hulton-Deutsch Collection/CORBIS/Corbis via Getty Images; **210** (tl) Keystone Pictures USA/Alamy Stock Photo, (br) Steven Blocker Warden (Hair Ball Builder) - Salon owner, stylist. Adam Green - Photographer. Blockers Studio, Cambridge, Ohio; **212** Edoardo Tresoldi, Archetype, Abu Dhabi 2017 © Roberto Conte; **213** (t) Neil Setchfield/Alamy Stock Photo, (b) Julian Stratenschulte/picture-alliance/dpa/AP Images; **214–215** Jeff J Mitchell/Getty Images; **215** (bl) Jane Barlow/PA Images via Getty Images; **216** Tim Anderson/Caters News; **217** (tr) Chronicle/Alamy Stock Photo, (br) JOE KLAMAR/AFP/Getty Images; **218** Wakeland E. Branz along with his father, Timothy D. Branz, climbed Mount Kilimanjaro in 2017, making Wakeland the youngest to ever sleep in the crater after summiting at the age of ten; **220** HANDOUT/EPA/REX/Shutterstock; **221** (t) 100%純污水製冰所/Cover Images; **222** (l) Fox Photos/Getty Images, (tr) George Skadding/The LIFE Picture Collection/Getty Images, (br) © Hulton-Deutsch Collection/CORBIS/Corbis via Getty Images; 223 (tr) Dallas Public Library, PA87-1/19-59-210-10, (b) Keystone Pictures USA/Alamy Stock Photo; **224** (t) Franck Fotos/Alamy Stock Photo, (bl) JOHANNES STEHLE/AFP/Getty Images; **225** Caters News; **226** Xinhua/Alamy Stock Photo; **227** (t) Courtesy of วิไลวรรณ บ้านขนมไทย via Facebook, https://www.facebook.com/Wilaiwan01/, (b) © SWNS.com; **228** (t) © PerPlex, Wikimedia Commons//CC BY-SA 4.0, (b) Jeff J Mitchell/Getty Images; **229** Caters News; **230–231** (dps) Romy Arroyo Fernandez/NurPhoto via Getty Images; **231** (bl) Sean Gallup/Getty Images, (br) Paul Fearn/Alamy Stock Photo; **232** (bc) Bettmann/Contributor via Getty Images; **233** (tr) Public Domain {{PD-US}}, (b) Public Domain {{PD-US}} Daily Telegraph, Pictures of first person to undergo plastic surgery released, 28 August 2008; **234** (tl) Jonathan Ryan/TipperaryPhotos/Cover Images; **234–235** Email: s.rangnekar01@gmail.com/peepalandme@gmail.com, Facebook: peepal&me, Instagram: peepalandme; **236–237** (dps) Michael DeFreitas Central America/Alamy Stock Photo; **237** (bl) Danita Delimont/Alamy Stock Photo, (br) Lucy Brown (loca4motion)/Alamy Stock Photo; **238** (tr) Courtesy of the Odette Centre for Sculpture, York University, ON, Canada, (l, c) Maskull Lasserre 2017, www.maskulllasserre.com; **239** DARREN MELROSE/CATERS NEWS; **240** Haziq Qadri/Barcroft Media; **241** (tl) David G. Marks, (tr) Dylan + Jeni, (b) Glasgow Science Centre/Cover Images; **244** (t) Solar Egg/Caters News; **245** NEWS CRUNCH/CATERS NEWS; **Master Graphics** Exhibit Tags: © Nils Z/Shutterstock.com; Background Elements: © keren-seg/Shutterstock.com
Infographics Icons made by Freepik//CC 3.0 BY, Gregor Cresnar from www.flaticon.com//CC 3.0 BY, Smashicons from www.flaticon.com//CC 3.0 BY

Key: t = top, b = bottom, c = center, l = left, r = right, sp = single page, dp = double page, bkg = background

All other photos are from Ripley Entertainment Inc. Every attempt has been made to acknowledge correctly and contact copyright holders and we apologize in advance for any unintentional errors or omissions, which will be corrected in future editions.

Connect with Ripley's Online or in Person

30 ZANY LOCATIONS

There are 30 incredible Ripley's Believe It or Not! Odditoriums all around the world, where you can experience our spectacular collection gathered during our century of strange!

Amsterdam
THE NETHERLANDS

Atlantic City
NEW JERSEY

Baltimore
MARYLAND

Blackpool
ENGLAND

Branson
MISSOURI

Cavendish
P.E.I., CANADA

Copenhagen
DENMARK

Gatlinburg
TENNESSEE

Genting Highlands
MALAYSIA

Grand Prairie
TEXAS

Guadalajara
MEXICO

Hollywood
CALIFORNIA

Jeju Island
KOREA

Key West
FLORIDA

Mexico City
MEXICO

Myrtle Beach
SOUTH CAROLINA

New York City
NEW YORK

Newport
OREGON

Niagara Falls
ONTARIO, CANADA

Ocean City
MARYLAND

Orlando
FLORIDA

Panama City Beach
FLORIDA

Pattaya
THAILAND

San Antonio
TEXAS

San Francisco
CALIFORNIA

St. Augustine
FLORIDA

Surfers Paradise
AUSTRALIA

Veracruz
MEXICO

Williamsburg
VIRGINIA

Wisconsin Dells
WISCONSIN

Stop by our website daily for new stories, photos, contests, and more! **www.ripleys.com**
Don't forget to connect with us on social media for a daily dose of the weird and the wonderful.

/RipleysBelieveItOrNot

@Ripleys

youtube.com/Ripleys

@RipleysBelieveItorNot

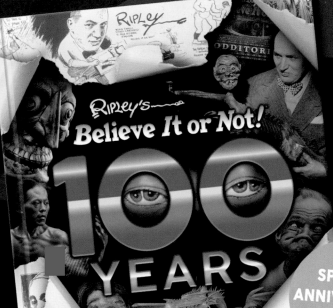

COLORS AND SHAPES

Learning colors and shapes has never been so much fun with these two new board books featuring easy-to-understand, real-life examples, silly characters, and colorful, engaging illustrations!

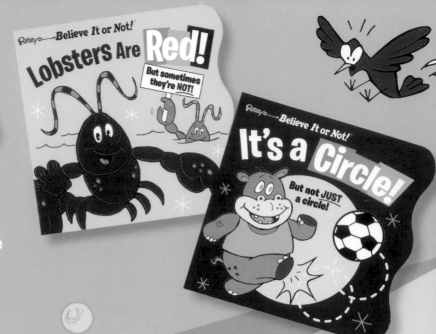

SHARKEE AND BREMNER

Captivating new picture books feature two favorite Ripley's Aquarium mascots—Sharkee the sand tiger shark and Bremner the puffer fish. Filled with expressive illustrations, silly situations, and lovable characters, kids and parents alike will be enchanted by each of these charming "tails"!

SHARKEE and the Teddy Bear
Jessica Firpi • Illustrated by John Graziano

BREMNER and the Party
Carrie Bolin and Jessica Firpi • Illustrated by John Graziano

PLAY IT LOUD!

The newest edition to the best-selling Fun Facts & Silly Stories series is packed with amazing stories, unbelievable facts, eye-catching photos, and wacky games and puzzles.

UNBELIEVABLE!

SILLY!